Date Due

Blue Monday

Blue

The Loss of the

Monday

Work Ethic in America

ROBERT EISENBERGER.

PARAGON HOUSE   New York

First edition, 1989

Published in the United States by

Paragon House
90 Fifth Avenue
New York, NY 10011

Copyright © 1989 by Paragon House

Library of Congress Cataloging-in-Publication Data

Eisenberger, Robert.
    Blue Monday : the loss of the work ethic in America / Robert
Eisenberger.
        p.   cm.
    Bibliography: p.
    ISBN 1-55778-133-8
    1. Work ethic—United States.   2. Work—Psychological aspects.
I. Title.
HD8072.5.E38   1989
306'.36—dc19   88-26780
                                                              CIP

Manufactured in the United States of America

To My Mother

Contents

Introduction

One of the reasons the United States became a great economic power was, quite simply, the industriousness of its people. Most Americans believed that hard work and profits (more so than prophets) provided a righteous and worthwhile life. The American vision involved not simply economic betterment but a willingness to work diligently toward that more prosperous future. As America became affluent, a preoccupation with leisure and sensual pleasure began to replace traditional work values, making managers, workers, and students less willing to undergo the self-denial required to achieve long-term goals. Society's emphasis on getting ahead by hard work disappeared before most of today's Americans were born. More than ever before, Americans view school and work as an unpleasant interlude in their relaxation and entertainment, to be gotten out of the way with a minimum of effort.

A rise in the worship of wealth, accompanied by weakened work values, has made short-term financial gain prized over the long-term economic well-being that results from skill, professionalism, and morality in job performance. Managers and employees alike show a growing predisposition to sacrifice the quality of goods and services to achieve immediate profits. Little heed is paid to the effects of such shortsighted greed upon the country's long-term prospects.

This book examines the loss of the work ethic and the pursuit of leisure by contemporary Americans and the forces that have destroyed traditional work values. To understand today's pervasive indolence, we must analyze the factors that produced a strong work ethic in the past and the conditions that led to its historic decline. We must consider how affluent Americans are trained to be lazy by parents, teachers, employers, and the entertainment media. We must also study the widespread lethargy among many poverty-stricken Americans who, unlike previous generations of the poor, make little attempt to improve their situation.

To restore America's sense of purpose and economic competitiveness, it will not be sufficient simply to eliminate conditions that foster laziness. In order to promote industriousness at school and work, we need to understand the nature and causes of strong work values. What accounts for the fact that some students voluntarily spend hours studying each night whereas others refuse to open a book? Why do some employees work hard in uninteresting jobs for poor pay while others manage to accomplish little in high-paying jobs that allow creative expression? Why do some unemployed people keep searching for jobs month after month when others are satisfied by unemployment insurance or welfare?

To gain a clearer picture of cultural influences on work values, we must consider the causes of greater diligence generally found among Japanese students and employees than found among Americans. To understand how individual parents, teachers, and employers reinforce positive or negative attitudes toward work, we must examine those carefully-controlled psychological experiments that have yielded new insights concerning the learning of laziness and industriousness. To comprehend how individuals acquire distinctive styles of industriousness, we must study the stories of individuals who work steadfastly toward long-term goals, of others who rise to the occasion with intense, concentrated effort, and of still others who pursue goals flexibly, continually searching for more efficient ways to reach their objectives. We will then be in a position to understand the practical steps that parents, teachers, employers, and legislators can take to restore America's strong work values.

Although this book considers a variety of evidence on laziness and industriousness, I have excluded almost all opinion polls. Most polls mislead more than they inform. When asked about an issue that has moral overtones, many people try to impress the interviewer by claiming they behave in socially acceptable ways. For example, near the close of the 1986 Congressional campaign, ninety-four percent of those questioned in a large, representative sample of American adults eligible to vote stated they would definitely vote or were highly likely to vote. In fact, only about one-third of the public voted. Laziness is not something about which a majority of the adult population is willing to tell the truth.

People feel comfortable agreeing with work values that sound good in principle while not forcing them to admit laziness to themselves or others. Would you agree with the statement that "Working hard on the job is important to the economic future of the United States?" A nice sentiment, but *important* compared to what? And what does *working hard on the job* entail? Putting forth greater effort then one's fellow employees? Greater than one's parents? Greater than the Japanese? Greater than one's own effort last week?

Pollsters sometimes try to escape the difficulty of interpreting the replies to their vague questions by reporting the change in sentiment from one year to another. Say eighty-five percent of those questioned five years ago agreed that hard work was important for the nation's future, and now only seventy-eight percent agree. Does this mean the work ethic is suffering a decline? Not necessarily. The number of people agreeing with the statement tells us nothing about the individual's strength of belief or actual job performance. A decline over the years in the proportion of people agreeing with a pro-work statement might disguise an increasing commitment among those who continue to respond affirmatively.

Attitude questionnaires can be used effectively to infer work values if carefully worded to allow respondents to express strength of agreement and if demonstrated to predict actual job performance. We will consider questionnaires that measure the strength of agreement with work values, paying special attention to questions that have been shown to predict actual performance at school or work.

Any writer who tries to deal seriously with important public issues faces the problem that the media explosion of the last decade has encouraged novelty and sensationalism rather than substance. I have attempted to discuss a diversity of evidence on the nature and causes of laziness and industriousness by steering a middle course between the convoluted jargon of the textbook and the bombast of the "how to" book or the "sky is falling" book. I have also tried to keep in mind Steven Jay Gould's criterion for a solid piece of scientific work:

Everyone appreciates a nifty idea or an abstraction that makes a person sit up, blink hard several times to clear the intellectual cobwebs, and reverse a cherished opinion. But science deals in the workable and soluble, the idea that can be fruitfully embodied in concrete objects suitable for poking, squeezing, manipulating, and extracting. The idea that counts in science must lead to fruitful work, not only to speculation . . . no matter how much it stretches the mind![1]

CHAPTER 1

Americans Used to Try Harder

Older people living now grew up during an era when the Protestant Ethic, with its emphasis on hard work and little play, was particularly strong. Many researchers assume that the Protestant Ethic still affects the attitudes of older people. . . .

Karen Hooker and Deborah G. Ventis

He saw that she was tall and handsome, and decked out in gay finery, with her cheeks a bit too red to look natural; and she said to him: "Young man, I see you are in doubt what to do, and what path of life to follow. I invite you to follow me; you shall have the easiest and pleasantest life in the world, no hard work and no dangers; you shall eat, drink, and be merry, others shall work and you shall have the enjoyment, and you shall be as happy as the day is long." And Heraclês said, "What is your name?" The woman answered, "My real name is Pleasure, but my enemies call me Vice."

W. H. D. Rouse

The Protestant Ethic prodded the early settlers of America to **work** strenuously for the glory of God and the well-being of the **com-munity.** John Winthrop, who became the first governor of **Mas-sachusetts,** told the newly-arrived Puritan immigrants:

We must be knit together in this work as one man, we must entertain each other in brotherly affection. We must be willing to abridge ourselves of our superfluities, for the supply of others' necessities. We must delight in each other, make others' condition our own, rejoice together, mourn together, labor and suffer together, always having before our eyes our commission and community in the work, our community as members of the same body.[1]

The Puritans espoused the Calvinist belief that Heaven was preordained for a select group of believers. Ethical behavior would not clear the path to Paradise. But hard work and charity helped convince oneself and neighbors of personal membership in the elect. Not that the Puritans were as stuffy and straight-laced as they are popularly portrayed. Enjoying the fruits of one's labor was permitted since the Bible directed: "You may labor to be rich for God, though not for the flesh or sin."[2] Vigorous recreation that sharpened one's wits or strengthened one's body was entirely proper. Idleness rather than recreation was the enemy.[3]

The combination of abundant, easily-tapped natural resources and a free-enterprise economy taught positive work values by rewarding high effort. Protestant ministers found that sermons stressing diligence and the divine justification of material wealth were well received by those reaping the benefits of hard work. The incorporation of industriousness as an essential component of a righteous life became widely accepted during the eighteenth century by middle-class Americans, including farm owners, merchants, artisans, clerks, and teachers.

Initially, tenant farmers, unskilled laborers and others in the working class generally did not view work as morally uplifting. But they were willing to work hard to scrape up enough bare necessities to make life tolerable. Members of the upper class, the landed gentry, initially retained a preference for leisure inherited from their European forebears.[4] Slowly, a belief in the moral and instrumental value of work spread from the middle-class majority to the lower and upper classes.

American farmers were taught positive work values by the strong relationship between hard work and bountiful harvests. The American frontier, continually shifting westward, allowed poor people to own land. For the price of transportation, tenant farmers from the East or immigrants from Europe might settle on the frontier where land was free for the taking, the soil was rich, and there were no taxes. Gone were the crushing rents for the privilege of tilling a small plot. Moreover, American soil was often more fertile than Europe's, not having been drained of nutrients by centuries of cultivation without adequate crop rotation. A French immigrant wrote of the settlers:

> Here individuals of all nations are melted into a new race of men, whose labors and prosperity will one day cause great changes in the world. Here the rewards of his industry follow with equal steps the progress of his labor; this labor is founded on the basis of *self-interest*; can it want a stronger allurement? Wives and children, who before in vain demanded a morsel of bread, now fat and frolicsome, gladly help their father to clear those fields, whence exuberant crops are to arise to feed them; without any part being claimed either by a despotic prince, a rich abbot, or a mighty lord. . . . From involuntary idleness, servile dependence, penury, and useless labor, he has passed to toils of a very different nature rewarded by ample subsistence. This is an American.[5]

Large numbers of European artisans, unable to find steady work, indentured themselves to pay for the trip across the Atlantic. Many were sold on the Maryland auction block to large land owners. After working perhaps four years to earn freedom, a blacksmith or tailor was likely as not to ignore the demand for his skills in the Eastern cities. The dream of being one's own boss was often enough to cause tradesmen to take up farming on the frontier.[6]

On the farm, the husband plowed, planted, and hunted. The wife butchered the meat, salted and smoked it to be preserved, and rendered the fat for lard.[7] She faced a backbreaking set of daily household chores. She would grind the wheat or corn to make flour for use in baking. For fuel, if the family lived in grasslands, she would search for chunks of dried dung from cows or buffalo. The wife typically fetched water for drinking, cooking, and cleaning by carrying bucket after bucket from a nearby well. If the couple had been unlucky enough to settle on arid land, she might have to trudge a mile or more to the nearest stream or well, making repeated trips with a large wooden barrel or bucket. To make soap for washing and laundering, the wife would collect scraps of fat and ashes. These would be cooked down with lye. Clothes were washed by placing them in iron kettles filled with soapy water, scrubbing and pounding the garments, and then hanging them out to dry.

Since ready-made clothes were usually unavailable, long hours were often devoted to sewing basic items such as women's skirts and men's pants. Animal skins would be fashioned into coats, hats, and shoes. The wife might be required to produce her own yarns and wools from sheepskins. And she would improvise. Clothes lines often seen in Kansas suggested that sacks containing "I. M. Yost's High Patent Flour" could be sewn into excellent undergarments.[8]

The wife cared for her husband and children when they became ill. Without modern medicines, measles might send a child to bed for a month; pneumonia for six weeks. The death rate was high from such diseases as diphtheria, whooping cough, tetanus, measles, mumps, tuberculosis, smallpox, cholera, malaria, and polio.[9] Other pioneers were killed by Indian attacks or simply found conditions too inhospitable, and returned East. For those who had little experience farming, the heavy work seemed almost unbearable. Over the years, however, most settlers learned to abide the drudgery and monotony that filled their lives. They developed an industriousness and resilience that enabled them to withstand privations and overcome hardships, and they took pride in their success.[10]

Children growing up on frontier farms learned to work diligently since the whole family cooperated in the fight for survival. One of six daughters recalled the difficult labor and noted that "sometimes there were unpleasant things to be done but we never thought of shirking them."[11] Parents encouraged teachers and clergymen to reinforce children's strong work values; sons and daughters who worked hard would help the family prosper and earn the respect of the community.

Youngsters attended school only when farm chores and weather permitted. The curriculum involved reading, writing, grammar, spelling, and arithmetic. Discipline at school was strict. The subject matter was often tedious, including memorization of grammar rules and history dates. But most children had been inculcated by their parents with the value of education and were accustomed to carrying out assigned tasks with diligence and vigor. These values were reinforced by McGuffey readers, when available, that taught that industriousness was the mark of an upright citizen, as well as a way to advance one's material success. Teachers later remembered with great fondness the earnestness of most of their students.[12]

In growing cities and towns, craftsmen worked long hours in small shops at a measured pace, the production rate not yet dictated by the machine. An artisan would simply lay down his tools when he wished to socialize with a fellow worker. Proud of their skills, craftsmen felt free to move on if dissatisfied with their current job. The pleasure of carrying out work skillfully and the satisfaction in a job well done, values that stemmed from Europe's Renaissance, supplemented the moral and instrumental merits attributed to work. These interlaced attitudes made craftsmen the hardworking counterparts of industrious farmers.[13]

Pride of accomplishment in occupations such as law, medicine, and teaching took the form of professionalism. Such occupations gradually developed standards of education and conduct. As standards were raised and formalized, professional identity became a source of pride and a motive for carefully performing one's duties.

America's industriousness bemused European travelers and recent immigrants, one of whom observed:

> There is, probably, no people on earth with whom business constitutes pleasure, and industry amusement, in equal degree with the inhabitants of the United States of America. Active occupation is not only the principal source of their happiness, and the foundation of their national greatness, but they are absolutely wretched without it. . . . Business is the very soul of an American: he pursues it, not as a means of procuring for himself and his family the necessary comforts of life, but as the fountain of all human felicity . . . it is as if all America were but one gigantic workshop, over the entrance of which there is the blazing inscription, *"no admission here, except on business."*[14]

Nineteenth century Americans who espoused the utility and morality of hard work also valued recreation for providing rest and enjoyment. The industrious German immigrant farmers showed other Americans that entertainment on Sunday did not portend moral corruption or self-indulgence. The German farmers were much respected for their diligence. Other farmers might cut down trees without removing the stump, but the Germans laboriously dug out the stump and roots.[15] The dances, picnics, and other active amusements enjoyed by the Germans on Sundays convinced other settlers that a well-balanced life involved both prodigious work and refreshing entertainment.

The pioneers found time for horseback and sleigh rides, ice skating, hunting for sport, taffy pulls, group sings, literary society meetings, and amateur theatrical presentations. They also looked for excuses for celebrations. Although July fourth came only once a year, there were weddings, impromptu festivities, and surprise parties in which the guests stayed the night eating and dancing. The ladies in Topeka, Kansas, once decided to have a community dance for no greater reason than to celebrate the leap year. And if necessity dictated simple daily meals, the settlers enjoyed hearty feasts at parties and community dinners.[16]

Youngsters led active lives of work and play. Children worked hard on farm chores. The prosperity and parental approval that resulted from increased effort taught them strong work values. But when the day's chores were finished, there was usually plenty of time for play. Store-bought toys were too expensive so a youngster created toys of her own: "Strands of prairie grass were woven into toy crowns, berries were strung into necklaces, and old twigs were whittled into dolls and whistles."[17] One woman, looking back at her pioneer past, noted: "In children the sense of comparative values is largely undeveloped, and I doubt very much if children of the present day, with the profusion of toys now attainable, derive any more joy from their expensive array than did we, with the less expensive and simpler ones which Santa Claus gave us."[18]

Never in history had so many common people been given the opportunity to become economically self-sufficient through their own industriousness. Patricia Cain Smith, a psychologist at Bowling Green State University, prefers the term "personal work ethic" rather than the "Protestant Ethic" because basic beliefs in the instrumental and moral values of work became stronger even as the hold of the church weakened. This socialization process instilled

6

positive work attitudes in Protestant, Catholic, Jew, and atheist alike. By the middle of the nineteenth century, the personal work ethic had three strong intertwined components: a perceived moral duty as a worthwhile person to work hard; a willingness to exert high effort to achieve material well-being; and a pride in one's work skills and in the quality of the product or service that resulted.

With the coming of the industrial revolution, workers applied themselves to the new machines with skill and care. Their union leaders believed, as most Americans, in the inherent nobility of work. Terence Powderly, the Grand Master Workman of the Knights of Labor from 1879–1893, proclaimed:

> In the beginning God ordained that man should labor, not as a curse, but as a blessing; not as a punishment, but as a means of development, physically, mentally, morally, and has set there unto his seal of approval in the rich increase and reward. By labor is brought forth the kindly fruits of the earth in rich abundance for our sustenance and comfort; by labor (not exhaustive) is promoted health of body and strength of mind; labor garners the priceless stores of wisdom and knowledge. . . . Labor is noble and holy.[19]

But early labor leaders also expressed concern that the excesses of the factory system were degrading the inherent value of work. Grand Master Powderly argued:

> To glorify God in its exercise, to defend it from degradation, to divest it of the evils to body, mind and estate, to which ignorance and greed have imposed; to rescue the toiler from the grasp of the selfish is a work worthy of the noblest and best of our race.[20]

A minority of labor leaders complained that the workers' long hours of strenuous labor for low pay allowed factory owners to live in luxury and leisure. The Philadelphia Mechanics' Union of Trade Associations declared in 1826:

> Do not those who labor, while acquiring . . . only scanty and penurious support, . . . maintain in affluence and luxury the rich who never labor? Do not all the streams of wealth which flow in every

direction and are emptied into and absorbed by the coffers of the
unproductive, exclusively take their rise in the bones, marrow, and
muscles of the industrious classes? In return for which, exclusive of
bare subsistence . . . they receive not anything.[21]

America's industrialization made traditional skilled trades ob-
solete. In 1915, an unskilled factory worker produced fifty times
the quantity of most products that had been turned out by a skilled
tradesman twenty years earlier.[22] Similarly, motorized farm equipment, better fertilizers, and insecticides resulted in overproduction
of food, causing farmers to migrate to the cities. Factories greatly
improved the average standard of living for workers and consumers,
but brought longer hours of uninterrupted work, a frenetic pace,
and unemployment during economic slumps.

Henry Ford showed the way to mass production with the introduction of the world's first continuously moving assembly line. The
body of the Model T car passed before stationary workers, each of
whom was responsible for a limited sequence of repetitive actions.
The assembly line increased the speed of production of a great
variety of goods and became the backbone of the industrial revolution.

Engineers under the leadership of Frederick Taylor divided tasks
into their smallest elements in order to study how each element
could be performed most efficiently and with the least variability
in the final product. The plan was to define tasks and set production
standards on the basis of job analysis and time-and-motion research.
In one celebrated study, Taylor increased the amount of pig iron
loaded by an immigrant laborer named Schmidt from twelve and
one-half tons a day to forty-seven and one-half tons. Another study
found that the most efficient shovel load was twenty-one pounds,
meaning that a larger shovel was better for ashes than coal. This
led to the concept of tool standardization.[23] In the art of metal
cutting, Taylor conducted over 30,000 experiments using 800,000
pounds of steel and iron.[24] Applied to the assembly line, such
studies led to efficiencies in which each worker rapidly performed
a repetitive and fragmented task.

Mass production and standardization meant that a worker had
to do the same small operation over and over again. "The man who

places a part does not fasten it," said Ford proudly. "The man who puts in a bolt does not put on the nut; the man who puts on the nut does not tighten it."[25] The lack of skill involved in most assembly line jobs minimized pride of accomplishment. Laborers whose self-esteem had previously depended on their ability as artisans or farmers found little fulfillment in their new status as a machine's helper. Echoing the time-honored complaint of assembly line workers, a Chicago spot welder would later observe:

> I stand in one spot, about two- or three-feet area, all night. The only time a person stops is when the line stops. We do about 32 jobs per car, per unit. Forty-eight units an hour, eight hours a day. Thirty-two times forty-eight times eight. Figure it out. That's how many times I push that button. . . . Repetition is such that if you were to think about the job itself, you'd slowly go out of your mind.[26]

The fractionation of tasks allowed managers greater measurement and control over the individual worker's speed of performance. Competitive pressures and the desire for greater profits led manufacturers to lengthen the work day and speed up the production line at a cost to product quality. The line worker was usually not given enough time to perform his trivial task carefully. Charles Madison, a worker at the Ford factory, complained in 1913 that the only way he could meet his production schedule was to work for eight straight hours without a break and that "no allowance was made for lunch, toilet time, or tool sharpening." When Madison learned to keep up with his machine by working as hard as he could, he was told to work even faster.[27]

Karl Marx had previously argued that workers in a capitalistic society became alienated from what they produced, that the misery of the worker increased with "the power and volume of his production."[28] This prevented workers from developing their physical and mental capacities and made them "physically exhausted and mentally debased."[29] But the perceived efficiencies of industrialization transcended politics. Nicholai Lenin saw Taylorism as a powerful tool for increasing the efficiency of the Soviet Union's collectivized industries.[30]

Efficiency experts and managers were correct in their view that employees, if pushed, could work with incredible speed. But ignored for the sake of profit was the hard truth that relentless effort cannot be maintained too long without producing severe physiological and psychological stress-related disorders. The wife of an auto worker wrote Henry Ford in 1914, "The chain system you have is a *slave driver*. My God! Mr. Ford. My husband has come home & thrown himself down & won't eat his supper—so done out! Can't it be remedied? . . . ."[31]

Like pride of accomplishment, the belief in the instrumental value of industriousness was victimized by the assembly line. The unique American opportunity to earn bountiful rewards for increased effort was turned upside down. Faster performance on the assembly line brought demands for even greater speed with no greater pay. Increased effort also brought angry rebuffs from coworkers who saw themselves guarding against the speedup. Workers shunned and sometimes battered "rate busters," whose high performance provided an excuse for managers to demand greater speed from all workers.

The increased pace, repetitiveness, and fractionation of work produced boredom, frustration, and anger. Workers fought back. To avoid the speedup, they learned to make tasks appear to take more time than actually required. Employees formed unions that struck for better pay and working conditions, and cooperation between management and labor unions was replaced by an adversary relationship. In 1910, John Tobin of the Boot and Shoe Workers Union proclaimed the spreading union philosophy of "less work to more workers for better pay and shorter hours."[32] The unions demanded work rules that would limit the scope of the worker's job and the speed with which it had to be performed.

The moral value attributed to industriousness declined among factory workers. Laborers still looked askance at those who refused to hold down a full-time job. But working hard as a cog in the machinery created little feeling of moral uplift. Assembly line workers did not want to hear their preacher or priest proclaim that a righteous life was to be had in mind-numbing activity. Responding to their constituency, churches no longer emphasized, as part of sermons and Sunday school lessons, the moral uplift of hard work.

Before industrialization, leisure was viewed by most Americans as a refreshing rest from the main business of life, which was diligent work. By the 1920s, however, the fractionation of jobs and the speedup made work seem an unpleasant necessity, and idleness a luxury. Moreover, increasing prosperity and a desire for emotional release after the first world war made Americans receptive to an ethic of leisure and entertainment. Added to this mix was the need of manufacturers to find new goods to sell. As the production of such basic staples as shoes, cloth, and lumber became more efficient, supply began to outstrip demand. To tap the increasing affluence of Americans, manufacturers began producing nonessential items such as radios and automobiles, which were merchandised by stressing pleasure and diversion.

Teenagers and young adults who had never struggled to obtain the necessities of life viewed work as a discomforting interlude in socializing, sensual pleasures, and entertainment. The exaltation of entertainment and sensual satisfaction in advertisements and movies made self-denial and hard work seem dull and old-fashioned. The strong preoccupation with pleasure and entertainment made hard work during regular hours at school or job itself seem highly unpleasant. Devoting long hours to homework or overtime on the job was out of style, not part of the good life.

The number of people attending movies each week increased from an estimated ten million in 1910 to fifty million in 1926.[33] Sex magazines, confession tabloids and lurid motion pictures proliferated.[34] The confession magazine *True Story*, begun in 1919, had two million readers by 1926. Although the purchase of alcohol was banned by law, men and women began drinking together at petting parties. Being called a Puritan meant you were a "blue-nosed ranting spoilsport."[35]

Previously, assembly line workers had grumbled about the tedium of their jobs. Now, many white-collar employees and managers accepted the view that their own work was an unpleasantness to be gotten out of the way with a minimum of effort. Managers and clerks were usually less closely monitored than assembly line workers and found more opportunities to slack off and daydream. The traditional American balance of indefatigable work broken by short periods of exuberant entertainment was replaced increasingly by grudging work and unremitting pursuit of diversion.

11

In 1923, Henry Ford was still able to produce half the cars sold
in the world by relying on low cost and reliability and by garnering
free publicity in the press.[36] But that year, an epochal advertisement for a sports car offered romance, adventure, and excitement.
A hard riding cowboy pictured above a fancy roadster described
his fascination with a "bronco-busting, steer-roping" cowgirl west
of Laramie "whose face is brown with the sun when the day is done
of revel and romp and race. She loves the cross of the wild and
the tame. There's a savor of links about that car—of laughter and
lilt and light—a hint of old loves. . . ."[37]

The ad's success came at just the right time for Alfred P. Sloan,
the new president of General Motors, who sought to overcome
Ford's lead by using advertising to create a glamorous image for
those alterations of sheet metal and chrome disingenuously labeled
"new models." The emphasis on adventure and style helped GM
overtake Ford's sales, and encouraged other advertisers to appeal
to sensual desires.

Stanley Resor, who became a pioneer in the use of sensually
oriented advertising, was a student at Yale University and one of
many who flocked to the lectures of sociologist William Graham
Sumner. The professor characterized humanity as a faceless mass
driven by hunger, greed, vanity, and lust held in check only by
the bonds of culture.[38] After graduating, Resor formed a group of
investors who purchased a small advertising agency. Resor incorporated his teacher's views about human behavior into emotion-
based advertising appeals, and the J. Walter Thompson Company
soon became the largest ad agency in the United States.

To create effective appeals to consumers' wishes and desires,
Resor hired psychologist John B. Watson.[39] Watson performed an
experiment showing that blindfolded smokers were incapable of
identifying their favorite brand of cigarette. Watson proclaimed the
finding to indicate emotion, rather than reason, dictated consumer
preference.[40]

Before leaving academia, Watson had performed an experiment
with a one-year old infant named Albert who had no fear of small
animals. Watson presented little Albert a white rat. When the child
reached for it, Watson made a loud noise behind the child's head.
The process was repeated several times. Watson reported that the

child now cried at the sight of the rat and that the fear generalized to other animals. Watson argued that such an association process is responsible for the way in which emotions such as lust, fear, or rage come to be elicited to previously neutral objects.[41] To Watson, this meant that a client's product should be paired with themes that appeal to strong emotions. Although Watson did not work on the creation of specific ads at J. Walter Thompson, his prominent position at the company and his speeches to the ad industry's gatherings reinforced the use of the emotional sell.

Advertisements for a variety of products appealed to sensual appetites and a self-concern with sex appeal. Women were introduced to cigarettes with ads that showed alluring females asking men to blow smoke their way, and cigarette sales doubled during the 1920s. Woodbury Facial Soap pictured an elegantly-dressed couple in embrace, with the caption: "A skin you love to touch."[42] Helena Rubinstein claimed her hand cream "will make you beautiful. And to be beautiful is to be a woman."[43]

Applying color to ones face and finger nails had been considered immoral by many women before the 1920s. But by 1930, estimates indicated that annual sales in the United States amounted to a pound of face cream and eight rouge compacts for every adult woman in the United States.[44] By 1946, a sampling of 1,000 women revealed that "99 percent used lipstick, 95 percent nail polish, 94 percent face powder, 80 percent makeup base, 73 percent perfume, and 71 percent cleansing cream."[45]

The flip side of appealing to sensual desires was promoting fear of offending others by how one looked or smelled. New terms were coined to instill fear of social disrepute among the masses, such as halitosis ("Often a Bridesmaid But Never a Bride") and B.O. (body odor). Deodorant started as a women's product with the copy: "It is a physiological fact that persons troubled with perspiration odor seldom can detect it themselves."

In 1931, well into the Great Depression, a college professor named George Gallup observed that ads in magazines appealed most frequently to economy and efficiency. Interviewing 15,000 people, Gallup found little recall of such ads. It turned out that men remembered appeals to quality most frequently followed by sexually oriented ads. Women remembered sex first, then, vanity, and quality. Evidently, even in difficult economic times the public was attracted by sexual themes. Gallup received job offers from many ad agencies, one of which he accepted, and his findings caused the advertising industry to increase its use of nudity and sexual innuendo.[46]

The effects of the uninhibited 1920s on attitudes toward work and sensuality accelerated changes begun decades before. Millions of Americans continued to resist sensual preoccupations. Farm families and self-employed merchants still learned industriousness from the increased rewards received for high effort. The great majority of Americans still believed a job was a basic part of a proper life, and most felt they owed their employer a fair amount of work. Moreover, fear of job loss during the Great Depression slowed the decline of work values. But the corner had been turned.

In the 1930's, the general shortening of the work week from six days to five gave the majority of Americans, those who held steady jobs, more time for leisure activities. Ads continued to promote entertainment and leisure as an important part of people's lives.[47] The decay of work values produced by the excesses of the factory system and the promotion of sensual pleasure and entertainment would accelerate once prosperity returned.

During the first three decades following the second world war, an expanding economy produced a widespread increase in affluence. Discounting inflation, average family income doubled between 1950 and 1973.[48] Social security and other entitlement programs began to provide a greater financial cushion against poverty and helped pay medical costs of the elderly. From 1960 to 1981, social security coverage was extended from 60 percent of the elderly to 92 percent, and more liberal payments greatly reduced the number of senior citizens living in poverty.[49] Young Americans did not have to save as much since the government would partially provide for basic needs in old age. As affluence increased, most Americans came to believe that the continued personal and national economic gain would proceed without hard work.

Structural changes in the economy reduced the availability of jobs that previously had inculcated strong work values. Family-owned small farms and businesses ceased to afford a practical job possibility for most people. Farming continued to become more efficient, requiring fewer workers. The number of farmers dropped from a quarter of the population in 1920 to one-tenth that number in 1981.[50] Opportunities to own a small retail business were reduced; large chain stores undersold and replaced mom-and-pop businesses. The number of self-employed Americans dropped from 80 percent in 1800 to only 8 percent in 1970.[51]

The decline in the numbers of farmers and merchants meant that work values would no longer be strengthened by a strong connection between effort and the size of reward. A factory worker's salary depended on union—management contracts rather than how hard he or she worked. For white collar employees in large companies, pay raises and advancement were more often the result of longevity or office politics than diligent work. Few Americans who worked in factories or chain stores possessed the same dedication to jobs as their parents, who owned small farms or retail stores.

The emphasis on entertainment and sensual pleasure begun by manufacturers and advertisers in the 1920s, became a more dominant theme in the popular culture. Magazines and the entertainment media increasingly stressed diversion and sensual satisfaction as more important than hard work. Before 1950, articles in popular magazines claimed a variety of benefits for industriousness in school and on the job. Some authors had stressed God's ordination of labor. Others noted the importance of diligence for success in school and the influence of such attitudes on subsequent pride of accomplishment on the job. Industriousness, the reader might also be told, would develop character, bring business success, increase national productivity, and produce happiness.[52]

After 1950, the benefits of industriousness were rarely mentioned in magazines. The importance of enjoying life and pursuing pleasure began to be emphasized in the 1940s and especially after 1960.[53] A careful observer of changing work values, David Cherrington, noted:

> It is uncomfortable for an author to swim against the tide of popular opinion, and it does not sell magazines. Proselyting for diligence, industry, and frugality was unfashionable and unpopular. Consequently, the work ethic was not taught or passed on to succeeding generations as enthusiastically as it had been in earlier years.[54]

Advertisers' emphasis on leisure and sensual enjoyment made the self-denial required to achieve long-term goals all the more discomforting. This increasing glorification of sensual satisfaction is exemplified by cosmetics ads. By 1960, Helena Rubinstein was advertising in the New York Times with a picture of herself next to the statue of the Venus de Milo and the caption: "The same female hormones found in Ultra Feminine Face Cream gave Venus her form."[55] Estee Lauder suggested that her new cream was worth $115 a pound in 1960 dollars because it made a woman look "younger, fresher, lovelier than you ever dreamed possible." Women were invited to become sensually irresistible by smearing themselves with Lauder's creme advertised to contain turtle oil and the jelly that worker bees brought to their queen.[56]

At the same time that sensual pleasure and entertainment were being promoted by magazine writers and advertisers, the portrayal of families in weekly television series in the 1950s and 60s denigrated the value of working-class jobs. Middle class parents (professionals, managers, and sales workers other than retail clerks) were shown more frequently in proportion to their actual numbers than working class parents (craft workers, laborers, and most service occupations).[57] The economic concerns of working class families, such as worrying about making ends meet or saving for the future, were seldom shown.[58] From 1950 to 1980 there were two dominant themes in television series concerning working class family life:

> . . . the working-class father and husband [appeared] inept, dumb, or bumbling, a characterization which seldom appeared in middle-class family portrayals; and upward mobility not only economically into middle-class occupations but also in terms of acquiring, or identifying with, middle-class lifestyle. The inept husband theme predominates in the 1950s working class series, while the upward mobility theme has prevailed in the 1970s. Both themes—taken together with the underrepresentation of working-class family life —serve to weaken the dignity and legitimacy of working-class family lifestyle by both emphasis and omission. The first theme is built upon slapstick humor which laughs *at* rather than with the working-class characters. The second theme usually appears where the working-class family is given some dignity. It represents working class-

ness as a one-generation phenomenon and as a condition to escape from rather than as a way of being-in-the-world which has desirable features that a working-class family might not want to relinquish as the price of economic mobility.[59]

The fractionation of work, the speedup, the denigration of manual labor by the entertainment industry, and the emphasis on leisure and sensual satisfaction by advertisers and entertainment programmers led factory workers to view their jobs as having little value other than pay. Owners and managers of large manufacturing companies became locked in an adversary relationship with their unionized employees who disdained hard work. Demands by unions for high wages and for inefficient work rules to guard against the speedup could be granted in basic industries without producing a competitive disadvantage because the major companies acted in concert to pass these costs to the consumer.[60]

The steel industry led the nation in complacency that resulted from vast profits achieved with little competition. In 1956, the major steel companies signed a contract with hourly workers that surrendered management's right to make changes in established labor practices. This meant that job responsibilities, once assigned, could seldom be expanded, altered, or eliminated to conform to changing needs. The past-practices rule became an excuse by laborers to remain idle while collecting the highest wages in the nation. William Heil, a former draftsman in Bethlehem Steel's plant in Pottstown, Pennsylvania, remembered:

> It was common to see a job where two or three guys were standing around because of work rules. In beam fabrication, one guy would come along and set up the location of the angle, the other guy would come along and tack-weld it, and a third guy would be needed to check it. In a nonunion plant, one guy did all the work. There wasn't the luxury of doing one particular job.[61]

Union contracts gave Americans more time to enjoy their new affluence. The eight-hour workday became standard, vacations were extended to two or three weeks for most workers, and there were an average of nine paid holidays.[62] The standard of living

17

continued to rise since mechanization in most industries increased productivity even more quickly than wages, and the inferior products of foreign manufacturers provided little competition.

As large American manufacturing firms became middle-aged, the entry of new companies into the market was discouraged by the enormous expense of plant and equipment that would be required to match the economies of scale achieved by the older companies. With limited domestic and foreign competition, managers grew indolent. Executives created their own small empires within a company by increasing the number of managers and white collar workers far beyond the number actually needed. Middle level managers in the bloated bureaucracy at Chrysler Corporation mindlessly prepared reports whose purpose had been forgotten long before.[63]

Salaried employees became less willing than their predecessors to work nights, weekends, or vacations, and the quality of their work no longer served as a source of pride. This lethargy encouraged pastimes on the job that had previously been considered non-job related leisure. At Bethlehem Steel's corporate headquarters:

> Upper-level executives found copies of the *New York Times* and the *Wall Street Journal* on their desks when they came to work. Reading them commanded the highest priority during the first hours of the morning. The lower ranks brought in the local papers to catch up on the community news, ball scores, and race results before beginning their own labors.[64]

If working-class television viewers were taught that their jobs were laughable, the work ethic among well-educated professionals such as college professors, teachers, clinical psychologists, physicians, and lawyers was assaulted by the human potential movement. Given an early impetus by psychologists Abraham Maslow and Carl Rogers, the new philosophy preached "experiential learning" by getting "in touch" with one's own feelings.[65] Individuals were taught to attribute dissatisfaction with their jobs or personal lives to a failure to behave "authentically": "the belief that there is a 'real self' inside the individual who is not getting a chance to express himself. The surface person, the one who is behaving in the world every day, is not that real person."[66]

Attempting to understand feelings and emotions through an undefined nonintellectual process was stressed over the self-denial and effort required to pursue materialistic goals. Human potential practitioners employed T-groups and sensitivity training in which people would be placed in an unstructured situation and encouraged to engage in "here-and-now" emotional experiences. Some companies used such training to make managers more sensitive to employees' "feelings."[67] Laboratory manuals used for organizational-behavior courses in business schools and college psychology departments included pseudo-scientific exercises designed to make students more aware of their feelings. Terms like self-actualization, self-fulfillment, and self-realization were used to connote a state of bliss to be gained by communion with one's essence. From this viewpoint, there was something inherently wrong with working hard toward conventional goals.

As the availability of good-paying jobs for skilled laborers and college graduates began to be taken for granted in the 1960s, young people reared in an era that glorified self-concern and sensual pleasure became ever less willing to work hard at school or the job for the high standard of living to which they felt entitled. Student radical leaders during the campus rebellions of the late 1960s denigrated any work that did not bring "self-fulfillment". Pride of accomplishment and financial rewards were discounted in favor of schooling or work that promoted self-discovery or social benefit. Mario Savio, the student leader at Berkeley, helped lead the nationwide student rebellion by arguing:

> . . . the schools have become training camps—and proving grounds—rather than places where people acquire education. They become factories to produce technicians rather than places to live student lives. And this perversion develops great resentment on the part of the students. Resentment against being subjected to standard production techniques of speedup and regimentation; against a tendency to quantify education—virtually a contradiction in terms. Education is measured in units, in numbers of lectures attended,

in numbers of pages devoted to papers, numbers of pages read. This mirrors the gross and vulgar quantification in the society at large—the *real* world—where everything must be reduced to a lowest common denominator, the dollar bill. In our campus play-world we use play money, course units.[68]

The counterculture college students believed they were rejecting the prevailing system of American values. They failed to understand that their search for self-expression matched the self-indulgence of business people or that they were acting in concert with the advertising industry and entertainment media to squeeze the remaining life out of the traditional American work ethic. Many prevalent beliefs of the counterculture were *exaggerations* of the sensualism that had begun in the 1920s and had been inculcated in later generations by television and the movies.

The counterculture also drew on the human-potential movement, accepting primacy of feeling over thought, and living for today rather than working for future goals. Many students attempted to get "in touch" with themselves by meditating. They tried to share their inner being with others by touching, hugging, gazing into each other's eyes. The counterculture students' major beliefs were aptly portrayed by pollster and social critic Daniel Yankelovich, including the following.

- To place sensory experience ahead of conceptual knowledge.
- To de-emphasize aspects of nature illuminated by science; instead, to celebrate all the unknown, the mystical, and the mysterious elements of nature.
- To embrace the existential emphasis on *being* rather than doing or planning.
- To devalue detachment, objectivity, and noninvolvement as methods for finding truth; to arrive at truth, instead by direct experience, participation, and involvement.
- To reject mastery over nature.
- To dispense with organization, rationalization, and cost-effectiveness.
- To reject mores and rules that interfere with natural expression and function (e.g., conventional sexual morality).[69]

By the early 1970s, the campus rebellion lost its support among the majority of students. Only a small minority of counter-culture proponents followed their affirmation of the sensual pleasure to the logical extreme of dropping out from college or a well-paying job. The mental self-destruction of drug cultists like Timothy Leary hardly seemed a good advertisement for a complete devotion to pleasure. But millions of college and high school students struck a compromise weighted toward immediate gratification. The sensual pleasure of drugs joined that of alcohol as an escape from reality.

The focus on a pleasant present promoted by advertisers, the entertainment industry, the youth counterculture, and the human potential movement seeped into middle class attitudes and discouraged the self-denial required to pursue long-term goals. Yankelovich found on the basis of careful polling, accompanied by in-depth interviews, that self-fulfillment became an important concern for a majority of Americans.[70] He noted most of those interviewed did not seem to be clear on what self-fulfillment meant, but that they knew it did not involve persistent effort. The emphasis on "finding oneself" and immediate gratification reduced the willingness of young Americans to work hard for the materialistic pleasures that formed a large part of their muddled definition of the good life.

The minority of managers who took pride in their work, who viewed with alarm the obsolescence of manufacturing equipment and the decline of product quality, tried to call attention to the growing threat of foreign competitors. Meeting a solid wall of opposition, they acquiesced, quit their jobs, or were fired. Ambitious executives, unencumbered by traditional work values, sought to satisfy stockholders and earn hefty bonuses by maximizing their company's short-term profit at the expense of future gains. To show immediate profits, top managers reduced the quality of their products and lessened investment in research and new equipment.

Executives welcomed new M.B.A.s fresh out of business school who believed they could manage any industry based on "scientific principles" of finance and production without having to find out much about products or production processes. Talented finance people such as Robert McNamara, who eventually came to run

Ford, increased profits by eliminating funds for the modernization of production equipment and facilities, by sacrificing product quality, and denying funds for research projects.[71]

The strategy was a great short-term success. American industry earned increasing profits with shoddier products:

> During [the] get-rich-quick 1960s, the cult of New Greed infected American industry. As sales volume increased, once-sturdy appliances were built with their internal workings fabricated from the cheapest of stampings. Furniture appeared with flimsy fiberboard backings and drawer bottoms. Staples replaced nails, metal screws were substituted for nuts and bolts, cheap die-castings made forgings obsolete and suddenly everything, from the grilles on our automobiles to the clock radios at our bedsides, was make of plastic. . . .[72]

Steel and car manufacturers, America's richest industries, set the pattern for the others. Despite increasing foreign competition, major American steel companies continued for decades to play the lazy and greedy game of milking short-term profits at the expense of research, investment in new equipment, and product quality. Because of economies of scale, promoted by increased production during the second world war, America could manufacture steel more cheaply than the Japanese or Europeans. However, the large American steel companies refused to modernize as more efficient production processes were introduced overseas and in small specialized American steel plants. The steel executives also gave in to union demands for large pay increases and restrictive work rules. With a shared monopoly over American sales, the large domestic steel producers sat back, raking in huge profits without worrying about modernization.

By about 1960, the production cost advantage of American steel over foreign competitors had been reversed by the failure to replace outmoded equipment, by bloated numbers of employees at all ranks, by inefficient work rules, and by high salaries and wages. America changed from an exporter to an importer of steel.[73] Despite this clear signal of impending crisis, the steel industry retained its short-term outlook. Corporate executives, having grown accustomed to huge profits and bonuses, refused to believe that their comfortable world could go astray. They made few changes as the cost disadvantage of producing American steel worsened for another two decades.

The crisis finally became apparent in the late 1970s when a quarter of the steel used in America was produced by foreign concerns. Employment in the domestic steel industry plunged from 700,000 in 1978 to 140,000 in 1986. The steel companies lost a total of $11 billion from 1982 to 1986.[74] In 1986, the second largest steel company, LTV, declared bankruptcy.

The laziness, complacency, and emphasis on short-term profits of the steel companies were shared by the automobile manufacturers. In the early 1970s, oil prices increased to many times their prior level. The greater price of energy raised the cost of producing a car's body and engine components. It was clear to many observers both within and outside the auto industry that the higher prices consumers had to pay for gas and standard size cars would increase the market for small, fuel efficient models.[75] Since larger cars earned much greater profits, the American auto makers used their shared monopoly to ignore the public's changing needs.

Even before the oil crisis, the tiny Volkswagen car, imported from Germany, sold well in the United States. The VW was getting 32 miles to a gallon of gas in the 1950s.[76] From 1968 to 1973, *before* the Arab oil embargo, sales of large American cars increased only 10 percent, compared to 122 percent for small foreign cars.[77] But because GM, Ford, and Chrysler dominated the American auto industry as a shared monopoly with little foreign competition, there was little market pressure to force modernization of plant and equipment or the production of fuel-efficient cars.

GM was not willing to exert the effort and spend the money even to match the advances in car design being made overseas. In 1973, Pete Estes was a top executive at GM who would soon rise to its presidency. He received a report indicating that Europeans had made an important engineering breakthrough with the introduction of front-wheel drive. By eliminating the drive shaft necessary to power the rear wheels, front-wheel driven cars would be lighter and more fuel-efficient than present models. Moreover, drivers found such cars easy to handle. Estes rejected the suggestion to begin working on front-wheel technology by relating the following story:

> When I was at Oldsmobile, there was something I learned that I've never forgotten. There was an old guy who was an engineer, and he had been at GM for a long time, and he gave me some advice. He told me, whatever you do, don't let GM do it first.[78]

The GM principle was to let others work industriously on technical innovations which, if successful, would then be incorporated into the company's cars. Previously the world's leading innovator in automobile technology, GM became lackadaisical and unwilling to match competitors' breakthroughs except when clearly necessary to retain market share. Oil crisis or not, Detroit continued to build big, expensive cars that brought much greater profits per unit than small, fuel-efficient compacts.

Auto makers refused to expend much effort working to develop small cars until the fuel-efficient Japanese compacts garnered a quarter of American auto sales. One half-hearted stab at the small car market was the Ford Pinto, a poorly-engineered subcompact introduced in 1970 that was thrown together cheaply and quickly. The Pinto was infamous for high repair bills and safety problems.[79]

Another example of Detroit's complacency and refusal to work hard on new technology was the failure to design a fuel-efficient bus with a capability to carry disabled passengers. There was a strong demand for such a bus both in the U.S. and overseas. The federal government was willing to provide financial support for bus re-design. But GM used its virtual monopoly over bus sales in America to keep producing buses with the same old chassis and engine.[80]

The result of the car companies' indolence and arrogance was a great loss of sales to innovative foreign manufacturers. In 1981, twenty-nine percent of cars sold in America were manufactured overseas.[81] Steel and autos, America's largest basic industries, had sown the seed of their own destruction.

By the mid 1980s, the three foundations of Americans' traditional strong work values were gone. Although holding down a job was still valued for respectability and income by most Americans, the fractionation of jobs and emphasis on short-term profits had destroyed the moral basis for industriousness as well as pride of accomplishment. Family-owned farms and businesses had been replaced by jobs in large organizations where increased effort no longer brought greater reward. Life styles involving sensual pleasure and entertainment dominated over positive work values.

Managers were using computer-programmable machinery to replace human skill in the remaining minority of industrial jobs that engendered pride of accomplishment, further damaging the work ethic. Automated equipment requires careful attention to prevent malfunctions that may damage products and the machinery itself. Managers want the operators to use the new, expensive machinery carefully. But the elimination of skill requirements reduces pride in work and promotes inattention and sloppiness.

One might think such automation simply substitutes one group of skilled employees for another. After all, engineers and technicians are needed to design and program automated equipment. It is true that some new forms of technology have increased pride of accomplishment by enhancing human creativity. The design of computer hardware and writing computer programs require great skill and reward innovation. Computer-aided design gives engineers an instant three-dimensional representation of an evolving plan for a car, airplane, or building. Computerized word processing allows rapid revisions in manuscripts. Computer spread sheets give managers a better understanding of the relative rates of production of an array of products that would maximize profit.

But most new technology is designed to speed production and lessen the involvement of human skills.[82] Managers have increasingly opted to make the jobs of engineers and programers themselves less skillful through standardized programs. One computer-aided program used to design tools that was developed by McDonald-Douglas eliminates the programer completely and reduces the options of the engineer by providing a "menu" of simple two-dimensional shapes that the engineer assembles on the computer screen just as one would use an erector set.[83]

The blind rush to substitute machine skill for human skill continues to lessen pride of accomplishment and detract from America's advantage over Japan and other competitors in worker skill and innovation. The drawbacks of completely separating the planner from the workers who are knowledgeable about the product and skilled in the implementation of engineering designs may be illustrated by an anecdote from a British aircraft factory:

> A young engineer designed the igniter for an aircraft turbine engine using the latest in computer-assisted design. The design was then produced on an numerical-control [computerized] machine tool. Somewhere in the process, a decimal point was accidentally moved one place to the right, resulting in a monster igniter, ten times normal size. When a worker lugged this giant igniter into the engineering office, the designer reportedly looked it over and commented on how good the design appeared, apparently unaware of the error. What is comical when it is this outrageous mistake could be devastating in countless more subtle ways when the error is more difficult to detect and therefore might go into use unnoticed. [84]

To catch up with the Japanese, General Motors invested billions of dollars in robots, computers, and telecommunications equipment during the last few years. Manufacturing costs nevertheless remained high, and for the first time in decades GM's profits dipped below Ford's. [85] GM failed to choose machines that complemented operators' current skills or to properly train operators. One engineer privately complained that he was required to teach operators the computerized control of robots even though he had little knowledge of the machines himself. [86]

The problems caused by skill-killing automation are becoming more severe for American companies that station their management and engineers in the U.S. and their factories overseas. The purpose is to take advantage of cheaper foreign labor costs. But new technology that provides instant audiovisual contact between stations thousands of miles apart is not a substitute for the cooperation between planners and skilled workers. The erector set factory in a foreign country, manned by an inexperienced work force and directed by planners in the U.S., fails to provide valuable interaction between engineer and skilled worker, and deadens the work ethic of all concerned.

The love affair of managers with speed of production at the

expense of product quality is now being extended to the service industry. There is an increasing use of the power of the computer to monitor worker performance in order to enforce greater speed. The time that telephone operators and service representatives spend per phone call is now recorded by many companies. Pride of accomplishment is destroyed for workers ordered to get callers off the line as soon as possible.

Two hundred reservation agents at Pacific Southwest Airlines in San Diego are expected to average 109 seconds per call and 11 seconds between calls, during which time they are required to complete paperwork.[87] The emphasis on speed reduces quality of service by operators and service representatives who try to maintain the required pace. Spending the time to look up answers to any but the simplest questions would cost the individual his or her job. It is much safer to give incorrect or incomplete information.

The tedium and exhaustion produced by the speedup of the production line is matched by the experience of clerical workers who sit hour after hour at a computer terminal obeying a simple set of rules used to tally a consumer's credit purchases or to maintain a myriad of financial records. Of the 17 million office workers who operate video display terminals, an estimated 20 to 40 percent are monitored by computer.[88] Credit card companies, banks, and stock brokers, caught up in America's craze for short-term profits, frequently provide inadequate numbers of back room staff to handle paperwork and continually demand greater speed.

As with assembly line workers who learned tricks to defeat the speedup, clerks have learned to sacrifice quality of performance to meet management's demands. Under time pressure, consumer questions about bills are often ignored and letters are sometimes thrown away unanswered. Employees of the Internal Revenue service were discovered in 1985 to have discarded thousands of tax returns. This constitutes only a small percentage of the total number of returns, but would no doubt have been much greater if employees did not fear getting caught.

John Gardner pleaded for making "technology serve man not only in the end product but in the doing."[89] Workers must be allowed to employ greater skill if pride of accomplishment is to be placed in the service of maintaining high product quality. The time

27

is passing when America's economy can be sustained with junk goods and careless services.

A variety of forces have combined to weaken Americans' work ethic over the last century. The bountiful rewards for increased effort provided by a capitalist economy and plentiful natural resources were destroyed when family-owned farms and businesses were replaced by large companies. The fractionation of jobs and the speedup, first in the factory and more recently in the service industry, reduced pride in work. The promotion of leisure and sensual satisfaction by manufacturers, advertisers, and the entertainment industry lessened managers' and laborers' willingness to forgo immediate satisfaction in order to work industriously toward long-term goals. The worship of wealth and power created an emphasis on short-term profits at the expense of the quality of goods and services.

Ambition and materialism remain as strong as ever in today's America. But compared to past generations and much of the current industrialized world, most Americans must be considered lazy and pleasure-seeking. In 1986, the nation celebrated the two-hundredth anniversary of the Constitution with speeches that glorified America's freedoms. Americans must realize that the nation prospered not merely because we were free and possessed vast natural resources but because we were the most industrious people on earth. Foreign critics claim that American individualism and freedom are incompatible with self-discipline. Let us hope they are wrong.

CHAPTER 2

Laziness Among Affluent Americans

During the 1870s, some 200 members of the British aristocracy and gentry settled in the barren lands of central Kansas. Their ranches were stocked with excellent breeds of draft horses, English rams, and short-horned cattle.[1] These settlers called their community Victoria after the home country's monarch and practiced leisure more than work. Surrounded by pioneers struggling to procure life's necessities, the wealthy Victorians recruited these others to run ranches, cook meals, wash clothes, and attend to all the mundane chores of everyday life while they themselves concentrated on cricket, fox hunting, banquets and parties.

French satins and English tweeds were the proper dress. Adorned in traditional British hunting attire, the Victorians chased rabbit and coyote as they had chased fox in England. Afternoons were frequently devoted to cricket for the men, while wives chatted over tea and crumpets. Evenings were reserved for banquets, balls, and parties. Sumptuous dinners, served on long tables, might include "baked buffalo, antelope and quail, mince pies, plum puddings, and tipsy cake, and after the dinner a dance that lasted till morning."[2]

The Victorians amused and bemused Kansans. One observer

noted, "The colony was composed principally of gentlemen's sons who had been taught no occupation but sent out with their pockets full of money, which they spent freely, knowing that in due time another remittance would arrive."[3] But even a sheltered and luxurious life on the prairie seemed too difficult for the Victorians. Within a few years all of them returned to England.

Hardworking pioneers laughed at the airs and indolence of the Victoria colony, as today the industrious peoples of Switzerland, Japan, Hong Kong, and Canada dismiss an America they view grown lethargic and complacent. The decline of the work ethic has produced a majority culture of affluent Americans who will not work hard to maintain their comfortable standard of living, and a minority culture of poor Americans who will not persevere to overcome their impoverishment. The aversion to labor that permeates American life will, unless reversed, continue to erode our nation's economic strength. Like the Soviet Union, the United States will be considered a world power primarily because of military might, not for any economic superiority.

Americans today show less capacity than previous generations to forgo instant gratification in order to pursue long-term goals. The ethic of leisure, entertainment, and sensual satisfaction, promoted by advertisers and the entertainment industry, has replaced a strong personal work ethic. More than ever in America's past, diligent work is viewed as an unpleasant interlude in the socializing, sensual pleasures and entertainment that preoccupy most people. Such continual desire for a pleasant present decreases the willingness to exert high effort at school or on the job.

The appetite for immediate gratification promoted by the leisure ethic has caused American consumers to spend well beyond their means. At this writing, consumer debt has reached an astounding 83 percent of income, up from 37 percent five years ago.[4] The nation's personal savings rate has dropped from a meager 7.5 percent five years ago to less than 4 per cent today.[5] It is true that older Americans can afford to borrow more than in the past because of the appreciation of real estate and stock. But the reduction in savings is due almost entirely to the carefree spending of young Americans born after 1940. Among the younger populace, savings have declined to a minuscule level of three percent of earnings. According to Michael J. Boskin, an economist at Stanford University who demonstrated the profligate spending of younger Americans, "The first explanation that springs to mind is the 'Me generation.' "[6] In short, younger Americans have become increasingly self-indulgent.

Because of fierce competition for new customers, most credit card companies now mail out pre-approved applications based not on an individual's creditworthiness but where the consumer lives as indicated by zip code. In 1986, 105.5 million card holders held 731 million cards, about seven cards for every card holder. Many people whose applications would have been rejected as a poor risk five years ago now hold multiple cards.[7] Borrowing increased by 18 percent in 1985, and 11 percent in 1986.[8] Bankruptcies and delinquencies began to soar as consumers found it more difficult to pay off their debt. There were 569,000 personal bankruptcies in 1986, up by a third from the year before.[9] Although part of this increase stems from the worsening markets for farm and oil products, most of the rise appears due to freer spending habits.

Why should the majority of Americans who spend imprudently expect their government to act differently? The American public, caught up in rapacious consumption, is content to receive the benefits of the government's deficit spending and to mortgage the nation's future. Combined federal, state, and local government outlays have reached $19,000 annually per household.[10] The national savings rate, which combines personal, business, and government savings, is now running one-half to one-third that of European nations and one-fifth that of Japan.[11] Since savings provide funds for investment in research and development, the nation's future economic competitiveness will suffer.

We have gone from the world's greatest creditor nation to the greatest debtor.[12] Although the increase in debt is no longer accelerating from year to year, the total amount owed continues to rise massively. It would not be so bad if this money were an investment in the future. But we are borrowing primarily to keep taxes low, allow high consumer spending, and make interest payments. Interest paid on the federal debt during the last five years doubled from $69 billion to $136 billion.[13] Because of self-indulgence, our children will have to lower their standard of living to pay off the principal and compounded interest on the huge debt.[14]

England provides a model of the negative effects of devoting too large a share of economic resources to personal consumption rather than investment in the nation's future. In 1860, British hourly employees earned two and one-half times as much as their German counterparts. For a century, investments in plants and equipment remained less than that of other economically successful nations. Market forces kept British employment high and exports profitable as workers' growth in real wages slipped. By 1980, hourly wages in Germany were double those in England.[15] The British do have a much higher standard of living than a century ago because they import foreign technology and inexpensive, high-quality goods. But Britain surrendered its economic leadership.

The increased concern with sensual satisfaction and entertainment by recent generations of Americans has contributed to the weakening of the three foundations of the personal work ethic: the moral value attributed to hard work, the willingness to exert high effort in order to achieve material gain, and the pride in skillfully accomplishing one's job. Most children grow up accepting the sensualistic values promoted by advertising and the entertainment media. Parents and teachers who care little about hard work are not inclined to inculcate strong work values in the nation's youth. Individuals who do possess a high work ethic are often hesitant to transgress against the popular view that children should be left to find their own values.

Because large numbers of parents, educators, and students view hard work at school as unnecessary, American education at all levels has become lax. The typical American school year lasts 178 days, compared to 220 days in England and 240 days in Japan.[16] The U.S. school day is two hours shorter than in many European countries and filled with easier courses. Japanese teachers assign seventh grade students an average of 4.7 hours of math homework per week, in comparison to 2.9 hours in the U.S.[17] A small minority of American elementary school teachers assign homework over summer vacation, in comparison to two-thirds of the Japanese teachers.[18]

As a result of mediocre education, one out of every five Americans is illiterate, compared to one out of every 150 in Japan.[19] American students beginning in elementary school perform worse in science and math than European and Japanese students.[20] Japanese factory workers are much better equipped than their American counterparts to understand graphs and charts and deal with mathematical formulas.[21]

The poorer school achievement of American students relative to Europeans and Japanese is not simply the result of foreign students becoming better. American students are working less hard than in the past. American elementary school students are less attentive during classroom lessons than are Japanese students. One study found the American students listened only 46 percent of the time in comparison to 65 percent by Japanese students.[22] Two-thirds of American high school students spend less than an hour a night on homework, and students show poorer average scores on standardized tests than when Sputnik was launched twenty-six years ago. The number of high school students opting for easy "general track" courses rather than vocational and college preparatory programs increased from 12 percent in 1964 to 42 percent in 1979.[23]

Television is a prime culprit taking up time that American students could spend studying and reading. Active television-watching usually begins when children are about two and one-half years of age and increases through the preschool years. Elementary school children watch an average of four hours every day of the week.[24] Heavy television watching has been found to reduce the time some elementary school children spend reading.[25]

By age sixteen, most children have spent more time before the TV set than at school.[26] Most continue to spend long hours watching television through high school. By reducing the amount of time devoted to reading and homework, television retards children's development of reading ability and lessens school achievement. The negative effects of television on industriousness go beyond school work. As will be demonstrated in Chapter 4, the act of watching television and the nature of entertainment programing produce a generalized laziness and decrease the capacity to delay current pleasures for future rewards.

As students' school achievement has declined, grades have risen.

33

In order to satisfy the demands by parents of college-bound young-sters, high-school teachers now give inflated grades for inferior work. Bright students have an easy time breezing through high school courses. Getting good grades for little study teaches an indolence that gets many students into academic difficulty once they enter college.

Bill Larson, now a twenty-six-year-old student at a technical college, provides an example of how laxness in American education contributes to the decline of the work ethic among the brighter students:

> Grade school was very easy for me. I was the only kid who could read well in first grade; I was the only one they would let read a-loud to the class. I got in trouble in 3rd and 4th grades a lot, be-cause I was bored and restless. It wasn't like I had to devote a great deal of my concentration in order to do the work that was assigned to me.
>
> School was never a challenge for me. I never studied for anything in grade school or high school. I always got A's without trying. On standardized tests I always scored in the 98th or 99th percentile. In high school, when I came across a challenge I just wouldn't do it, because there was no need to. I didn't have anything to prove, because everyone told me how smart I was.
>
> My first year in college I hung in there because I didn't have to do any homework. I never had to study in the past. It would be pretty silly for me to begin studying in college when I received good grades for 12 years without having to put forth much effort. After that I just didn't put enough effort into it. It was a lot harder than high school and my grades just didn't concern me.
>
> I soon realized that I wasn't going to be able to breeze through college without working, but studying wasn't a priority. In fact, not studying was actually reinforced by the group of people I associated with. It was cool to go out every night. But I was in Engineering, so my curriculum was far more difficult than my friends'. My grades began to fall, and I considered studying. But it was just safer not to study. Why should I take the risk of failing? You see, getting poor grades without studying is not failing, because you are expected to fail if you don't study. But getting poor grades while studying

would be a failure, because you'd have no reason to get poor grades. I didn't want to take the risk of having nothing to blame my poor grades on. So I flunked out because I didn't even try.

I think that if I was pushed when I was younger I would've appreciated what I had. Grade school was like running a race against people that all have one leg. I'd jog around the track and stop to read the paper and wait for them to catch up and then I'd jog through the finish line. Everyone would slap me on the back and say "great race" when I wasn't doing anything.

I think that when you're never really pushed to reach your potential as a child, it has a negative effect on your self-esteem and confidence. When you get older, you're going to be afraid to re-try some things, because you don't know if you're going to fall on your face.

Bill's poor college performance resulted from the ease with which he obtained high grades all during his prior schooling. Succeeding with minimal effort, Bill became lazy and developed the arrogant belief that his innate ability insured high achievement. Such pride offered a comfortable shell until, in a difficult college major, lackadaisical study no longer succeeded. Initial failure in college made Bill question his ability. He feared that hard study might still result in failure, demonstrating his pride was unwarranted. A reluctance to work hard for fear of showing one's incompetence is called "self-handicapping" by psychologists. When a student learns to attribute success to innate ability alone rather than effort, a few failures are enough to destroy confidence and lead to self-handicapping.

After flunking out of one college, Bill was delighted to find another where he could succeed without work. Despite his poor grades, Bill was admitted to a respected technical college. Bill's study habits have not improved, but he is doing well because of lax grading standards:

I'm going for an electronics degree. I got A's in all of my classes except one. I got my only B in this English class that was a joke of a class. This class was ridiculous. I aced all of the tests, and I got a B in the class because I wouldn't do the homework. I was getting penalized for being smart enough not to have to practice. This class was about as meaningful as picking up a pile of sand and moving it to the other side of the yard, and then going out the next day and moving it back. What the hell was the sense of me doing this stupid homework that involved picking out the topic sentence. I'm not going to move a pile of sand just so this woman would be happy. I guess I really didn't study for any of my classes I've taken at the college yet. I think maybe I will study if I feel that the class is useful; I don't know right now.

College students increasingly shy away from majors that provide lucrative careers but require hard work. American universities are granting only about half as many doctoral degrees in physics as they did in the early 1970s. Foreign students are happy to fill the chairs left empty by Americans. In the last decade the proportion of foreign full-time engineering and science students in U.S. universities doubled to thirty per cent. Today, half of all students receiving Ph.D.'s in science and engineering, as well as forty percent of the math students, are foreign.

The scarcity of scientifically trained Americans has forced research and development laboratories to hire foreigners to fill one out of every five positions. As some of these foreign scientists return home overseas, they will supply America's economic competitors with acquired skills and advanced technological information. The Defense Department fears that the pool of American scientists available for classified research will soon be inadequate and worries about the danger to national security of hiring foreign scientists.[27]

Many of the college students majoring in business, education, and the social sciences are attracted by what they see as the easy curricula. The declining college-age population has made higher education a buyer's market. This factor, together with greater student activism on issues of self-interest, has put colleges under strong pressure to relax standards in order to attract students and keep them happy. During the last decade, most colleges made their curricula easier by reducing the number of required courses. Students are thus given a greater opportunity to choose easy electives. The difficulty of the courses that are still required has been reduced and grades are inflated.

Some pressure for lax standards comes from teachers themselves. Since the 1960s, psychologists and educators in the human potential movement have emphasized the primacy of self-discovery over external evaluation. Students, we are told, should be allowed to choose whatever courses they wish to take, should determine the objectives of each course, and should decide how those objectives will be reached. To stimulate a positive climate, the teacher should not: "determine lesson tasks, specifically require readings, give lectures (unless requested to do so by the student), volunteer criticisms or evaluations (unless requested), give formal examinations, or assume sole responsibility for assigning grades."[28]

A number of the 1960s counterculture students who embraced these views completed their graduate education and became college professors in the early 1970s. Some of the new professors rejected the assignment of grades for students' work. Forced to assign some grade, they insisted on giving all or most of their students As. On occasion, even students who dropped out of courses before the end of the term were given As.[29] These professors were generally given the choice of following more standard grading practices or being fired. Many found a successful compromise, grading just hard enough to get by.

There remains a large minority of high school teachers and college professors in the social sciences and humanities who are beloved because they "relate to" students rather than teach. Readings are assigned from the simplest texts that often include exercises that help the student understand how his *feelings* relate to various issues. Students may be asked to keep a diary tenuously related to the course's subject matter, so that they can record their *feelings* about various events in their lives.

Such teachers select topics for lecture and class discussion on the basis of popular appeal rather than importance to the area of study. Complex issues are oversimplified, and facts are distorted for dramatic effect. A single position on controversial issues is presented by teachers anxious to be viewed on the "students' side" and who wish to satisfy student desires for a set of simple facts and simple opinions to regurgitate on tests. Every student comment in class is treated as equally valuable and true on the grounds that truth is relative and that feelings are more important than understanding difficult subject matter.

By the end of such a course, the students have no inkling that they have learned only one-tenth of what they should have learned or that much of what was taught distorted the facts. All the students know is that the teacher cared about them, helped place them "in touch" with their own feelings, or helped them discover "something special" about themselves. The students believe the teacher has taught them a great deal since their grade for the course is so high.

Perhaps a larger number of high school teachers and college professors who would prefer high standards are intimidated by student pressure. At most colleges, the sole measure of teaching effectiveness is a numerical average of anonymous evaluations filled out at the end of the course by students. Students exert direct and effective force on professors to "dumb down" courses and give higher grades. For example, in the psychology departments of many colleges, the assignment to teach the undergraduate statistics course is the kiss of death for any untenured teacher who takes the job seriously. Statistics, often required of all psychology majors, is not fun for most students; it necessitates hard work. The greater the rigor of the course, the more negatively the instructor is viewed by the majority of students.

Many students believe that they should receive high grades for a vague verbal understanding of statistics. The conscientious statistics teacher who does not buckle under student pressure receives very low course evaluation scores from the students. The teacher thereby gains a poor reputation among other faculty and the administration.

Teachers know that evaluations depend, in part, on convincing students the teacher thinks each one is a special individual. Moreover, students are receptive to learning something about their "unique personalities." The teacher also knows that students are pleased by having the path to an academic degree eased by simple exams and inflated grades. Avoidance of difficult subject matter, oversimplification and dramatization of issues, and non-judgmental emphasis on the value of each student's "feelings" are tempting to teachers who care about tenure, promotion, and pay raises.

The promotion of introspection and emotion-laden social relationships by the human potential movement alienates individuals from a commitment to hard work in the pursuit of long-term goals. Teachers who accept these values may influence students' subsequent attitudes toward their jobs and the organizations for which they work. Employees who express a concern that they must find their "genuine" self have been found more likely to believe that they are powerless pawns in the grip of external events, and they resent the lack of responsiveness by their employers to these personal concerns.[30]

Young adults trained by parents, school, and television to be lazy and desirous of instant gratification enter the world of work with a solidly entrenched indolence. A nation that once took pride in the work ethic now views hard workers as "workaholics," social misfits who are to be pitied rather than emulated. Managers and the news media frequently decry the laziness of laborers. But workers at all levels of the corporate hierarchy are less industrious then their predecessors.

It used to be common for managers to work evenings or weekends. Today, driving past the parking lots of corporate headquarters at night or on a Saturday, one is likely to find only the guard's car. Executives traveling to Asia are frequently surprised to find business offices open on Saturday and important business meetings held on weekends.[31] In a younger America, managers frequently took only part of their vacation time, a rare happening today despite longer vacations.

To assess work attitudes, Psychologist David Cherrington administered a carefully-constructed attitude questionnaire to three thousand workers in fifty-three companies of various kinds throughout the United States. About half the employees were production workers, another twenty percent were supervisors, and the remaining thirty percent were clerks or middle-level managers. Cherrington found, and I quote:

- Younger workers do not believe hard work and pride in craftsmanship as important as older workers believe them to be.

- Younger workers have less favorable attitudes toward their jobs, the company, and top management than do older workers; these differences cannot be entirely attributed to the kinds of jobs they are assigned.
- Younger workers are much less committed to the company than older workers, and they report less favorable attitudes about its role in the community and the economy.
- Younger workers are more concerned than older workers about having their fellow workers like them; they feel it is more important to get along with friends than to work hard on the job.[32]

Cherrington judged that young workers have learned less favorable attitudes toward hard work than previous generations. Such a conclusion, based on questionnaire results, is usually open to a number of criticisms. Older workers might give more positive responses on work-related issues simply because they received better treatment by the company. After all, older employees are more likely to occupy positions of higher status and authority and receive greater pay. Moreover, older employees have usually been with the company longer so that their ranks have been thinned of disgruntled employees who left the company after a year or two of employment. Older employees also tend to have a somewhat lower degree of education than younger employees who may desire more meaningful work. And finally, older employees contain a larger ratio of men to women so that the findings may simply be due to gender differences in attitudes.

Cherrington's claims deserve special attention because he dealt effectively with each of these complications. He used sophisticated statistical techniques to examine the effect of age on work attitudes, removing the influences of occupational level, income, seniority, education, and gender. The results strongly indicated that younger employees have less positive attitudes toward work than older employees.

Of course, no single study can rule out all plausible alternative interpretations. It is possible that some variable other than the way today's young workers are brought up is responsible for their less favorable attitudes toward work. But it seems likely that Cherrington is correct in his interpretation that younger workers have been taught weak work values.

Indolence taught by parents and teachers is reinforced on the job. Managers increasingly are rewarded for lazy and improvident behavior which generates short-term profits but damages the company's future prospects. The improvement of quality control, the modernization of plant facilities and equipment, and the development of new products through research all take persistent work that may take years to pay off. Working hard for such long-term gains is discouraged by the demands of stock holders and top managers for immediate profits.

Since the 1960s, large institutional investors such as mutual funds, insurance companies, pension plans, and brokerage houses have become responsible for a growing percentage of purchases and sales of corporate stocks. For example, such institutions hold forty percent of GM shares.[33] These groups jump in and out of stocks with impunity in an attempt to achieve quick profits that will attract and hold customers. Companies' profits every three *months* are now carefully scrutinized.

Until recently, laziness among chief executive officers (CEOs) of corporations was encouraged by their lack of accountability for company performance. Boards of directors consisted of company executives whose future depended on their commander-in-chief's beneficence, joined by outside directors with limited knowledge of the industry. When CEOs made poor decisions, their subordinates took the heat.[34] The current corporate buy-out mania has put the fear of God in many CEOs but, unfortunately, has not resulted in any greater emphasis on product quality or greater orientation toward the development of new products. On the contrary, in order to keep a company's stock price high, which will discourage corporate raiders, CEOs are ever more tempted to sacrifice future gain for present profit.

As Avon's CEO, Hicks Waldron, observed:

There is a fixation and I think it's terribly unhealthy. . . . Seated in your chair ten to fifteen times a year is a securities analyst quizzing me on the company and trying to make a judgment on the company and whether to recommend the stock. And you can't get those people to think ahead more than six months. . . . It's highly possible to manage earnings. Example: Run a quarter-end promotion that will steal money out of the next quarter . . . cut out a research-and-development item. . . . It really gets to be a pressure pot.[35]

The managers of most large companies receive incentive stock options, the right to buy the company's stock within a specified time limit at a price usually fixed near the current level. They can keep their bosses and stock holders happy, and drive up the value of their stock options, by showing high short-term profits at a cost to future productivity. Managers and stock holders temporarily gain by managers' continued stress on short-term profits, but America's future loses.

In the mid 1980s, the laziness of American workers and managers brought our chickens home to roost wearing Japanese kimonos. Between 1950 and 1980, the United States' share of the world gross domestic product was cut in half, from 40.3 percent to 21.8 percent. Our country's share of world exports went from 16.7 per cent to 10.9 percent.[36] In 1986, the value of West German exports surpassed the U.S., with Japan a close third.[37]

America is losing out to Germany and Japan despite this nation's far greater population and superior natural resources. The decline has been greatest in the basic manufacturing industries. For example, American car manufacturers' share of the world market has dropped from 79% to less than 30%.[38]

How has American industry changed its way of operating in reaction to the flood of imports from Japan and such developing countries as South Korea and Taiwan? Managers tried to reduce employee salary increases and fringe benefits. Such concessions, granted by many unions, together with the fall in the value of the dollar, have increased the competitiveness of America's manufactured products. Moreover, employees in a few threatened industries are working somewhat harder than previously because of the fear that foreign competition will eliminate their jobs.

As a sop to workers who endure boring jobs and declining real wages and as a public relations ploy to enhance the quality image of products, many American companies have recently adopted a facade of interest in employees' well-being and in suggestions by employees for improved productivity. As glorified by Howard K. Smith in numerous spot ads on radio and television, some 500 American companies have instituted "Japanese" quality circles, that are actually an American invention successfully adopted by the Japanese.[39]

In the quality circle, small groups of perhaps eight or ten representatives of management and labor from the same work area may meet an hour a week to suggest improvements in the quality of the products or services with which the workers are involved. Quality circles have generally been successful when companies carefully train the participants and obtain the full cooperation of managers and unions.[40]

In a majority of cases, however, such programs have been introduced halfheartedly with only a small number of employees. Quality circles are not easily established in American companies because managers and workers generally accept our culture's assumption that management will lead and employees will follow.[41] American managers usually show little evidence of taking workers suggestions seriously. This suits many union leaders since worker integration into the management process eliminates the gulf between labor and management upon which unions thrive.

Overall, the response by management to the superior quality of many European and Japanese products has been disappointing. Some large companies, such as Xerox, have cut costs and dramatically decreased the percentage of defects found in their products.[42] But most executives no longer care about the quality of their company's products and are unwilling to work hard to develop new products. Large companies with shared monopolies continue to act by implicit agreement to keep prices high and quality low. After all, items that self-destruct quickly are cheaper to produce and require replacement sooner.

As inexpensive high-quality foreign imports of steel, autos, and other products began to cut into American companies' profits, industry trade organizations lobbied for import quotas and tax breaks. American automobile manufacturers exerted political pressure that resulted in the current "voluntary constraints" on the import of Japanese cars. This allows the auto makers to sacrifice quality while keeping prices high.

In 1979, the National Highway Traffic Safety Administration recalled six and one-half million cars manufactured in this country. Japanese cars made up 14 percent of cars sold in America that year but less than 4 percent of the recalls.[43] In the same year, General Motors introduced with much fanfare its answer to the Japanese challenge, the X-car. By 1983, almost a million of the vehicles had been recalled for defects that ranged from faulty clamps on fuel tanks to cracked steering gears. A suit filed by the Justice Department claimed that GM knew the X-car had serious brake problems, failed to notify car owners, and lied to the government about their knowledge of the defects.[44] *Consumer Reports* continues to report better repair records for Japanese than American cars.

Current television commercials would have you believe that Detroit has seen the light and is working day and night to produce cars equal to or better than the Japanese imports. In that case, why is it that all ten of the most fuel-efficient 1987 models were produced by the Japanese?[45] Near the end of 1986, GM announced plans to lay off about one-third of its engineering staff and reduce planned production of its much touted import-fighting Saturn subcompact by half.[46] GM seems content to act as a selling agent for fuel-efficient Japanese cars such as the Chevrolet Sprint, ER, and the Pontiac Firefly. Does this sound like a company taking up the Japanese challenge?

Chrysler Corporation Chairman Lee Iacocca complains: "It's not Japan's fault if we want to be a doormat. They're going to take advantage of us—and why not?" But Chrysler imports the Dodge Colt from Japan and has introduced a Mitsubishi engine as an option in its vans, recommended to buyers who want quality performance. The auto makers are importing the engine and in some cases the entire car from Japan, knowing that the public will snap up the import because of the inferior quality of American-produced cars. Selling Japanese cars rather than working day and night to bring technology up to par is an easy and ultimately self-destructive course for the American auto makers.

This concession of technological superiority to the Japanese will only increase the public's preference for foreign cars. The practice of using foreign companies to supply one's own products is also carried on by steel companies that import some kinds of foreign steel to re-sell in the United States at a higher price. Such behavior makes sense only if one owes allegiance to short-term profits rather than to the longer-term gains that result from innovation and hard work.

Major companies have used tax breaks and profits created by import restrictions to diversify into fields outside their major competence. The purchase of new businesses reduced U. S. Steel Corporation's sales of steel to only about one quarter of its total sales. In 1985, the company's steel production was operating at only sixty-four percent of capacity. Just after Independence Day in 1986, U. S. Steel announced it was changing its name to USX Corporation and reorganizing to reflect the acquisition of oil and gas companies that now provide the bulk of the company's business. As justification for the reorganization, Chairman David M. Roderick asserted at a news conference that "steel has been a major cost to the organization. . . ." Rockwell said that if such losses continued in the future, the steel unit "will shrink drastically."[47]

Rather than fight foreign technological advances with hard work to improve its own production processes, USX Corporation chose the easy, self-indulgent path of using cash to purchase established companies that have nothing to do with the production of steel. The X in the new name of the company is fitting. In algebra, X is the unknown factor. For the USX Company, X represents the unknown benefits of expanding into technologies outside its expertise. Where has patriotic dedication to keeping America as a viable manufacturer of basic goods gone? Such is the repayment to the American people for allowing a small number of companies to dominate the manufacture of basic goods and to give them substantial tax breaks when foreign competition became intense.

The indolence and short-term orientation of American managers is by no means restricted to the automobile and steel industries. One easy way to earn quick profits is by trading advanced technology to foreign firms in return for sales. A survey of 154 military contractors revealed that from 1980 to 1984, almost half of overseas sales were accompanied by "offset" agreements in which the seller sent technology or provided some other side benefit.[48] American companies also transfer technology by setting up subsidiaries jointly owned with foreign companies, licensing agreements, and manu-

facturing arrangements. RCA licensed it's color television technology to the Japanese decades ago only to find its own sets outsold
in America by Japanese models. Often, Japanese companies back
out of joint ventures after acquiring American technology and then
become competitors.[49]

The aerospace industry today shows the same nearsightedness
that many previous manufacturers did by providing foreign companies the tools that aided their own destruction. Robert Rosati,
a recently retired Pratt and Whitney executive involved in jet-
engine technology-sharing deals, claims: "I don't see the Japanese
or anyone else developing competitive technology by associating
with us. They don't have the design or development capability to
do any kind of engine, and they're not going to get them."[50] When
McDonnell Douglas sold the F-15 fighter plane to Japan, the offset
involved supplying the Japanese with advanced technologies. According to the General Accounting Office, the deal will come back
to haunt the domestic airplane manufacturers by furthering Japan's
plans to capture control of thirty percent of the world's aerospace
market.[51]

"A strong case could be made that these contracts and contractors
are in fact de-industrializing the United States," argued John Din-
gell, chairman of the House Energy and Commerce Committee.
"Although the amounts involved run into the billions of dollars
each year, it appears that no one really looks at these matters or
understands their consequences with regard to jobs, employment,
and opportunity of the American people."[52] Corporate executives
that sell advanced technology are the institutional equivalent of
drug addicts willing to do anything to obtain a quick high and
thinking nothing of the future.

Laziness and complacency have produced a cavalier approach
by U.S. companies to foreign markets. Following the second world
war, most American manufacturers paid little attention to tailoring
their products for export. The needs and tastes of foreign consumers
were ignored. If other countries wanted to buy our products as
designed for the American market, all well and good. If not, the
manufacturer simply supplied American consumers.

The spunky Apple Computer Company crashed the American

market in the 1970s with its consumer-oriented personal computer. In 1977, Apple began selling personal computers in Japan without a single competitor. But Apple neglected to develop a computer with the Chinese characters that are employed in the written Japanese language. Apple even failed to provide Japanese-language instruction manuals.

In a nation that regards corporate alliances as very important, Apple wheeled and dealed by giving exclusive distribution rights to one company only to allow other companies subsequently to distribute its products. Apple could have become a major force in Japan's personal computer market. But by 1984, its estimated sales accounted for less than one percent of the personal computers sold there.[53]

Americans take their patriotism during times of peace less seriously than the Japanese. Most Americans are willing to work harder for the welfare of the nation when an external military threat is perceived. But, as we shall detail in Chapter 5, patriotism in Japan influences economic behavior during peace time as well. Americans consider a company to be successful if it earns great profits. The Japanese venerate companies that gain a large share of the world market. Profits are important to the Japanese, but they understand the necessity of obtaining a large portion of the world sales in order to maintain the nation's economic prosperity. Japanese companies are willing to forgo the goal of high short-term profits that is destroying the long-term prospects for American industry.

And subordinates take their cues from managers. It is a common observation by American visitors to Japan and by Japanese visitors to America that Japanese workers are more industrious than Americans. For example, in many Japanese factories no more automated than our own, per capita car production is twice that of American plants. A General Motors assembly plant worker, laid off after two-and-a-half years, told automobile journalist Brock Yates:

> We worked half an hour on, half an hour off. That way we could make the work last maybe a couple of hours before our shift ended. If we worked too fast, it was a problem dodging the foremen and

supervisors. To be honest, I'm not the most ambitious guy in the world, but I could easily have done the work for myself and the two men next to me in an eight-hour shift and still have had an easy day. Based on what I saw, I'd estimate the entire plant could have operated easily with less than two-thirds of the work force before the layoffs began.[54]

Because of lax supervision, institutions such as government buildings, hospitals, and universities are often a haven for lazy custodial and service staff. I once knew a painter named Allen who was a master of slow motion, taking five months to paint the small entrance hall of a university building. He would ever so gradually lower his brush into the paint bucket, lift the brush with determined sluggishness, very carefully tap the end of the brush against the side of the can to remove excess paint, and s-l-o-w-l-y paint a swath 8 to 12 inches long. Then Allen would step back and admire his new patch of color. He would light a cigarette, deeply inhaling drag after drag and basking in nicotine sensuality.

After his smoke, Allen would stare at the students and professors entering and exiting the building. When someone wearing unusual clothing or having an odd mannerism happened along, Allen would crook his head to the right side, as if trying to understand what had driven the traveler to such deviance. Faced again with the painful thought of his burden, Allen would sigh. The paint brush would descend slowly into the bucket. Allen would then use the brush to gingerly dab the edges of his last swath with such care that even the most inattentive observer knew that here was a man who would not be rushed.

Some lazy employees frequently stay home from work. Absenteeism figures are not available for the majority of American workers. One study of 500 firms found that absenteeism records were kept on fewer than two-fifths of the employees.[55] Available evidence indicates that Japan has the lowest absence rate among industrialized countries, perhaps 2.0 percent, in comparison to 3.5 percent in the United States. Although not up to the Japanese standard, the U.S. figure is still respectable compared to Germany at 7.7 percent, France at 8.3 percent, and Italy at 10.6 percent. The Netherlands, Sweden, and England underwent substantial increases in absenteeism during the late 1960s and now appear to equal or exceed Italy's level.[56]

Records available for the period from 1967 to 1974 indicate fairly stable absenteeism in the U.S., perhaps increasing at a tenth of a point every two years.[57] This modest increase in absenteeism is not so favorable in view of two factors that should have reduced the incidence of absenteeism. Older U.S. workers, who increase the absence rate with long illnesses, have been retiring in recent years at a younger average age. This means that the rate of absenteeism among younger workers has been increasing at a faster rate than the overall figures show. Also, vacation time and paid holidays continued to increase during the period measured, giving employees more time for relaxation and taking care of personal business.

Nevertheless, the average of one day missed for every thirty-three is a good record. Absenteeism in the United States may be lower than in Europe because of less stringent sick leave policies there. Showing up to work is strongly influenced by sick leave policy and may not reflect how hard one works on the job. In a large office of the postal service studied by my students and me, management kept absenteeism low by allowing time off only for severe and well-documented illness. Despite the low absence rate, virtually every non-management employee expressed a profound dissatisfaction and an anger toward management that was unequaled in over forty companies we investigated. The employees picked their own ways of getting even with a management they viewed as imperious and uncaring, which sometimes involved reducing effort in ways they knew would escape detection. Possible disciplinary action effectively reduced absenteeism but did not produce hard work on the job.

Absenteeism levels are more influenced by the work ethic in organizations in which there is no threat of disciplinary action or loss of pay, or where such threats can be circumvented. Several studies have found that employees who are frequently absent have weaker work values, on the average, as measured by carefully constructed questionnaires.[58] At Ford, the number of employees staying home from work on a given day doubled during the 1960s.[59] A few years ago, the Chrysler factory in Newark, Delaware, instituted stringent penalties against repeated unexcused absences. But employees had their own way to defeat the system. One line worker confided: "Say you don't want to come in for a couple of days. You know from your friends which doctors to go to. For six or seven dollars they'll give you a written medical excuse."[60]

Absenteeism records are usually not kept for salaried employees, making it easy to take time off without the justification required of hourly workers. Two decades ago, white-collar workers used to brag about never missing a day of work in ten or twenty years. Not any more. If you work in any large business or government agency, try keeping a month's absenteeism tally of salaried colleagues. The true absence rate is likely to be far greater than the supposed national average of one day in thirty-three.

Many lazy people don't mind coming to comfortable jobs in which they can socialize rather than work. In general, the higher one's position in the organization, the less closely one is supervised and the greater the opportunity for avoiding work. Ford Foundation sociologist Robert Schrank notes that much time on the job is wasted "schmoozing": gossiping, joking, and discussing such topics as baseball, boxing, politics, and sex. In small doses, schmoozing can be an excellent relief from the pressures of the work place. The problem is that many Americans who fail to take pride in their work spend most of the time on the job schmoozing. Employees whose job tenure is protected by contracts, contacts, or custom may have to be flattered or cajoled into work.

As a result of the continual pressures toward the speedup, factory workers have learned a multitude of ways to make work seem to take longer than it actually does:

> The experienced worker does everything possible, including purposely springing frames and burning up drills to put time-study men off their calculations and set a slower time estimate for the job. No mean dramatic ability comes to the fore in the effort: the worker jumps around the machine, steaming and sweating at every pore. Once management's man is out of range, the job goes back to the pace the workers themselves have decided to keep. They set a job at a certain pace, or fix an output quota, not only to keep from being speeded up but to avoid having their pay rates lowered.[61]

One automated manufacturing company with a high frequency of work stoppages among skilled laborers found that:

> When the operator wanted a break from his routine he would decide that the tool was dull, stop the machine, remove the tool, and walk clear across the shop to the toolroom where he would apply for and receive a similar freshly sharpened tool. He would then proceed back to his machine and install it. Detours past the coffee machine were not infrequent.[62]

Industrious employees are frequently resented and mistreated by fellow employees. Consider American postal workers. Their political clout produces such a high salary that the waiting list of well-qualified applicants is invariably many times greater than the number of positions available. One postal union official struggled to retain his composure as he angrily described the supervisors' periodic observation of mail carriers to determine whether individual routes could be enlarged. The union official had justified concerns about an unreasonable speedup. But several postmen in the same office said that their current routes were short enough to be completed at a leisurely pace.

One mail carrier expressed surprise on the first day on his route to be finished in time to return to the post office before noon rather than at 2:30 in the afternoon as the job "required." His fellow workers were enraged. "Never, never act that way again," they told him. Rate busters would not be tolerated. He would have to learn to "take it easy" if he expected to get-along well with his co-workers.[63]

Both speed of production and product quality have suffered from the inattention and sometimes outright maliciousness of workers who take no pride in their work and are bored with their jobs. A Newark, Delaware, auto worker complained: "The noise on the line is so intense you can't talk. You do exactly the same job hour after hour. To break the monotony some of the fellows begin leaving off a few bolts or misaligning a part."[64] One loyal worker purchased a new Chrysler only to have the steering wheel come off in his hands as he drove home. A co-worker had left out a crucial bolt. Other forms of worker diversion which have the added benefit of asserting one's machismo include filing unreasonable grievances and calling wildcat strikes out of all proportion to some minor slight.

If laborers wreak vengeance on rate busters, it is only fair to point out that management provides its own punishments for quality busters. "Whistle blower" is a term for an individual who risks his or her career to reveal waste and fraud by the employer. The term is a bit misleading. As in the case of rate busters, most of these individuals do not realize they are starting trouble but are simply trying to do a good job. Myron and Penina Glazer made a study of fifty-five recent whistle blowers. Most of these individuals did not understand that the consequences of their actions might involve strong retribution, including "transfer, demotion, firing, blackballing, personal harassment, and intimidation."[65] One whistleblower, Demetrios Basdekas, an engineer who worked for the Nuclear Regulatory Commission, refused to license a plant that he believed was unsafe. His punishment began with isolation:

> I was put in an office with no windows and no heat controls, a building that used to be the FBI storage building. That would be OK if there was no other space available. But right across the hall from me there was a nice office with windows, heat controls, desk, chairs, table, the whole works. And it was empty.[66]

Basdekas was refused a promotion for eleven years. Compared to the fate of most other quality busters, he was lucky not to have been fired. When confronted with decisions by top executives to sacrifice quality for the sake of profit, most lower level managers say nothing. Management culture that places loyalty over product quality is no less harmful to the long-term interests of the company than the mistreatment of rate busters by co-workers.

Indolence extends to a wide variety of jobs. As America's basic industries began to lose their domestic and overseas markets to more efficient foreign producers, newspaper and television editorials pointed with pride to the American superiority in advanced technology. That lead is rapidly disappearing because managers in American high-tech companies are rewarded for short-term profit just as in basic industries. Thus, the Japanese have drawn even with the U.S. in sales of semiconductor chips, which are used in computers and control systems in everything from cars to appliances.[67]

With high tech being overtaken by foreign competition, the editorial writers fell back on farm production as an example of America's continued economic strength. What other country besides the U.S. could serve as the world's wheat basket? Farmers were not only able to supply the ample diets of American consumers but produced a ten-billion dollar surplus of exports over imports.

The American farmer symbolized the durability of American skill and hard work. No more. The U.S. now imports more food than it exports. The variety of foods that are now cheaper to import than buy domestically includes tomatoes from Mexico, potatoes from Canada, apples from Chile, cantaloupes from Mexico, lemons from Spain, and beef and lamb from Australia.[68] The dollar value of food exports fell from a high of $44 billion in 1981 to about $27 billion in 1986.[69]

It is true that the overpriced value of the dollar reduced overseas sales. So the recent reduction of the dollar's value against most foreign currencies should help. But another major part of the problem is the federal government's subsidization of farm products. Small farmers have been starved out because they lack economies of scale, while large farmers have grown complacent and lazy on a glut of federal subsidies.

Federal farm subsidies reached nearly $26 billion in 1986, up from $4 billion a few years ago. In 1985, seven percent of the farmers received about seventy percent of these handouts.[70] Warehouses are bulging with billions of dollars of surplus wheat, corn, soybeans, and cotton. Government subsidies encourage large farmers to produce the same old products in the same old way rather than becoming more efficient and diversifying into products that have a strong international market.

There is one class of farmers who, free from debilitating government subsidies, has responded to market forces by becoming more efficient and productive—the marijuana growers. Since growing marijuana is against the law, farmers have to make it on their own. Here, the balance of payments is improving. Domestic marijuana production has increased from zero ten years ago to about twenty-five to thirty percent of the American market today.[71] Improvement in techniques for marijuana production abound. Taken away from the trough, American farmers can recapture their industriousness and ingenuity.

Laziness has even spread to professional sports players who do not work as hard as their predecessors. The public prefers that major sports such as baseball, basketball, and football be played in separate seasons so that each game can be given undivided attention. But is that any reason to limit practice to a few weeks before the start of a half-year season? Baseball is popular in both the United States and Japan, but Japanese training is much more vigorous. Steve Ontiveros, a Chicago Cub, who went on to play for almost six years in Japan noted:

> I've never seen anything like the Japanese training camp. In the American majors, we were on the field from 10 till 2 every day, and we were ready to start the season in three weeks. In Japan, we're all out there from January, seven to eight hours a day, with lectures and indoor workouts in the evening. It's incredible.[72]

The decline in the personal work ethic has not been accompanied by any lessening of Americans desire for material rewards. This mismatch between avarice and willingness to work has increased the tendency to take advantage of dishonest shortcuts in pursuit of difficult goals. In a study to be discussed in more detail later, college students whose answers to an attitude questionnaire indicated a weak personal work ethic were found to work less hard on a difficult task and cheat more than those with a strong work ethic[73].

The decline of the personal work ethic has contributed to the willingness by Americans to sell military secrets to Soviet Union. A rarity in the past, such spying is becoming increasingly common. Senator Bill Roth dubbed 1985 the "Year of the Spies." Twelve Americans were charged with carrying out espionage for foreign countries. According to Roth; "What was sickening is that in all these cases there has been one common motivation—making a fast buck by selling U.S. secrets to our adversaries."[74]

In the most serious security breach ever to hit the United States, John Walker and his accomplices spent two decades providing Soviet agents every major code used in secret naval communications, as well as technical manuals that enabled Soviet engineers to build copies of coding machines used by all the armed forces, the State Department, CIA, and FBI.[75] Walker was ready to do anything to make money as long as it did not involve hard work. As a teenager he committed four burglaries and joined the navy to escape punishment. A communications specialist, he had access to the navy's secret codes and manuals. When Walker had financial difficulties, he drove to the Soviet Embassy in Washington D. C. and sold stolen classified information. Walker kept on selling secrets to pay for a mistress, a Cessna plane, a houseboat, and properties in Florida and North Carolina.[76] It was easier to sell military secrets to the Russians than to work to maintain his expensive life style.

Jerry Whitworth, one of the Walker spy ring's central members, had failed a number of courses while attending a small California community college.[77] This evidence of lack of diligence and responsibility did not stop the Navy from training Whitworth as a communications officer. Giving up the Navy, he once more tried school unsuccessfully.[78] Returning to the Navy, Whitworth was a valuable source of naval codes after Walker's retirement. Whitworth was sentenced to 365 years in prison by U.S. District Judge John Vukasin who claimed the spy "believed in nothing."[79]

The judge was wrong. Whitworth cared a great deal about being liked and was offended by Walker's boorish manners.[80] He tried to impress others as an intellectual, talked about Ayn Rand's books, and attended Libertarian meetings. He enjoyed the freedom of modern America and he needed money to finance such hobbies as scuba diving and stunt flying in Piper Cubs.

Whitworth was afraid of getting caught for spying.[81] But he lacked the tenacity to work hard for what he thought were the good things in life. Without patriotism or a strong work ethic, it made sense to Jerry Whitworth to take the small risk of getting caught for the large amounts of cash the Russians supplied for naval secrets. Whitworth was like most recent spies caught in America. They spy not for ideological reasons but simply because they desire a good salary, and their fear of getting caught is less aversive than working hard to achieve economic goals.

The American scientific community has shown increasing concern about the fabrication of data. Some researchers allege important discoveries, based on concocted evidence, because they cannot sustain the long, careful work often required to shed light on complex scientific issues.[82] In 1974, William T. Summerlin was a 34-year-old immunologist with a respected position as a senior scientist at the world renowned Sloan-Kettering Institute for Cancer Research in Manhattan, New York. He was appointed by Robert A. Good, the director of the Institute and a prominent scientist who had appeared on the cover of *Time* magazine. Good had brought Summerlin in his retinue of fifty researchers when he moved from the University of Minnesota to his new position at Sloan-Kettering. Good supported Summerlin's research with substantial grants received from both the federal government and private sources.

Summerlin came under increasing pressure to obtain his own funding. In March 1973, hoping to obtain newspaper and television publicity that would increase his chances for obtaining a grant from the American Cancer Society, Summerlin announced a major scientific breakthrough. He had found a way to transplant skin from one animal to another without the rejection normally produced by the recipient's immune system. The research made headlines because the body's rejection of implants is a major medical problem and because understanding the immune system may help provide more effective treatments for cancer.

Robert Good, Summerlin's boss, traveled a lot and was in demand by many researchers at the Institute. Summerlin found it very difficult to get much time with his mentor to discuss research. But by co-authoring Summerlin's scientific articles and expressing faith in Summerlin's work, Good reduced suspicions by other scientists who were unable to replicate successfully the experiments that Summerlin had reported with mice.

By March 1974, people working in Summerlin's laboratory were having trouble reproducing his results. Good was thinking of retracting some of the claims made in scientific publications. To convince Good that such a retraction was unnecessary, Summerlin showed him some white mice with transplanted skin from a black-skin mouse. Unfortunately for Summerlin, a lab assistant noticed that the black patches were the result from Summerlin's use of a felt-tip pen.

Lewin Thomas, the president of Sloan-Kettering, announced that Summerlin was not responsible for his actions because of emotional problems and put him on medical leave for a year at his full $40,000 salary. His career ruined, Summerlin complained of pressures to report significant findings. [83]

But an unwillingness to work diligently toward his goals appears a major source of his dishonesty. Other staff had previously complained of Summerlin's "sloppy habits—appointments broken, letters unanswered, and written reports containing obvious errors in arithmetic."[84] Moreover, Summerlin had acquired a considerable staff, including four secretaries and a number of scientists, who might have been expected to help him with preparing grant applications. [85]

Summerlin claimed to be kept busy with patients at the Cancer Center. But a nurse said, "We saw very few such patients, and when we did, he would talk to them about future plans and new treatments but in reality none of them existed. After a number of months, though, the patients began to ask for explanations. Their hopes had been raised and nothing was forthcoming."[86] Summerlin's failure to give his full effort was also noted by a doctor who had worked with Summerlin soon after Summerlin had graduated from medical school. [87]

Summerlin had been on the fast track in cancer research. Prestige and promotions depended on publishing scientific findings in prominent scientific journals and obtaining research grants from the federal government. The pressure Summerlin felt is not unusual. Universities and research institutes press their scientists to obtain research grants because the institution receives a substantial portion of the funds as overhead. Having achieved a prestigious scientific position with little effort, Summerlin lacked the resilience to keep working honestly and conscientiously during dry periods in his research. For some individuals, like Summerlin, the fear of ostracism by other scientists may be less powerful than the rewards contingent on impressive sounding fictional results.

Child and parent, student and teacher, laborer and manager, farm hand and farm owner, laboratory assistant and scientist—Americans embrace materialism as greatly as ever. They value the free-enterprise system that produced great prosperity. But acceptance of a present-oriented life style involving sensual gratification undermines their tolerance for the hard work needed to achieve long-term goals. Most Americans no longer view industriousness as intrinsically worthwhile, take pride in the quality of their work, or are willing to exert high effort for material gain. Everyone blames someone else for America's economic decline without considering his or her contribution.

CHAPTER 3

Laziness Among Poor Americans

William Jones is a short, slightly-built man, aged twenty-three, who works as a janitor in a large, east coast city. The cleaning company that employs William is contracted by large office buildings to wash floors, clean bathrooms, and remove trash. William is poorly paid but is satisfied with his earnings and job. He lives alone and has no steady girlfriend although he would like to marry in the next year or two. William has a strong affection for his mother but feels estranged from his father, whom he remembers as seldom being at home and showing him little affection.

On his meager salary, William can afford a shabby apartment located in a poor section of the city. From the single, small window in his room, he has a view of a garbage-strewn alley. William must walk to the other end of the hall to use the floor's one bathroom. His apartment is poorly heated. During the winter, frost forms on the inside of his small window, and he finds it difficult to stay warm. In the summer, the pavement and the apartment building absorb the sun's rays throughout the day, creating sweltering evenings. By pushing with all his might, William can force his window open the three inches that may bring a faint breeze. He has no stove and gets his supper from a take-out around the corner.

At work, William's supervisor usually leaves him alone. On occasion, however, William has been chastised for what he believed to be perfectly good work. He has never received a single word of praise from the supervisor.

The shoddiness of his apartment and low status of his job don't seem to bother William much. He considers himself lucky to have any kind of work and applies himself diligently. From the moment his job begins at 8:00 AM until 5:00 PM when he finishes, William scrubs and polishes quickly and carefully. He attacks dirty offices like a whirlwind, grunting approvingly as he brings a gloss to the surface of a floor or desk top. He always works until the job has been completed meticulously, even if requires overtime without pay. William takes great satisfaction in being an expert janitor.

William's real name is Kenji and he is a typical working-class resident of Tokyo, Japan. Kenji is satisfied with his job and his life, for degradation is in the mind of the beholder. The inattention from his father during his upbringing is typical of Japanese families. Crowded housing, lack of heat, shared toilet and bath facilities are not much minded in Japan because such conditions have always been the way the majority of people live.[1] Criticism for imperfections and absence of praise for good work are standard management practice. Kenji is satisfied with his job because he believes that as a janitor he provides a service to the community. Poor performance on the job, not the job's low status, is a source of shame.

A janitor's work in Japan is respected because keeping offices clean contributes to the occupants' productivity, health and comfort. Expertise in any job that helps the community, including janitorial work, is valued.[2] Kenji may be near the bottom of Japan's social hierarchy, but his work helps the community and he expects to be treated with courtesy and respect.

Social class is more frozen in Japan than America, but America gives its working-class citizens less respect. In the U.S., the worship of wealth increases the significance of differences in salary, housing, and creature comforts as indications of a person's worthiness. Those with "menial" jobs feel degraded not because there is anything inherently demeaning about their work, but because those with better-paying or more prestigious jobs look condescendingly at the poor.

Well-paying jobs are scarce for unskilled workers. Many of those refusing low-paying jobs fail to identify work as a source of pride. A low paying job earns one little more respect in America than being out of work. Such attitudes diminish the desire of many poor people to seek work.

Needy Americans hold diverse views concerning their ability to overcome poverty by working hard at school, by persevering in the search for a long-term job, and by laboring industriously once a job is found. The *work-oriented poor* embrace the traditional view that having a "decent" job is essential to being an upstanding citizen. They believe that with enough effort they can pull themselves up from poverty. The *work-avoiding poor* believe themselves unable ever to obtain permanent jobs that pay well. They view work as a peripheral part of their lives and show limited motivation to search for a job or retain it for very long. They work sporadically even when job opportunities are good. The greatest rejection of the instrumental work ethic, the readiness to work hard toward desired goals, is found among the *helpless poor*. For this group, sometimes called the underclass, dependence on welfare has become ingrained, passed on unquestioningly from one generation to the next.

Among the *work-oriented poor* are many migrant farm workers whose jobs are seasonal and affected by such uncertainties as the weather and replacement by new harvesting machinery. In addition to native-born Americans, millions of poorly educated, hard working Mexicans and Central Americans have entered this country illegally to try to better their lives. They typically receive low wages for farm work, unskilled manufacturing jobs, or other occupations considered menial by the general population, such as washing dishes and collecting trash. To these escapees from nations stricken with great poverty, a low paying job in the U.S. is a godsend.

Many additional *work-oriented poor* are mothers with young children who have been divorced or simply abandoned by the father. These women would prefer to work but find it very difficult to do so while raising their youngsters.

The ranks of *work-oriented poor* are being swelled by hundreds of thousands of blue-collar workers laid off from America's declining basic industries. Only about a fifth of American jobs remain blue collar, about equal to the number of service jobs. The remaining six in ten jobs are white collar. The great difficulty that displaced blue collar workers experience trying to find jobs suggests poverty is becoming as American as apple pie.

Most welfare recipients can be counted among the *work-oriented poor*, managing to obtain jobs within two years after going on the dole.[3] An example of this type of short-term unemployment, common in affluent parts of the country, is provided by Suffolk County in Long Island, New York. The western portion of the county is a bedroom suburb for many commuters who take the Long Island railroad to work in New York City. The eastern area depends on farming and agriculture, raising sheep, and fishing. The country also provides many high-tech and service industry jobs. The majority of county residents who receive unemployment insurance or welfare payments keep looking for a job until they succeed.

Brian Ackerman, who was a social worker before becoming a developmental psychologist, described to me the nature of unemployment in Suffolk County, and the problems many *work-oriented poor* face trying to obtain jobs:

> The dominant value was to work; to be self-supporting. Most people felt stigmatized by being out of work. Most preferred not to have someone looking over their shoulders concerning how they spend their money. Most people seemed willing to work. And if you gave them the opportunity—had a wage better than they could get on welfare—they would work. Most were not second- or third-generation because Suffolk county was a growth area. There were opportunities to get off welfare. There wasn't a history of ghettos or unemployment, and the people I saw were newly poor.
>
> Some of my case load consisted of migrant workers. I certainly don't know that you could call the migrant workers lazy. It was really a question of periodic work; work was available only at certain times. At other times they'd be out of work. A lot of them stayed around. A lot of them moved south. Their problem was work availability.
>
> The bulk of my clientele were divorcees; a lot of mothers with children; a lot of lower middle class whites and blacks. These women were situationally unemployed. There wasn't any day care around

population centers. You had to have a car; these women did not have cars and did not have transportation into the population centers. There was no bus system, no infrastructure of transportation. All the transportation went east-west—into New York City and out on the train. There was no transportation north-south, and that's where the day care centers were. It was really difficult to get these women to the centers where they could take care of the kids while they were working. So independent of laziness or anything else there were a lot of impediments to working. They just couldn't afford cars on their welfare allowances.

The Work Incentive Program always seemed to do well because they trained women specifically to be teachers' aides, nurses or nurses aides, or practical nurses. Those were highly mobile jobs; there was a lot of turnover. You could almost always place someone. There were also some kinds of secretarial training they could get. I had a lot of young women in their early twenties who seemed to do well. They presented themselves nicely. Maybe that was instrumental in their being success stories.

Men were being trained to be carpenters, auto mechanics, and for road work. They weren't taught computer skills or typing or those kinds of skills. They were all high school drop-outs. So they weren't exactly training them to be teachers. I think those jobs trained go-fers. You couldn't train skilled craftsmen because the trade unions wouldn't employ them. The construction industry was really tightly closed out there, really strongly unionized. You had to have an entry. You had to know someone to become an apprentice on the job, such as your father. So they were being trained for menial jobs.[4]

The Work Incentive Program (abbreviated WIN rather than WIP, for obvious reasons) works well, as Ackerman suggested, when the recipients have a good enough education to benefit from training in occupations that are in demand. It fails when participants' education is insufficient, when jobs are artificially limited by union restrictions, when the programs are incompetently or corruptly run, or simply when the economy is in a slump so that few jobs are available. Ackerman's observation that welfare mothers obtain jobs more easily than single men is true nationally.[5]

Just as the vigor and persistence of work by America's economically advantaged citizens has been reduced by indulgence, so millions of America's poor have become reconciled to sporadic jobs
and welfare. Because one inadvertent effect of welfare payments
is the reward of low effort, chronic unemployment reduces the
personal work ethic. There are about nine million *helpless poor*
who are permanently unemployed, about seventy percent of whom
are black.[6] There are, in addition, a much larger number of *work-
avoiding poor* who alternate between meagerly paid jobs and welfare or help from family and friends.

Lack of job opportunities over many years has produced large
numbers of people with negative attitudes toward work in Appa-
lachia and the deep South. Ken Auletta examined poverty among
white people in Preston County, West Virginia, where in 1977
almost a third of the population was classified as poor, compared
to eleven percent nationally. Few blue collar jobs were available,
and less than a third of the male adults had completed high school.

Many adults showed little interest in a permanent job, sought
work only sporadically, and were not disturbed by being on welfare.
The culture of laziness was passed from one generation to the next.
Without regularly-employed role models, these individuals did not
know how to look for a job and failed to understand the importance
of coming to work regularly and on time. Unaccustomed to following orders or working consistently, they were often quickly fired
because of a surly attitude toward supervisors.[7]

Although nationally more than twice as many whites as blacks
are poor, black unemployment deserves special attention because
the percentage of the black population living in poverty is about
three times greater than whites.[8] During the past two decades,
millions of black Americans made great strides toward employment
in well-paying jobs. From 1972 to 1981, the percentage of blacks
who held jobs as accountants, computer specialists, chemists, and
medical doctors roughly doubled to reach about the same level as
the proportion of blacks in the general population (11.6 per cent).
Moreover, blacks' level of employment grew to exceed their proportion of the population in less lucrative skilled positions such as
nurses, health technicians, social and recreational workers, elementary school teachers, heavy equipment mechanics, industrial

checkers and inspectors, welders, assemblers, and meat packers and wrappers.[9]

Unfortunately, there are not enough of such good-paying jobs available for most poor people even if they did possess the necessary education. The decline in the available unskilled jobs and the increased disinclination to accept such jobs has increased poverty and unemployment among poorer blacks. Despite the gains made by blacks in good-paying jobs, the average amount of money black families earned in the 1970s as a proportion of white income dropped from 61 per cent to 57 percent.[10]

In the past three decades, the percentage of black males without jobs rose at all age levels.[11] The increase in joblessness among black young-adult males was particularly severe, rising from 23 percent in 1970 to 40 per cent in 1985.[12] Some of the increase in unemployment among young blacks can be explained by such factors as increased numbers entering military service and remaining in high school, but most of the increase appears due to low job availability and poor work attitudes.[13] Since habits of industriousness or laziness are strongly influenced by work experiences in youth, the high rate of unemployment among black youth is tragic.

America's ghettos are perfect training grounds for inaction and dependency. Poor blacks are heavily represented in the ghettos of large cities such as Detroit, Chicago, New York, and Washington, D.C. Many of the residents' parents or grandparents are descendants of Southern sharecroppers. There, racist laws and customs kept the poor black tenant farmers uneducated and dependent on the landowners. Moving north provided enough opportunities in education and jobs to allow a majority of blacks, those whose ambition and tenacity had somehow survived, to move into the broad American middle class.

Blacks who obtained decently paying jobs left the ghettos in large numbers to find better housing and escape crime. The poverty-stricken blacks who remained lost role models whom they could emulate by completing their education and applying themselves industriously on the job. Moreover, as the surge of jobs during and immediately following the second world war dried up, it became more difficult for even highly motivated ghetto blacks to break the bonds of poverty.

Nicholas Lemann has described the flight from Chicago slums by blacks who entered the middle class, leaving a self-propagating culture of poverty, crime, and welfare.[14] In such areas, role models are gang leaders, crooks, pimps, and prostitutes. There are few legal jobs that pay well or provide year-round employment. A minority of ghetto blacks are *helpless-poor*, having given up work completely, and a limited number are *work-oriented poor*, who hold permanent full-time jobs. The majority are *work-avoiding poor* who sporadically take low-paying jobs that generally are part-time or seasonal.

The giant, ugly concrete apartment buildings and broken-down wooden apartment houses occupied by the poor in America's cities mark these people as failures by the rest of society and themselves. The same kinds of housing in Japan contain apartments that are clean and well-kept by people who may have been selected by lottery because of the great scarcity of city housing.[15] Appreciating a place to live and caring for one's home are simply not a part of the culture of most ghetto residents. The degradation that the poor feel is not an attitude they have adopted out of thin air, but it is an acceptance of the derogatory view of them held by society.

The *work-avoiding poor* and *helpless poor* frequently fail to keep their apartments in good repair, reflecting an orientation toward the here-and-now and a rootlessness that denies the home as a central part of self-identity. Cyndi Curland spent nine years as a social worker and social-work supervisor in Salem County, New Jersey, where there are large pockets of white and black poverty. According to Curland:

> All of the screen doors in housing projects eventually get torn out. If you forget your key they charge you a dollar as a motivation to remember your key. They'll come on over with a master key. But the residents don't want to spend a dollar so they tear the screen and they put their hand in to get inside. Some break things. They stop up the sink because their apartments have no trash container. Decent housing doesn't make decent people.
>
> [The ghetto resident has] lived hand to mouth all her life. She doesn't know you take care of property and it shows. She doesn't own anything that's lasted her long. So we talk about having some

educational program for these people to teach them how to care for a place. There must be collective pressure to take care of a place. That's why public housing fails. Because some of the people don't have the will or the motivation to care for property. Its not part of their background or lifestyle. It was the belief that if you take them out of this wretchedness they'll be so appreciative. They'll take care of their places. Unfortunately, this was really misguided. They didn't know how to take care of the place.[16]

Edward Banfield has written of the culture of immediate gratification and lack of persistent, job-oriented effort that he contends maintains poverty:

The lower class individual lives from moment to moment. If he has any awareness of a future, it is of something fixed, fated, beyond his control: things happen *to* him, he does not *make* them happen. Impulse governs his behavior, either because he cannot discipline himself to sacrifice a present for a future satisfaction or because he has no sense of the future. He is therefore radically improvident: whatever he cannot consume immediately he considers valueless.[17]

Such attitudes among the poor reduce their chances to escape poverty by lessening the fortitude required to obtain an education, look for a job, and display the job-related behaviors necessary to keep a job (regular attendance, respect for authority, sufficient work effort). Of course, as we noted in the last chapter, affluent Americans also are increasingly showing a present-orientation, albeit not so severe as claimed by Banfield for ghetto residents.

In addition to the cultural transmission of faulty work values from one generation to the next, the helplessness and hopelessness of the *work-avoiding poor* and the *hopeless poor* result from each generation's own experience of repeated failure. The *work-avoiding poor*, who make up the majority of ghetto residents, have no clear-cut path to success to kindle optimism. They typically are illiterate or can barely read or write. They lack skills that will land them decent, paying jobs. The temporary jobs they hold for brief periods bring no new skills or contacts that will enable them to obtain better jobs.[18]

The low-paying jobs that *work-avoiding poor* male ghetto residents periodically hold include trash collection, washing dishes, serving as short-order cooks or busboys in restaurants, mopping floors, cleaning rest rooms, working part-time in small retail businesses such as liquor stores and take-outs, and selling sex, drugs or stolen goods. Some are night watchmen and delivery men. Unskilled construction work provides many temporary jobs, but the work is seasonal and too strenuous for the old or the infirm. And one has to have the cash to pay for union membership in order to obtain many construction jobs. Non-union construction jobs tend to be more plentiful in the suburbs, but getting there on public transportation, when possible, often involves a trip lasting hours.[19]

Most residents of the ghetto do not view their jobs as permanent, let alone leading to anything better. They see their low-paying jobs as menial because they accept the American identification of status with wealth. (Witness how most such workers are treated by their employers and regarded by society at large.) Although dissatisfied with temporary jobs, they do not have the ambition, training, or persistence to achieve something better. As Elliot Liebow noted in his classic study of the social structure of *work-avoiding poor* men, work is a peripheral part of their lives:

> Putting aside, for the moment, what the men say and feel, and looking at what they actually do and the choices they make, getting a job, keeping a job, and doing well at it is clearly of low priority. Arthur will not take a job at all. Leroy is supposed to be on his job at 4:00 P.M. but it is already 4:10 and he still cannot bring himself to leave the free games he has accumulated on the pinball machine in the carry-out. Tonk started a construction job on Wednesday, worked Thursday and Friday, then didn't go back again. On the same kind of job, Sea Cat quit in the second week. Sweets had been working three months as a busboy in a restaurant, then quit without notice, not sure why he did so.[20]
>
> Lethargy, disinterest, and general apathy on the job, so often reported by employers, has its street-corner counterpart. The men do not ordinarily talk about their jobs or ask one another about them. Although most of the men know who is or is not working at any given time, they may or may not know what particular job an

individual man has. There is no overt interest in job specifics as they relate to this or that person, in large part perhaps because the specifics are not especially relevant. To know that a man is working is to know approximately how much he makes and to know as much as one needs or wants to know about how he makes it. . . . So much does one job look like another that there is little to chose between them.[21]

Liebow wrote of a group of *work-avoiding poor* black men whose central meeting spot was a take-out shop, a quick-food spot open long hours, in a Washington, D.C., ghetto. But he could also have been writing about the street corners, social clubs, record shops or other spots in America where the *work-avoiding poor* congregate. The *work-avoiding poor* men who take part in such street-corner society seek warm friendship with other men and form romanticized intimate bonds. Strong friendships often lead others to believe that two men are blood relations, a view that the two may encourage. Such friendships meet emotional needs for belonging and affection and have practical value for times when a man may need help of some kind.

These men think of work primarily as a way to make a few dollars when needed rather than an important part of their lives. They have accepted the view of the larger society that they are failures whether they are unemployed or hold down a menial job. With no prospects for improving their lot, they concentrate on present pleasures and social relationships. The atmosphere is oriented to the present rather than shared past experiences or future hopes. Thus, many relationships between men are both intimate and fragile, easily broken over a great variety of possible disagreements.

The indolence bred by lack of available work and the inclination to refuse low-paying jobs is not confined to the black ghettos, as illustrated by the previously-discussed low work ethic among many white males in Preston County, West Virginia. Moreover, the high levels of unemployment among young black males outside the ghetto indicate that the lack of available jobs, as well as community values, is a major cause of poverty.[22] The repeated failure to find a job produces a learned laziness in or out of the ghetto.

Adolescent females in the ghetto frequently further reduce their economic mobility by becoming pregnant. There has been an over-all decline in the birthrate among all classes of society during the last twenty-five years.[23] But among women who bear children, the proportion of illegitimate births has been increasing. The proportion of black illegitimate births rose from a worrisome 25 percent in the early 1960s to nearly 60 percent today.[24]

Among the *work-avoiding poor* and *helpless-poor*, fathers usually take little responsibility for their offspring. Although the father may take pride in his manliness for producing a child and in seeing his physical likeness in another, raising the child is usually considered entirely the mother's responsibility.[25] The father feels little social pressure from the community to marry or support the unwed mother. To marry or move in with the woman usually establishes a financial burden and emotional ties that the father usually seeks to avoid. Living a present-oriented life with no hope for a better future makes a man shy away from a commitment to the mother and child.

A minority of fathers do live with the mothers of their children, sometimes in marriage, but they almost invariably leave within several years. The man's strong emotional ties are reserved for his own mother or whichever woman raised him. The most the woman who bears a man's child may generally hope for are his occasional contributions of small amounts of cash and periodic visits. The more illegitimate children a woman has borne, the more hesitant a new man is to become her lover. Children are not only an unwanted economic burden for the man, but they may resent the intrusion of this newcomer.

The unwed pregnant black teenager typically drops out of school and goes on welfare to support herself and her baby. Taking care of the child usually ends the mother's further schooling or job seeking. She is likely to have additional illegitimate children in the future. Many social workers encourage birth control. But the reaction of one resident who had received birth control pills from the family planning clinic is typical: "I was on the pill but it just didn't work," she said. When questioned more closely, she said: "Well, I don't know, I just stopped taking them. I figured I'd just get pregnant anyway. What was the use."[26] Without perceived career options or the likelihood of stable marital relationships, unwed pregnancy does not interfere with long-range plans.

There are distinct benefits of unwed motherhood for an adolescent girl living in the ghetto. Former social worker Curland notes:

> Handing women the pill is not enough even though a very young woman may face the strain of childbirth and the care of the child and supporting the child. You and I would think that this would be motivation enough never to do it again. But of course, in reality, the motivation is not there because they have a very poor self-image, a limited view of their potential. So they have less motivation to stay not pregnant.
>
> Its very easy to say, "If you stay in school, you can find a job." But many people don't stay in school. You're dealing with people who aren't really used to following through on things. These are people who often missed school, who often were late for school. Part of it is self-image. If you don't think much of yourself, you don't care what happens.
>
> There is now strong social pressure against abortion. The message to the pregnant teenager is: "If you want an abortion we consider you a murderess and we're not going to give you a cent, but if you get pregnant we'll give you food and care. We'll have you all signed up so that the day the baby is born all the medical bills will be paid retroactively." If you have these two choices, what is the woman going to do?
>
> Furthermore, you may have a young girl, and she might be sixteen, and she's not getting along with her mother and she's sexually active and out a lot. She's not doing her homework and she's cutting school. Having a baby is the best thing that could happen to her. Now I'm not saying that she's consciously making this decision, any more than older women have made a choice to get pregnant, to have seven or eight children in order to have a bigger grant. But there's no motivation to *not* get pregnant. Because if she does get pregnant and has that child and she makes a good enough case about what a horrible time she has with her mother, she can get her own place.
>
> We set her up in her own apartment. She finds a place. She gets

her own welfare grant. She is an emancipated minor in the eyes of the law. And so she can quit school if she's sixteen or older. And even if she's younger than sixteen, chances are the school system is not going to come after her. She'll claim. "Well, who is going to take care of my baby?"[27]

Other observers of ghetto culture have similarly noted the escapist benefits that result from unwed pregnancy: "In the absence of educational and work experiences which can provide young women with positive identities, motherhood is viewed as a certain path to maturity and immediate income."[28] The stigma against unwed pregnancy has been replaced in the black ghetto by the view that the welfare mother's rearing of illegitimate children is the normal role. As a field report from New Rochelle, New York, indicated:

> The girls' mothers were tolerant of their daughters' pregnancies in most cases. Many of the girls' mothers' friends had pregnant daughters, so that it was almost expected for their daughters to get pregnant. There seemed to exist a peer group of . . . young mothers."[29]

Unwed motherhood is viewed as a short-term escape from the teenage girl's everyday problems of attending school, setting career goals, and living in a possibly troubled home. These immature adolescents often bring up problem children. A child reared by a young single parent who is frequently on welfare lacks a role model with industrious work attitudes and habits that can be emulated. If the rate of unwed births among blacks is very high, it is equally disturbing that at a time when birth control methods are more available than ever before, unwed births by whites have risen to a national level of thirteen percent.[30] The teenage pregnancy rate in the U.S. is double that of Canada, England, and France, triple that of Sweden and seven times that of the Netherlands.[31]

Traditionally, unwed motherhood among whites and blacks was a stigma because premarital sex violated conventional morality. Today, there is no strong community criticism of premarital sex, and conservative religious groups have depicted abortion as a heinous crime. Thus, unwed teenage girls who are pregnant are encouraged to bear children. Poor white women, as blacks, often find advantages in bearing a child out of wedlock. A girl who is having difficulty in school and feels unwanted and unloved can often look forward to increased concern and attention by parents and relatives for her and her new baby. Counseling agencies, public and private, will help her adjust to motherhood. Welfare agencies will provide money.

Her life will be given new meaning and pleasure. No one will ever check up on the unwed mother to see how well she is bringing up the child. She will escape the persistent demands of the workplace.

A common stereotype presents the welfare mother as having a large number of children and staying on welfare forever. Welfare mothers do have more children than the national average.[32] The majority of welfare mothers do not stay on the dole forever since the average block of time the assistance is received is only 30 months, and only about ten to fifteen percent of single mothers who go on welfare continue receiving payments for eight straight years or more.[33] But many single women come from families that received welfare payments, and they go on welfare more than once.[34] Thus, many and perhaps most welfare mothers receive aid repeatedly, broken by intermittent periods of work or financial support by a man. Once on welfare, a single woman is likely to go on welfare again in the future.

The Manpower Demonstration Research Corporation reviewed the progress of unwed mothers taking part in a large federally-funded educational-training program. The women who successfully completed the program and obtained and retained jobs were generally those who "made a conscious decision to break out of a day-to-day existence and were doggedly determined to develop a skill or at least acquired the work experience they knew was necessary to enter the regular job market."[35] Among the poor, as with more affluent individuals, those who believe they can control their own future and actively set goals for themselves have been found to show greater gains in promotions and earnings than those who believe important changes in their lives are determined mainly by external causes.[36]

Without a culture that emphasizes the importance of work or

provides successful role models to emulate, few long-term ghetto residents develop the self-confidence or resilience for overcoming poverty. From a lifetime of failure, the *work-avoiding poor* typically lack the self-confidence to accept good jobs on the rare occasions when they are offered. Liebow tells of one man who while in the Army was caught up in confusion and doubt as the result of a minor promotion. Another man, a painter, was frightened off when asked to give a bid on painting a whole house. Unfortunately, as the percentage of illegitimate children continues to rise and as unskilled young adults fail to find jobs, the welfare culture becomes more widespread. The poor tend to shift from the status of *work-oriented* to *work-avoiding* or *helpless*.

Each new generation of welfare recipients born in the ghetto is trapped by lack of opportunity and negative attitudes toward work. Many ghetto residents fail to imbue their children with the desire for education that would make them eligible for better-paying jobs. Each generation, brought up in ignorance and poverty begets the next similar generation in the cycle. Attempts to educate the young in the inner-city ghettos are usually unsuccessful. Nicholas Lemann presents a tapestry of failed education in which students who care nothing for learning are matched with teachers who have given up trying to teach. He states that the following example from a Chicago high school history class is typical:

> In Joe Valenziano's American-history class, the students were finishing their homework from the night before which consisted of answering a series of questions by copying the answers out of textbooks. For handing this in the students would get five bonus points on their next exam. . . . A student put a paper on his desk. Some of the answers were copied correctly and others were not: who was George III? "He was a spy." Explain the role of blacks in the Revolutionary War: "forming of America." Valenziano glanced at the paper and wrote a 5 on it. "If it looks good and they answer the questions, they get five points."[37]

What this teacher was doing was literally worse than nothing. As we shall see later from experimental studies, such reward for low effort produces a generalized laziness. An education that leaves a person lacking the skills, self-confidence, and the perseverance necessary to obtain and retain a good-paying job does nothing to break ghetto poverty. One resident of the Washington, D.C., ghetto described his wasted education as follows:

> I graduated from high school [Baltimore] but I don't even know anything. I'm dumb. Most of the time I don't even say I graduated, "cause then somebody asks me a question and I can't answer it, and they think I was lying about graduating. . . . They graduated me but I didn't know anything. I had lousy grades but I guess they wanted to get rid of me.[38]

Nationally, one-third of black students and an even greater proportion of Hispanic students drop out of high school.[39] Most of these dropouts are not educated well enough to obtain white collar jobs. And there are simply not enough low-level blue collar jobs for many people who want to work. When ghetto children have as a role model a mother who subsists on welfare and a father who is seldom present and works only sporadically, they fail to develop either the persistence or the work skills necessary to complete school or hold down a job.

In the previous chapter, we noted that affluent students often fail to build up a reservoir of persistence because class work is trivial and easy. Ghetto students similarly fail to learn to work hard in school. The ghetto culture provides neither role models nor incentives for studying hard. Students are expected to perform at a minimal level.

People who have become accustomed to lives of leisure (including many rich people who inherited wealth) have not the persistence to tolerate the unpleasantness often involved in a regular full-time job. Many ghetto residents, to an even greater extent than the affluent majority, have come to value sensual pleasure and entertainment ahead of work and long-term goals. Alvin Gouldner, the sociologist, observed that the opportunity to "give up promiscuous sex, give up freely expressed aggression and wild spontaneity [so] you, or your children, may be admitted to the world of three square meals a day, to a high school or perhaps even a college education, to the world of charge accounts, of secure jobs and respectability" may not be very inviting.[40] As one student in a government-sponsored work-training program put it:

> Man, you go two, three years not working and hanging around and smoking reefer or drinking and then you get a job—you can't handle it. You do two, three years of idleness and after the first two, three weeks of working, you feel people are pushing you. You say, "I don't want to get up in the morning, get pushed and shoved. I'm gonna get on welfare." Unless a man sits down and gives it good thought, he's not gonna figure out how he got there. He's gonna fall into the same cycle. I'm twenty-eight, and have been working for fourteen years. Never the same job for more than one year.[41]

The ghetto student who drops out of school may later be induced to enter a government-sponsored or privately-sponsored remedial education program. A significant minority, perhaps a third of the students, do succeed in well-run remedial programs.[42] This figure overstates the overall percentage of success because in most parts of the country such programs are voluntary rather than required to receive welfare (no matter what the law states) and thus tend to enroll the more motivated students. Many of those sufficiently motivated to sign up for the programs would have found jobs on their own.

The true gain in private sector employment that results from mandatory job-training programs appears to be more like one in twenty.[43] The majority of those enrolled fail to complete remedial programs. They lack motivation, good work habits, and the resilience to withstand initial failure. As one teacher of welfare mothers noted, "I see it all the time. They feel they can't succeed. If they don't succeed once, their confidence is gone."[44]

The development of a class of poor Americans resigned to intermittent work and government handouts is not much of a drain on the federal government's resources. Because people other than one-parent households or the medically disabled receive minimal aid, less than one percent of the gross national product is spent on welfare. Various groups of financially well-off citizens, such as many thousands of affluent farmers, receive more than this in government handouts.

76

The greater financial loss is the potential productivity that the *work-avoiding poor* and *helpless poor* could add to the economy. Even this consideration pales beside the destruction of the American dream of working hard toward a more prosperous future. No nation can indefinitely retain the loyalty of citizens pushed aside from what they consider the opportunities of the majority.

Because a culture of laziness has taken root in the black ghettos and the pockets of white poverty is no reason for the American people to respond with pious demands for self-help. Poverty in America will not go away by ignoring or punishing it. It does not really matter whether we wish to assess ninety percent of the blame for persistent ghetto poverty on slavery and poor economic conditions and ten percent on lack of personal responsibility, or vice versa. The point is that most ghetto residents have poor work values that they are passing on to their children.

Since the majority of the poor receive little welfare aid, eliminating welfare is not going to solve the problem. On the other hand, since welfare encourages poor women to become pregnant and drop out of the school and the work force, it is also clear that greater welfare support would increase indolence. The government and the business community must spend more money on the poor in ways that will teach them stronger work values and give them hope for a better future. We will be able to consider how this might be done in the final chapter, after completing our analysis of the determinants of laziness and industriousness.

CHAPTER 4

Laziness Among Television Viewers

Judging by the amount of time people devote to it, television is America's favorite leisure activity. Adults spend more time watching television than at any other activity except work and sleep.[1] TV causes Americans to sleep less, attend fewer social gatherings, talk to each other less, read fewer books and magazines, and skimp on housecleaning.[2] This reduction in the time spent carrying out various activities is just the surface effect of television. The present chapter shows how television makes viewers lazy and increases their desire for sensual satisfaction, both of which interfere with hard work. Television researchers distinguish three kinds of outcomes of television viewing. The *act* of watching refers to the hours spent before a one-way entertainment medium. The *form* of programing concerns audiovisual techniques such as the pace of the action and the frequency of changes in scene and characters. *Content* refers to the explicit and implicit messages that are communicated. Each of these components of television contributes to viewers' indolence and reduces their willingness to work industriously at school or on the job.

*　*　*

The act of watching television teaches mental passivity and flightiness. Television is an information-poor medium that requires much less attention than reading. All the words spoken on a thirty-minute evening newscast will fit on the front page of a newspaper, with room to spare.[3] Even the "talking heads" that dominated programing in the early days of TV could provide only a very limited amount of information in comparison to the printed page. Television requires even less concentration than conversation since, as a one-way conduit of communication, it has the drawback of never responding to the questions, suggestions, or innovations of the viewer.

Television viewing is a mindless activity. The amount of thinking while watching television, in comparison to other activities, was studied by having adults record their conscious mental activity when signalled by a beeper at various times during the day and evening. These self-reports indicate that viewing involved less challenge, less skill, and more relaxation than working, reading, socializing, eating, waiting, or idling (sitting and not doing anything, staring out a window or daydreaming). Moreover, television was rated as involving greater passivity, less concentration, and less alertness than all other activities studied except idling.[4]

Like adults, children relax while watching television. When three- to five-year-olds were observed together with their parents in a laboratory that was set up as a living room, the children talked less often while watching television, were less active, and paid less attention to their parents.[5] Of course, even the minor degree of concentration required by TV may be a challenge to very young children. But youngsters soon come to understand the simple forms and content of television programing, after which they exert less mental effort comprehending most shows than they would reading, playing with other children, or doing their homework. Long hours spent passively before the tube accustoms viewers to mindless ease, a learned habit of mental indolence.

Television also teaches viewers to be flighty, switching their attention toward and away from the screen as the whim strikes. Television will never scold viewers for not paying attention; nor will it reward them for persistence in difficult physical or cognitive pursuits. While watching a program such as *Sesame Street,* for example, it is common for children to look away from the screen about 150 times an hour, usually for periods of less than 15 seconds.[6] Children become accustomed to being entertained by a machine that doesn't complain about being ignored or treated rudely. They learn to tune in and tune out information as the whim strikes.

The act of watching also makes viewers lazy by promoting a hedonistic life style. Hours spent before the screen provide a bland experience because the communication is one-way and because programing is designed to be simple enough to keep viewers from turning to other channels for light entertainment.[7] The viewer's mild titillation often is insufficient to maintain arousal at a comfortable level. Supplementary stimulation is needed.

Reading and prolonged conversation while watching would interfere too much with following the gist of shows. So watchers learn to complement viewing with sensual pleasures that require little attention. Conversation is replaced by cuddling with family members, eating, and in some cases at a later age, by smoking and alcohol consumption.

When the TV set is on, parents talk less to their children but touch and fondle them more.[8] Such touching and cuddling contribute positively to children's emotional adjustment. But when carried to the extreme of replacing most family discussion, tactual comfort retards the development of intellectual persistence.

Eating also provides a needed boost in stimulation while watching. The tendency to eat while viewing increases with age. By sixth grade, three out of four children eat while they watch. By tenth grade, the figure is up to nine out of ten.[9] Heavy viewers also smoke more cigarettes.[10] These supplementary activities combine with the mild titillation of programing to provide prolonged, if mild, sensory pleasure. Thousands of hours of womb-like comfort achieved by this mix of small pleasures accustom the viewer to continual sensual satisfaction.

Heavy watchers build a *shell of comfort* around themselves in which time goes by mindlessly as they receive mild pleasure from viewing, supplemented by the other minor stimulants. By comparison to the enjoyment experienced within the electronic womb, the experience of *trying* hard at school or job becomes more unpleasant. The desire for continual sensual pleasure instilled by television reduces the time students are willing to spend on homework and the concentration they are willing to exert at school. Concentration by workers on the job is similarly reduced.

Rapid changes of scene and topic, used to hold viewers' attention, interfere with the development of the ability to sustain concentration on complicated tasks. In TV's youth, competition for viewers produced experimentation with techniques for capturing and maintaining audience interest. Physical motion and changes in scene and sound intensity were found to be effective attention getters. Because of competition, programers continued over the years to speed up changes in person, scene, and topic until many of today's adult adventure and game shows, soap operas, made-for-television movies, and news programs proceed at a frantic pace. Even situation comedies jump from one scene to the next at frequent intervals.

With television producers and writers believing that pace is particularly important for retaining the attention of children, virtually all of children's entertainment programing has been segmented into small independent bits that are taped together to make a show. Children are exposed to rapid changes of topic and scene within a program and to numerous disruptions by advertisements and program announcements.

Public television, as with commercial programing, tries to capture a large audience and has adopted the traditional attention-grabbing techniques for children's educational shows. The most popular children's educational program, *Sesame Street*, has been a continuing success since it began in 1969. The show was designed "to improve the language, numerical, and reading skills of children between the ages of three and five."[11] Approximately forty short unrelated segments comprise a sixty-minute show. Each segment provides a change in characters, format, content, and the concepts being taught.[12]

The plan was to use the segments "as a bunch of quick, funny and entertaining moments—like a collection of the catchy com-

mercials that most young children chant around the house."[13] Even
the bouncy melody of the show's theme song was designed to grab
children's attention:

> Sunny day, keeping the clouds away
> On my way to where the air is sweet,
> Can you tell me how to get,
> How to get to Sesame street?

The theme's words are accompanied by quickly changing shots of
activities that appeal to preschoolers.[14] A large wagon drawn by
two horses carries a bunch of youngsters, followed by scenes of
children using a set of swings, feeding a lamb, playing soccer, and
running down a street.

The show's original director of research was Dr. Edward L.
Palmer who previously studied children's television watching habits as a research professor. Palmer explained, "Every element in
Sesame Street [must say to preschoolers] this is for you . . . The
answers we're looking for come from what [kids] indicate by their
behavior while watching a segment. We watch the children as they
watch."[15] The show's first executive director noted: "The children
we used for our appeal studies were all poor children in day-care
centers, but it turned out that all pre-schoolers have pretty much
the same concerns—and they're all conditioned by the same television shows: *Batman, Get Smart, Laugh-In.*"[16]

The rapid pace of children's programing inhibits the development of patience for concentrating on a single topic. Learning to
read and paying attention to lectures at school are thereby retarded.[17] As a letter writer to a newspaper warned almost two
decades ago: "To give a child thirty seconds of one thing and then
to switch it and give him thirty seconds to another is to nurture
irrelevance and to give reinforcement to a type of intellectual process that can never engage in sustained and developed thought."[18]

Anyone who has observed young children in a classroom knows
how difficult it is to maintain their attention. Students can actively
"interrupt an activity by getting out of the their seats, being disruptive, inappropriately calling out, or coming up to the teacher."[19]
Or they can passively daydream or doze off. It is only natural that

youngsters made inattentive and flighty by TV are uncooperative when asked to learn difficult academic subjects.

The mental passivity and flightiness produced by viewing television makes the teacher's job much more difficult. TV-fed children come to the classroom accustomed to attention-getting movement and quick changes of topic. By contrast, the concentration required by classroom lectures and homework seems too unpleasant to tolerate. Young students expect to be allowed to shift attention frequently or to daydream as the whim strikes. Kids talk, play, and fight during instruction at school partly because they are used to ignoring the TV set at will.

Teachers are often taught to deal with television-reared inattentive children by dividing activities into short segments in order to keep the children watching and listening.[20] Of course, briefly dipping into an academic subject is not a very efficient teaching method because the teacher cannot get far into the material before moving on to the next topic.

Unfortunately, little carefully-controlled scientific research has been carried out concerning the effects of television on children's passivity and flightiness. A number of studies have reported that beyond the fourth grade, there is a negative relationship between the amount of television watching and scores on various measures of educational achievement.[21] Such findings may indicate that television watching increases passivity and flightiness, but other interpretations are equally plausible.

For example, on the average, poor children watch more television and perform worse in school than middle-class children. Thus, the low school achievement by heavy television watchers could be either an outcome of watching or some factor related to poverty, such as the low quality of the schools that poor children attend or the insufficient emphasis placed by their parents on hard study. It seems likely that all of these factors are involved.[22]

One of the best-controlled studies examined the relationship between television watching and school achievement by El Salvadoran junior high school students over a three-year period before the subsequent military chaos. The poverty interpretation of poor achievement among heavy watchers was ruled out by controlling for parents' socioeconomic status and the children's initial reading skills. Youngsters who first acquired a television set some time during the three-year period studied were found to fall steadily behind their expected gain in reading skills.[23]

Additional evidence suggests that rapid changes in character, scene and topic in children's programing reduce students' task persistence.[24] The most extensive experimental study of the effects of television programing on children's task persistence and tolerance of delay examined the normal, everyday activities of ninety-seven four- and five-year old children enrolled during the summer in nursery school.[25] An instance of task persistence was scored each time a child encountered difficulty in a task and made three or more attempts to overcome the difficulty. Tolerance of delay was scored each minute that a child waited voluntarily to obtain materials or to receive the attention of an adult.

These behaviors were observed for three weeks prior to the introduction of television entertainment. Over the next four weeks the children were divided in three groups. One group watched a total of twelve episodes of the violent and quick-paced television cartoons *Batman* and *Superman*, another group watched the slower-paced and more prosocially-oriented *Mister Rogers' Neighborhood*, and a third group watched films that involved less aggression than the cartoons and fewer prosocial lessons than *Mister Rogers' Neighborhood*.

The change in behavior for each child during this period and two weeks after the last showing of these films was measured. Among the half of the children with the higher IQs, viewing *Mister Rogers' Neighborhood* produced the greatest persistence in classroom activities, and watching the fast-paced cartoons produced the least persistence. In addition, regardless of the children's IQ, watching the cartoons resulted in the least tolerance of delay.[26] The rapidly-paced cartoons had made the children intolerant of delay and unwilling to persevere on difficult tasks.

When *Sesame Street* was first introduced on Israeli television in 1971, an experiment was carried out in which children watched either *Sesame Street* or nature and adventure films one hour per day for eight days. Next, to test the children's perseverance, they were given a booklet filled with random numbers and told to cross out specified digits. The children were asked to work as fast and as long as they could. The children who had watched *Sesame Street* were far less persistent than the children who had watched the nature and adventure films.[27]

This disappointed the researcher who had hoped to find that *Sesame Street* made children more persistent but was instead forced to conclude that: ". . . it must have been the [children's] willingness to persevere that was affected by their exposure to the fast-paced, kaleidoscopic structure of the program."[28] Although much more research is needed to reach definitive conclusions, the preceding findings indicate that watching television reduces task persistence and tolerance for delay in the pursuit of goals.

The content of television advertisements and programs denigrates working-class and middle-class jobs, and promotes a hedonistic life style that discourages hard work. I noted in the first chapter that television programming in the 1950s and 60s disparaged working class occupations. Such portrayals have undermined the dignity of blue collar work and furthered the decline of the personal work ethic. These shows continue their negative message through reruns.

Jackie Gleason's portrayal of a lovable but foolish bus driver named Ralph Kramden shows a man who hates his job but is too incompetent to qualify for other work. His wild schemes to improve his lot always end in disaster, followed by his wife Alice saying, "I told you so." Ralph's buddy Ed Norton is a sewer worker who is portrayed as even more bumbling than Ralph. The idea of working in a sewer is itself the starting point of many jokes that make the occupation seem laughable.

The situation is getting worse. Working-class parents largely disappeared in series begun in the late 1970s. Re-runs of more recent vintage treat the working class as too unimportant to think about, let alone ridicule. Instead, television producers pointed their battering ram at the middle class. George Jefferson, the proprietor of a group of dry cleaning stores, is the middle-class equivalent of the 1950s' Riley (*The Life of Riley*) who always got himself into trouble through ineptness.

Welcome Back Kotter degrades teachers and education, helping to destroy the vestiges of civility and study habits in school. Teacher

Kotter can't control students; the message seems to be "why try?" In the old days, another teacher named Mr. Boynton was portrayed as socially inept on the *Our Miss Brooks* show, but at least there were no upstart students characters in featured roles who prevented his teaching.

In TV series beginning in the 1980s, even teachers and owners of small businesses were too unimportant to serve as principal characters. The newer shows concentrate on protagonists who are rich and/or have highly prestigious jobs. The father in the *Bill Cosby Show* is a medical doctor who lives very well even though he never seems to go to work. His wife is a lawyer who is financially successful enough to buy a painting on a whim for an amount of money equal to the yearly salary of many working class people.

Cosby's show is one of the few to employ a social scientist to review the material. The psychiatrist and Harvard professor, Alvin Poussaint, defends the characters' occupations by arguing:

> The American public has been so programed to seeing blacks as hip, jive talkers that they don't appreciate that some blacks are in the mainstream. . . . Actually it is the white critics who accuse us of becoming too 'white.' Black families can identify with the show.[29]

In reality, few middle class families can relate to the high economic status of these characters. The Cosby program has many fine qualities but saying something nice about the middle class is not one of them. The great financial success portrayed for both husband and wife is so far beyond realistic possibilities for the great majority of Americans that it emphasizes the lack of success of the working class and middle class.

Another series in which the protagonists have elite occupations is *Family Ties*. The father has an executive position at a television station and the mother is an architect. In *Dallas* everyone in the main family is an oil tycoon. In these shows, the people with high-paying jobs predominate; everyone else is background. No one else has status; no other jobs are worth bothering about.

It is a wonder that any of these protagonists are able to hold on to a job or fortune, as they hardly ever seem to work. I only saw Doctor Cosby work once. As a favor to his daughter, Dr. Cosby saw one of her friends. On *Dallas* the rich don't work except to make an occasional deal. Popular television series communicate the view that if you accumulate enough money to *stop* working, you're somebody. Otherwise, you're nobody. Why take pride in accomplishments as a teacher, truck driver, bank teller, or computer clerk when, according to most television programing, you simply don't exist?

The disparaging portrayal of working-class and middle-class jobs is accompanied by the promotion of sensual desires. The average television viewer is bombarded from early childhood until old age with thousands of hours of commercials and programs glorifying a hedonistic life style that is antithetical to hard work. Commercials convey the message that happiness is to be found in sensual enjoyment associated with novelty, excitement, sex, eating, alcohol consumption, and smoking and not by achieving long-term goals through diligent effort.

As the viewer comforts himself by eating and perhaps consuming alcohol or smoking while watching TV, advertisers encourage him to seek still more pleasure in these activities. Even the government puts in a plug for pointless excitement in the form of lotteries. The change in a person's outlook produced by advertisements goes beyond the choice of one brand of beer, candy, or VCR over another. The hedonistic doctrine promoted by television is generic, calling forth more time spent pursuing sensual pleasure.

The cumulative effects of four hours a day of ads and entertainment programing viewed throughout the average person's youth strongly influences the kinds of behaviors and social relationships considered desirable. Consumption-oriented advertising instills a hedonistic outlook that makes high effort at school or job highly unpleasant:

> There now exist more opportunities for immediate self-indulgence, and people are subject to innumerable messages urging them to consume and providing reassurance against any guilt they might feel in so doing. The complexities of this effort are infinite. One central feature of it is the repeated association—or the deliberate confusion—in advertising messages, of possession and enjoyment of many consumer goods with specifically erotic need and satisfac-

tion. Ready submission to felt need is projected as normal, rewarding and desirable.[30]

The inculcation of sensualism begins well before children are old enough, by about age eight, to distinguish commercials from entertainment programing and to understand that commercials are intended to sell a product. Most young children say they enjoy watching Saturday morning TV commercials.[31] When asked, "What is the difference between a TV program and a TV commercial?," the young children usually respond on the basis of perceptual cues such as: "Commercials are short and programs are long."[32] When asked, "Why are commercials shown on TV?," young children generally give incorrect answers.[33] The failure of youngsters to distinguish the intent of commercials is also suggested by the fact that they show less of a decrease of attention during commercials than do older children.[34]

Obeying the "limits" allowed by the guidelines of the National Association of Broadcasters, television stations devote between 9.5 minutes and 16 minutes per hour to advertising, depending on the time of day.[35] Children are bombarded by about 20,000 commercials annually.[36] Food advertising constitutes the majority of commercial announcements presented during breaks in programing aimed at children, with toys accounting for most of the remaining commercials.[37]

Children see an average of 5,000 food ads annually, over half of which involve high-calorie, high-sugar, and low-nutrition products.[38] Sugar was found to be the chief ingredient of forty percent of a sample of food products advertised in children's programing. When not the primary ingredient, it was the second ingredient in most cases.[39]

A substantial majority of food ads directed at children depict consumption of the product as a basic part of kids' fun. Youngsters are frequently shown laughing and playing in amusement parks. They sing and dance around the cereal and candy; they yell, tease one another, and consume the product while giggling and grinning. These scenes are also often accompanied by verbal assertions about the "fun" nature of the brand.[40] Candy/sweet ads also often associate their brand with energy or sporting ability in such activities as:

. . . skateboarding, basketball, skiing, tennis, volleyball, football and cheerleading, gymnastics and other vigorous activities. An example is the Cracker Jack commercial in which skateboarding and gymnastic abilities are demonstrated to the jingle—'What do you call a kid that can skate like that . . . you call that kid a crackerjack. . . .'[41]

Many ads associate cereal consumption with adventure. For example: "While eating the cereal, a child is attacked by a lion and a giant that come up from behind him. By spelling 'lion' and 'giant' in his spoon with cereal, the child is able to eat his attackers (Post Alphabits)."[42]

The message of cereal and candy ads is that it is normal and proper for kids to have a grand time gorging themselves with sugar. The message works. Advertisements for sugar-laced cereals and sweets produce not only a preference for a particular brand, but greater overall consumption.[43] Kids come to use and enjoy the sensual pleasures of overdosing on "candy, heavily sugared cereals, snack foods, soda pop, hot dogs, and empty calorie foods."[44] Extended exposure to food ads increases children's belief that sugared cereals and candy are highly nutritious, causes children to make more requests for the advertised products, and results in conflict when parents deny such requests.[45]

Advertising by fast food chains supplements the child's growing sugar addiction by creating habits of self-indulgence involving a wider variety of fattening foods. A sample of television commercials of chains like McDonald's and Burger King emphasized fun and happiness in one hundred percent of the ads, and energy and sporting ability in twenty-five percent.[46] Children who are heavy television watchers emphasize as important features of food products both the good taste and the fun of eating.[47]

Overeating is also promoted by adult advertising. Among high and medium income families, heavy television watching leads to an increased frequency of agreement with the statement: "I'm not concerned about weight, I eat whatever I want, whenever I want." Low income families show little change in such nutritional complacency as a result of heavy television viewing. Most already are very complacent about overeating and remain so.[48]

The sugar addiction and the identification of eating with enjoyable activities are a strong opening wedge in the creation of a hedonistic outlook on life. Adolescent viewers are taught by commercials to take a greater interest in how people look and smell. Advertising increases fourth- to seventh-grade students' use of deodorants, mouthwashes, and acne cream. Heavy viewers are twice as likely to use these products as light viewers.[49]

Adolescents learn what kinds of behavior are normal and enjoyable from watching television commercials and programs. About one-third of all teenagers questioned admit to often getting ideas about dating behavior and trying them out based on what they observe in entertainment shows.[50] A hedonistic outlook is also encouraged by the increasingly widespread use of sexual eroticism in advertising.

In Van Huesen shirt ads, the voyeuristic camera pans up a woman's bare legs until the viewer sees that the woman is wearing only a shirt which reaches just below her crotch. Using her most seductive manner, she says that the shirt belongs to a man friend. Just so the point is not missed, the viewer sees a repetition of the suggestive sequence involving another woman. Such ads promote a preoccupation with sex and carry the message that casual sexual relationships are common and socially acceptable. Television programing and advertising contributed to a two-thirds increase in the number of sexually active teenagers during the 1970s.[51]

Major companies selling inexpensive men's cosmetics use overt eroticism in their magazine and television commercials, leading to increased sexual preoccupation. Jovan's TV commercial for Musk includes three hands clasped on a bronzed thigh and a wet-kiss in a shower.[52] Launching an ad campaign for a new scent called Obsession, Calvin Klein used women's magazines to show hazy images of nudity and group sex.[53] An ad for five-dollar cologne by English leather features:

> . . . a sketch of a man and a woman right out of the *Kama Sutra*. Old Spice's couple appeared to be on the way to the bedroom. . . . Some of the bottle ads had bottles that were designed so . . . that they could have been launched not at Bloomingdale's but at Cape Canaveral.[54]

Upscale men's cosmetics advertising uses "tasteful" advertising that carries the message that casual sexual affairs are the norm. One television commercial shows a handsome and well-dressed man unexpectedly meet a woman friend outside what is meant to be recognized as the New York Plaza hotel. She happens to be, you guessed it, a beautiful and well-dressed woman. She notes that he still uses Aramis fragrance. They have planes to catch but when asked what she is doing now, she replies, "I think I am missing my plane."[55]

The increased eroticism in magazine and television advertisements for clothing and perfume is being matched by the introduction of sexual titillation for such ordinary household products as detergent, salami, and pianos.[56] Such ads encourage interest in sensual pursuits at the expense of the self-control needed to pursue long-term goals. The ads promote the view that personal satisfaction is closely related to sensual pleasures and that there is something abnormal about people who fail to devote a large portion of their waking hours to sensual enjoyment.

Students who work hard on homework and employees who put in extra hours to do a careful job are made to feel they are missing out on the good life. Why work hard to achieve distant goals when present sensual pleasure is the ideal?

Entertainment programing carries the same message that a continual concern with sensual satisfaction is the norm and the ideal. In soap operas and weekly series, self-denial in order to achieve long-term goals is seldom displayed. Studies of television programing reveal the virtual absence of instances showing an individual deciding to withstand the temptation to satisfy urges and desires, whether or not the behavior is approved of by society.[57] An analysis of over 300 television programs showed that the number of instances involving "postponing a small reward for a larger one and/or spending additional time or effort on a task so that a goal may be reached or a product made better" averaged about two per hour, far fewer than the frequency of altruistic acts, aggression, or expressions of sympathy.[58]

In order to appeal to sexual desires, women are often presented in erotically enticing clothing and portrayed as using their bodies seductively. Camera angles and close-ups are used suggestively. Males are frequently shown as interested in women only as sex objects.[59] Soap operas depict numerous scenes in which unmarried partners lay on a bed or couch in passionate embrace getting more and more excited until, that's right, fade out to a commercial. But the viewer knows very well that IT happened during the two-minute commercial.

Such graphic depiction of sexuality with the strong suggestion but not the actual act of intercourse allows soap operas to attract viewers while escaping trouble with network sensors or private watchdog groups. Sexual innuendo can be highly arousing, sometimes surpassing the excitement produced by more explicit presentations.[60] Sexual promiscuity is encouraged on television by presenting allusions to intercourse more frequently involving unmarried partners than married partners.[61] Viewers learn that preoccupation with sex is normal, exciting, and admirable.

Situation comedies that supposedly poke fun at current mores and morals use sexual titillation to attract viewers. The audience sees that rampant promiscuity is the norm and a basic part of good living. Take the show *Night Court*. This program contains two-dimensional people in one-dimensional plots, and pretends little more. The comedy writers are good cartoonists and the show is amusing. But *Night Court* conveys the typical emphasis on sex.

Dan Fielding, the prosecuting attorney, demonstrates a ravenous sexual craving. Fielding lets prospective partners know that his interest in them is limited to sexual intercourse. And beautiful women respond to him as if casual sex was all there was to life. If Fielding's monomania is treated comedically, causual sex is glorified.

Fielding's sexual liaisons are presented partly for comedy, but more importantly for sexual titillation. Fielding scores frequently. *Scores*, a sports term, is the appropriate verb because Fielding wants conquests rather than friendships. In one episode, Fielding got a date with a curvaceous lady dressed in tight clothing who continually exaggerated the movement of her breasts and behind. As an introduction to their first date, she told Fielding that her biorythms caused her to be more and more sexually aroused as midnight approached, after which she would rapidly lose interest.

Later into the evening, the lady's *heat* intensified. The "comedic" aspect of this subplot was that circumstance would interfere with the opportunity for consummation until after midnight, when the lady would no longer be interested.

The unbelievable plots involving Fielding's lust change from episode to episode, but the implicit message does not. Sexual desires can be satisfied by using others as objects, not in a cruel way to hurt anyone, but simply as partners in a brief liaison who happily agree to a relationship consisting of a quick coupling. Preoccupation with sex is taught as normal and satisfying.

A smaller number of entertainment programs treat sexuality in a more responsible manner. In *The Bill Cosby Show* the husband and wife enjoy flirting with each other as part of a warm, loving relationship. Sexual interest is treated as normal and enjoyable. Not hidden from the television cameras but also not presented excessively or voyeuristically.

No one presentation of a television show or movie is going to make much of an impact on most people's sexual desires and habits.[62] But thousands of hours of programing with a sensualistic message can have a major effect on what viewers consider normal behavior and the good life. Watchers of movies, television entertainment shows, and ads learn that continually feeding one's body with food, alcohol, and sexual partners is society's ideal.

The individual who works hard for greater achievement at school or job is made to feel he or she is missing out on a truly satisfying life that results from continual sensual pleasure. Together with the denigration of working-class and middle-class jobs and the mental passivity and flightiness produced by viewing, television is a strong force for laziness.

Marx was wrong. *Television* is the opiate of the masses.

CHAPTER 5

Industriousness Among the Japanese

In the late 1930s, State Department officials expressed alarm at Japan's strong militaristic sentiment. By 1941, half of Japan's national income was being spent on its armed forces. Secretary of State Cordell Hull delivered a conciliatory note to the Japanese that called for settlement of international disputes by co-operation rather than war, non-interference in internal affairs of other nations, and treatment of all nations as equals.[1] The Japanese government would have had some justification for calling the proposal hypocritical since America had frequently interfered in the internal affairs of other nations. But when the Japanese bombed Pearl Harbor, they responded to Secretary Hull in a different vein:

> It is the immutable policy of the Japanese government . . . to enable each nation to find its proper place in the world. . . . The Japanese Government cannot tolerate the perpetuation of the present situation since it runs directly counter to Japan's fundamental policy to enable each nation to enjoy its proper station in the world.[2]

The American State Department had failed to understand the Japanese culture, which held no place for egalitarianism. Secretary

Hull's proposal contradicted the Japanese ideology that relations among nations, as among individuals, should be organized as a hierarchy with the most virtuous at the pinnacle. Immutable laws of nature dictated that the superior "race" of Asia, as the Japanese identified themselves, would rule the region and neighbors.

The devastation of years of war, including the American bombing of Tokyo that left 90,000 dead in one day's bombing, did not destroy the Japanese' determination to defend their homeland against foreigners they viewed as barbarians.[3] But the atomization of Nagasaki and Hiroshima finally induced the Emperor to take a stand against the militarists and ask the armed forces to lay down their weapons. Such was the tight discipline of the hierarchically structured society that, unless the jingoists were willing to place the Emperor under their "protection," warriors and civilians alike were constrained to accept the imperial edict without complaint.

The defeated Japanese resigned themselves to the same murderous treatment they had meted out to prisoners of war and the civilians of the nations they had conquered. Strong anti-Japanese, prejudice that existed in the U.S. before the war was intensified by Japanese atrocities. Many of America's military commanders, angered by Japan's torture and starvation of prisoners of war, favored vengeful policies, and few officials in the Truman Administration disagreed.

Most Americans, as President Truman, could justify the annihilation of Japanese cities in order to bring the war to a speedier finish. But Americans could not understand the pervasive brutality of the Japanese army toward war prisoners and civilians in captured territories. The use of torture without any strategic purpose created a lasting distrust of the Japanese by Americans and the peoples of southeast Asia.

The Japanese were accustomed to an authoritarian society and expected cruel treatment by their new sovereign, General Douglas MacArthur. Simply by inaction, MacArthur could have allowed thousands of Japanese to starve to death. Perhaps because he wished to enhance his image as a statesman prior to a Presidential bid, MacArthur declined to punish Japan. He told an American writer:

If we exert [our] influence in an imperialistic manner or for the sole purpose of commercial advantage, then we shall lose our golden opportunity; but if our influence and strength are expressed in terms of essential liberalism we shall have the friendship and the cooperation of the Asiatic peoples into the future.[4]

Defeat at war effectively discredited the militarists in the eyes of the Japanese people, and MacArthur got off to a good start attempting to democratize the Japanese government and economy. He forced large landowners to sell plots to tenant farmers. He also began removing the leaders of giant companies who had collaborated with the militarists. Unfortunately, there were no moderate or liberal political groups with whom MacArthur could work. He therefore placed in power conservative leaders who had opposed the militarists but who were committed to maintaining the traditional hierarchical society. The Prime Minister from 1946 to 1954 was Shigeru Yoshida who slowed MacArthur's reforms.[5]

MacArthur dictated that Japanese workers be given the right to form unions and took great pains not to interfere with the union activities even when they conflicted with American objectives. Because of pre-war suppression of labor organizations, a cadre of militant communists found it easy to establish their leadership. In 1947, there were severe food shortages, the economy teetered on disaster, and the government printed money to pay its debts. The labor unions challenged MacArthur's tolerance by calling a general strike that would have brought economic and political chaos.

MacArthur refused to allow the strike and moved firmly to strip the unions of their communist leaders. Many unions permanently lost their power and independence, falling under the control of company management. By 1948, the Truman Administration feared a communist takeover in China, and MacArthur came under strong pressure to stop his purge of businessmen collaborators. With the American electorate turning more conservative and MacArthur still contemplating a campaign for the Presidency, he allowed the reestablishment of much of the pre-war economic hierarchy.

MacArthur's beneficent policies caused most of the Japanese public to view America not as an enemy but as a strong older brother to be obeyed and emulated. But no brief military occupation could crack the bedrock Japanese ideology that hierarchical power was part of the natural order and that the Japanese people were a superior race. With MacArthur's liberalization policy brought to a halt, post-war Japan failed to develop an egalitarian philosophy of international relations. Today, as before the war, the Japanese government emphasizes its traditional faith in "harmony" rather than fairness in international trade.[6]

The equipment needs of the American military during the Korean war provided considerable help in restoring the Japanese economy. Later, Japan's productive power gained from the nation's readiness to adopt modern Western technology and to support universal high-quality education. For three decades following the second world war the Japanese worked tirelessly to rebuild their economy, using a variety of restrictive measures to limit foreign investments and imports that could have threatened the budding domestic industries.

Japan's growing economic strength and the concurrent stagnation of the American economy have caused the Japanese people to reconsider their family relationship with America. The United States has been demoted, in the Japanese view, from Strong Older Brother to Weak Sister.

The Japanese believe that their destiny is to lead the world, if not militarily, then economically. Exports have given Japan the second largest gross national product in the world.[7] About one-third of America's trade deficit comes directly from Japanese imports, and many additional billions are the result of Japanese competition in overseas markets.[8]

The ability to incorporate Western scientific advances into practical technology has greatly contributed to Japan's success. The introduction of modern equipment, for example, has enabled the Japanese to manufacture steel, cars, and computer chips more cheaply than American companies. Japanese workers on the shop floor are much better than American workers at understanding graphs and charts and using complicated mathematical formulas.[9]

But the role of technology should not be overemphasized. Some Japanese industries were highly successful prior to the introduction of advanced technology. Honda in 1980 had only five robotic machines, yet outperformed Toyota with 420 robots.[10] And we have previously noted instances of Japanese plants outperforming their more-mechanized American counterparts. The industriousness of Japanese workers at all ranks has been a key ingredient.

Twenty-five hundred years ago, Confucius formulated standards of behavior to try to restore order to a chaotic society in China. The traditional ethical code of Confucianism, which still strongly influences Japan, China, Korea, and Vietnam emphasizes hierarchy, discipline, family, education, and hard work. In Japan, there is intense social pressure on the individual to conform to society's strictures, including doggedly persistent work.[11]

The only American white collar executive recently stationed in the Tokyo offices of a large Japanese construction firm was scolded for receiving a private phone call. Such interruptions, he was told, would distract other workers and were an inappropriate use of time. He was also criticized for yawning since this would make the others feel tired. Disagreement with his boss produced the angry comment, "There is no place for insubordinate actions or thoughts here. I am your senior and you will do as I say. If you cannot accept this, you cannot work in a Japanese company."[12]

The inculcation of Confucian beliefs and conditioning to accept group control begin early in childhood. Fathers usually take little part in rearing young children, which is left almost entirely to the wife. Both husband and wife view the man's role as the breadwinner. When asked what they liked most about their husbands, Japanese wives consistently refer to his dedication to work and dependability as a provider.[13] Sometimes working late, often socializing with office companions at bars and clubs, and perhaps having to commute a long distance from work, the father often does not get home at night until after the child has gone to bed. A typical father spends so little time at home that he seems to foreigners an honored guest.

Most single Japanese women are strongly pressured by parents, especially the mother, to marry. Females are inculcated with the belief that becoming a "whole woman" requires having babies.[14] Although many women hold jobs before they marry, work following marriage is frowned upon by employers and relatives. Rearing children and taking care of the household, including handling the family's finances, are considered the wife's major obligations. Japanese mothers are reluctant to use baby sitters, and couples rarely leave the house without taking their children.

Mothers generally engage in much more physical contact with their babies than do their American counterparts.[15] Japanese mothers are devoted to their children and greatly indulge them. As a result, children develop *amae*, "a feeling of dependency coupled with the expectation of indulgence."[16] This smothering with love does not include the encouragement of individualistic traits. Rather, the mother uses the child's dependence to inculcate a concern for the opinions of others so that the child's behavior will not be an embarrassment.

When asked what their children should be taught before age six, Japanese mothers emphasized emotional maturity, compliance to adult authority outside the home, and courtesy. American mothers, in contrast, stressed verbal assertiveness and social skills.[17]

The Japanese mother usually makes little use of direct punishment. The child's strong emotional bond to her allows great power to instill the community's values. In contrast to the American mother's direct assertion of authority, the Japanese mother stresses to the child the potential disapproval of misbehavior by others outside the family.[18] She uses the threat of withdrawal of her love to induce conformity.

When another young child is brought for a visit, the mother may fondle it and say, "I'm going to adopt this baby. I want such a nice, good child. You don't act your age." The child's response is often to throw itself on the mother, fists flailing and crying, "No, No, we don't want any other baby. I'll do what you say."[19] A mother may pretend to give away a naughty young child to a visitor, saying "Will you take this child away? We don't want it."[20] The visitor acts out the role of taking the child from the house. After the terrified child cries out to the mother, she rescues it and exacts a promise to be good.

At a later age, when children learn that such threats are not to be taken literally, the punishment value remains strong by signifying ridicule and loss of love.[21] As the child grows older, threats of withdrawing love become more subtle. If an older child repeatedly refuses a mother's request to eat a helping of vegetables, Japanese mothers frequently say, "All right, then, you don't have to eat it."[22] In America such a statement means the child has won. In Japan, the same statement conveys the powerful threat of withdrawal of love that causes the child to obey.

Failing to honor one's family by appropriate public behavior is considered inexcusable. A child who disgraces the family name by poor school performance may be shunned by his parents.[23] Japanese mothers also use a good-guy/bad-guy technique to elicit conformist behavior, invoking punishment by the father who has a much weaker bond to the child. The mother may draw invidious comparisons of the child with others, or tell the child that others will criticize his behavior, which would cause both the mother and child to suffer.[24]

The child's dependence on mother's good love becomes transformed into a gnawing apprehension about the opinions of society. The development of conformity is encouraged by the "measuring community" (*seken*), which refers to the watchful presence of neighbors, kin, teachers and others who will hold the mother responsible for her child's behavior. Older children are taught by parents and teachers to subordinate their independence to the desires of the group.

In the United States, self-fulfillment connotes the individual's search for the good life; self-fulfillment in Japan means fitting in perfectly with the group. To speak of someone as acting "unexpectedly" in the serious conduct of life comes close to calling that person a fool.[25] The lessons in group identification and conformity that the child learns from the mother are reinforced in school. The Japanese people consider their self-described "race" to be homogeneous in a variety of traits, including intellectual aptitude, and believe themselves superior to foreigners. Therefore the individual's success or failure at school is attributed to diligence and perseverance, rather than innate intelligence. A recent study reported:

> In Japan, poor performance in mathematics was attributed to lack of effort; in the United States, explanations were more evenly divided among ability, effort, and training at school. Japanese mothers were less likely to blame training at school as a cause of low achievement in mathematics. . . . Their children generally shared this view of things.[26]

In pre-school and elementary school, group performance and the child's responsibility to the group are emphasized above individual achievement.[27] Elementary school classes are large, averaging forty-two students.[28] Children are formed into mixed-ability groups of four to six students, called *han*. If a child's work is not finished on time, the teacher says the *han* is not ready and leaves it to the *han* to pressure the wayward individual. A pair of students serve as monitors to enforce discipline. Since the assignment of monitor rotates through the class, all children have the experience of both obeying and enforcing discipline.[29]

Moral instruction in school emphasizes the importance of social order, cooperation and hard work. In elementary and junior high school, the children are continually urged to try harder. Anxiety created by failure to conform to hierarchical control and group opinions internalizes the motivation to work tirelessly. Almost every elementary school student has his own desk and study area at home, where he or she is expected by teachers and parents to complete homework diligently.

In junior high school, study is oriented toward passing the competitive admission tests for prestigious local high schools, a necessity for obtaining a good job after graduation. More prestigious jobs require a degree from a prominent college, admission to which is also based on a difficult entrance exam. A common motto among high school students is "four hours pass, five hours fail," referring to the maximum number of hours of sleep possible if one is to study hard enough to pass the entrance exam.[30]

Preparation for high-school and college exams involves years of intense study. Much of the study has little educational value, involving the memorization of large quantities of information. But the mountain of work serves a social purpose. Strong performance on a school entrance examination is taken by employers as evidence that a job applicant is industrious and conformist. A degree from a good college, which presupposes that the individual has spent years of diligent work required to pass the entrance exam, is an important criterion used by employers in hiring decisions.[31]

The conformity of the Japanese is not simply an outward display of behavior. The individual learns to take comfort in sharing the feelings and beliefs of the group. There is no worse punishment than to be laughed at by the community for displaying foolish, that is, individualistic behavior. Self-fulfillment becomes identified with satisfying the measuring community.[32] Since the measuring community favors the social norm of hard work, training in conformity produces individuals who work hard.

The child develops a strong identity with the self-styled race of Japan that makes self-sacrifice a much stronger force than in the United States. Parents and schools indoctrinate children with pride of race and the belief that ceaseless effort is necessary for Japan to reach its rightful place at the top of the world's economic hierarchy. Japanese children are also taught that the laws of nature dictate a limitless obligation to work (*gimu*). To fail to meet this obligation is a source of profound embarrassment.

Japanese society calls a person a success for carrying out any socially useful job carefully and well. The worth a person feels in Japan is less dependent on wealth, power, or fame than in the United States. The difference in wages across professions is much smaller in Japan than in America, reflecting a lesser emphasis on pay as a source of prestige. It is easier in Japan than in the United States for a sanitation or factory worker to believe he is valued by the community.

Although Japan has a more rigid social hierarchy than the States, those near the bottom of the hierarchy take pride in the social value of their work and are accustomed to being treated with dignity. Working-class attitudes are similar to those held by many servants in Victorian England. Knowing one's place in the social hierarchy and believing one's work is appreciated provides great comfort to most Japanese. The positive self-worth felt at various levels of the hierarchy contrasts with the American view that jobs that lack favorable pay or prestige are "menial." In contrast to the Japanese, Americans who hold "menial" jobs tend to adopt society's disdain and may take little pride in carrying out their work conscientiously.

The Japanese are inculcated with a doctrine of self-discipline that contains the ideal of total commitment to one's job no matter how humble it may be. The emphasis on learning to perform one's job expertly fosters the attitude that all jobs are important to the community.[33] It is taken for granted that Japanese workers, whatever their status in the hierarchy, will complete their tasks with the utmost care and diligence.[34] An American white collar worker in Tokyo noted, for example, that the day officially ended at 4:40, but employees often continued until 8 o'clock.[35]

The Japanese also take pride in self-discipline as a trait to be nurtured:

> The American assumption is that a man, having sized up what is possible in his personal life, will discipline himself, if that is necessary to attain a goal. Whether he does or not, depends on his ambition, or his conscience, or his "instinct of workmanship". . . . The Japanese assumption, however, is that a boy taking his middle-school examinations, or a man playing in a fencing match, or a person merely living the life of an aristocrat, needs a self-training quite apart from learning the specific things that will be required of him when he is tested.[36]

Occidentals and Japanese have different understandings of the nature of self-control. Americans, with their emphasis on individualism and freedom, speak of the willpower to complete a difficult task. Willpower connotes the concentration of the conscious self toward the task at hand. For the Japanese, self-control is expressed by the concept of *muga*, a state of expert training in which self-consciousness is eliminated, and the person's energy flows into the task.[37] The expert does not try consciously to *push* in carrying out a difficult task but, rather, attempts to lose self-awareness in the skillful performance of the task.

For the Japanese, the requirements of the task dictate expert behavior. A person becomes one with the task, letting the task take over his consciousness. To the Japanese, a metaphor for losing one's self-regard while performing a task is to be as if dead. A father whose child is worried about passing final examinations might tell the child to "take them as one already dead and you will pass them easily."[38] The child is being advised to let her energy flow into the task to such a degree that anxiety, a result of self-regard, will pass.

Another example of a Japanese concept of expertness is a housewife kneeling on the floor and making a formidable supply of rice cakes. She shapes the dough using quick, repetitive movements of such deftness that she seems completely absorbed by the task.

One Westerner observed: "As a personality in her own right, [the housewife] was easily overlooked; perhaps the distinction was no longer possible. It was difficult to see how the woman could be separated from the function."[39]

Influenced by ethnocentrism, American psychologists have emphasized the importance of one's conscious self-assurance and determination for dealing with difficult tasks. Americans say they *push themselves* to tackle difficult tasks; Japanese say they surrender their consciousness to the dictates of the task. These alternative views may result from the stress on conformity in Japan versus the emphasis on innovation in America.

When there is a clear standard of expert performance, the capacity to allow one's attention to be controlled by the dictates of the task helps a person gain mastery. For example, an expert ballerina will train until she can complete her classical movements with precision and little conscious thought. The expert math student will train until specific problems are quickly matched to a limited set of relevant rules. Such conformity to a standard is especially admired in Japan. The Japanese are comforted by knowledge that standards are limited and fixed.

In contrast, most Japanese are discomforted by innovation, which requires thinking of new ways to perform a task or new solutions to a problem that go beyond standard procedures. "Some Asian students come to Julliard and they just go crazy," says pianist Ken Noda. "They have been so disciplined that they have to let go. Actually, the best music is a strange dialogue between a dead composer and a live musician. You can't have that dialogue if you're too caught up in technique or too caught up in your own emotions."[40]

For the ballerina to invent variations of classical movements or for the math student to discover new logical systems requires the creativity and self-assurance to strike out on one's own. Self-confidence encourages persistence despite false starts. Americans admire innovation and understand the courage necessary to think creatively. The Japanese venerate the patterning of behavior to a standard, consistent with their conformist society.

The Japanese view the pursuit of sensual pleasure as a valued avocation so long as it does not interfere with business. Thus, the same Japanese who sits under a cold waterfall in the winter to strengthen his discipline also enjoys prolonged soaking in a hot tub.[41] Social drinking is the main release for the tensions that Japanese men feel in their conformist and rigidly structured lives.

Tens of thousands of small bars are kept afloat by regular customers seeking release after work from the day's pressures.[42] Such bars are typically run by a woman of late middle age, the *mamasan*, who provides a homey atmosphere. She employs a younger, good-looking woman to attract the clientele, drink with them, banter, and sing.[43]

Getting drunk after work with business associates provides an excuse for boisterous behavior, a temporary release from the hierarchical relationships, formality, predictability, and politeness required at work. Enjoying visual pornography, telling dirty jokes, singing ribald songs, groping bar maids (the greater the grope, the greater the bill) and visiting prostitutes are considered perfectly acceptable behaviors. But the Japanese almost invariably confine their drunkenness to the evening hours when they are away from work and home.[44]

Japanese economic progress is encouraged by the belief of the populace that the nation's future depends on each individual's willingness to work hard; that patriotism and self-interest require the highest industriousness. The Japanese have always feared foreign domination and viewed their independence as precarious. Inhabiting a small island nation poor in natural resources, the Japanese feel they must outdo the West in productivity in order to attain their natural place at the top of the economic hierarchy. Most Japanese are convinced of their "racial" superiority, but fear the imposition of trade barriers by the United States and invasion by the Koreans or Soviets.

The resilience of Japanese employees to discomforting work conditions is similar to that of hard-working Americans at the turn of the century. An example of determination of the Japanese worker to endure any hardship in order to complete his job is provided by the Toyota car company. There, the speedup reached proportions reminiscent of Charlie Chaplin's frenetic pace in the movie "Modern Times."

Japanese journalist Satoshi Kamata got a job on the assembly line at Toyota. He described work days that often reached twelve hours. Auto parts moved down the line at a speed too great for even agile, experienced workers to keep up. Kamata reported that a work shift was required to meet its production quota although this often meant working overtime. A worker who fell behind the required pace could press a button to summon a supervisor. But he knew that the supervisor would then tell him he was letting fellow workers down and that everyone will suffer as a result. Because group identification and subservience to authority are strong in Japan, this system kept production levels high at Toyota.

The cost to the physical and mental health of the workers at Toyota was great. No matter how hard workers tried, the pace required by the line simply could not be maintained. After the overtime required of workers to meet the production quota, they were usually too exhausted to do anything besides eat and sleep. Days off were taken up by sleep. Sexual desire and general zest for life decreased.

Old, unsafe machinery worked by tired men and women resulted in numerous accidents. A bloody gash on the head was considered too minor a discomfort for a sick call. The loss of fingers was a common occurrence. Workers were known to have healthy teeth pulled by dentists to provide a medical excuse for a few hours of needed rest. Chronic gastrointestinal disorders were common, with workers leaving the line to vomit. When a laborer tried to quit the company, his supervisor would tell him how much he was needed and how much more difficult his leaving would make working conditions for fellow employees. If the worker still insisted on quitting, the supervisor would try to wheedle whatever extra time he could from the worker—a month, a week, or even a single shift.

Why did Toyota impose inhumane working conditions? Toyota seemed to view employees as machines that were more expensive to maintain in good working condition than to replace when a part wore out. This suggestion is more than a metaphor. A detailed medical examination weeded out prospective employees with physical weaknesses. When stress-produced illness or physical injury impaired a worker's performance, the worker generally would be asked to resign. There was no place at Toyota for workers broken by the pace of the assembly line. Toyota justified the perpetual speed-up by telling employees about difficult domestic and foreign competition. But, in fact, Toyota is one of the most profitable corporations in the world. The goals of profit and market share simply crowded out human values.

Why did Toyota's workers tolerate these conditions? Many low-skilled employees, hired without any guarantee of long-term job employment, simply quit. Other employees to which the company made a long-term commitment, stayed on because they valued job security. Subservience to authority and identification with one's employer played a role. An employee with a long-term commitment from a company who quits has broken a strong social norm and finds it difficult to get another job in the industry. Japanese labor unions are weak and staffed by supervisory personnel who owe their high-status positions to management. Japanese industry, including Toyota, exerts enormous political power that is used to inhibit progressive labor legislation. And the economics of labor supply and demand weighs against the unskilled worker in Japan.

But working hard extends to the majority of companies that place less pressure on employees than does Toyota. At work, Japanese usually put in from 250 to 400 hours annually more than Americans.[45] Japanese middle managers and line supervisors often decline to take vacations. One important reason why the Japanese work long hours is the management policy of many factories, like Toyota, of failing to provide relief workers. If you are sick or take a vacation, others will have to take up the slack.[46] The Japanese workers' strong social dependence makes them feel traitorous for taking all their vacation.

Most large Japanese companies have a strong commitment to permanent employees. Managers must undergo seemingly-endless meetings and discussions with workers to obtain consensual agreement on important company policies. The identification of the employee with the company is strong both in the employee's mind and in the opinions of others. Even in the course of a Japanese Buddhist funeral ceremony, each mourner may be introduced by the name of the company for which he or she works.[47]

For the great majority of Japanese, one's roles in family, work organization, and nation are important components of self-identity. Other families, work organizations, and nations are seen as out-groups to be competed against. When rival political parties or businesses compete, obtaining power or sales for one's ingroup is weighed against the costs to both sides who belong to the larger ingroup composed of the Japanese people.[48]

Manufacturers normally at each other's throats are extremely susceptible to government requests for cooperation on issues having international implications. Extensive consultation with all parties involved in a business or governmental decision is an important social norm. Disregard of this etiquette brings strong disapproval. Such procedures slow decision making, but they encourage useful suggestions for increasing productivity and help insure commitment to company policies.

It is a truism that international discord would be reduced if we understood better the viewpoints of other nations. The liberal political tradition in America holds that the peoples of foreign democracies will treat us fairly if we treat them decently and if both sides discuss differences in an open and friendly atmosphere. Such beliefs have been sorely tested by the trade war with Japan. The Japanese have modernized by adopting Western methods of industrial technology. But the traditional Japanese concern with racial superiority, order, and hierarchical authority extends to international trade.

The Japanese take pride in the "racial purity" of their nation. Prestigious jobs and social approbation are open only to the dominant ethnic group that makes up a large majority of the population. Notably excluded are second- and third-generation descendants of Koreans brought to the country as forced laborers. Japan conquered and colonized Korea in 1910 and treated its people harshly for thirty-five years.[49] The Japanese of recent Korean ancestry are not Japanese citizens despite the fact that they and perhaps their parents were born in Japan. These people are still "Koreans" to the Japanese even though many look the same and speak as fluent Japanese as their fellow countrymen. Such "Koreans" must register with the police as long-term resident aliens.[50] When excavations in central Honshu suggested that the Imperial family might have Korean ancestors, the diggings were stopped. The "dirt" was literally swept under the rug.[51]

In order to keep their "race" unpolluted, the Japanese make

naturalized citizenship virtually impossible. Hundreds of books and articles are published each year in Japan purporting to show the superiority of the Japanese "race." Dr. Tadanobu Tsunoda has achieved prominence in Japan with his widely accepted theory that foreigners cannot become fluent in the Japanese language because of an inferior brain structure. Many Japanese are nonplussed upon meeting a foreigner who can speak the Japanese language well.

Of course, the Japanese do not openly flout the belief in their own superiority because bragging is foreign to the Japanese character and is unwise politically. As Atlantic Monthly editor James Fallows noted:

> The stated premise is that Japan has to give foreigners a break, so that it doesn't make needless enemies overseas. The unstated but obvious corollary is that Japan could crush every indolent Western competitor if it tried. Even the things some Japanese still claim to admire about America suggests racial condescension. Among the American virtues that Japanese have mentioned to me are a big army, a sense of style and rhythm, artistic talent and energy, and raw animal (and supposedly sexual) strength. In their eyes we are big, potent, hairy.[52]

Occasionally, the political leaders of Japan let their cockiness overcome their reticence and come close to saying what they really believe. In a widely reported speech in 1986 to junior members of his ruling Liberal Democratic Party, Prime Minister Yasuhiro Nakasone said:

> The American people have accomplished great things. But at the same time the United States is a multinational [read 'multiracial'] society and in some fields, such as education, there are points they have not reached. Japan is now a highly educated and fairly intelligent society, much more so than America, on the average. In America, there are quite a few black people, Puerto Ricans, and Mexicans. On the average, [education] is still very low. In America even now there are many black people who do not know their letters.[53]

In his clarification issued after these remarks received unflattering public comment in America, Nakasone said he had:

> . . . no intention of committing any racial discrimination or of slandering other countries . . . [The Unified States is] a multiracial society and had been making great progress as a democracy, overcoming education, social and other issues associated with such a background. . . . There are things the Americans have not been able to reach because of the multiple nationalities there. On the contrary, some things are easier because we are a homogeneous society.[54]

In response to angry attacks by American politicians and the prospect that Congress might use his speech as an excuse to erect trade barriers, Nakasone later apologized for his clarification and claimed he believed that diversity is one of America's strengths. Still later he apologized to the descendants of the indigenous peoples of Japan who are not part of the dominant ethnic group, although the "Korean" Japanese were not included in this small kindness. Despite this disclaimer of his disclaimer, a reasonable observer would conclude that the Prime Minister firmly believed, as most Japanese, that a homogeneous society works better than an ethnically mixed society.

But, of course, its more than that. The Japanese judge but will not say to foreigners that if the majority of Americans had Japanese ancestors, we would be better off than with the present mix of "brutish races." Why was Nakasone so interested in America's ethnic composition? Because the Japanese enjoy attributing their economic success to "racial" superiority.

The Japanese see white Americans of European ancestry in much the same way as most American whites used to view blacks. Of course, the Japanese view blacks and Hispanics as inferior even to white anglo-saxons, perhaps on the same level as the Koreans whom they perceive as bestial and more dangerous than the Soviets.

Many, if not most, Japanese are arrogant and apprehensive at the same time. Their national pessimism causes them to fear that without the utmost struggle, Japan's economic progress will somehow be swept away. Self-assurance often masks a strong concern that all Japan has accomplished might come crashing down. The Japanese still speak with great anxiety of the "Nixon Shock," when the United States temporarily imposed export restrictions on the sale of soy beans, a protein source widely used in Japan. The Japanese believe they have to maintain a strongly favorable export balance to keep their prosperity alive. They also worry that their children experience too few difficulties and will therefore fail to develop the self-control needed for demanding tasks.[55]

The success of the Japanese in such basic industries as steel and automobiles severely damaged American manufacturers and threw hundreds of thousands out of work. American politicians, industrialists, and labor leaders find it convenient to use the Japanese as scapegoats for America's poor economic performance rather than face discomforting questions about our own complicity. During the 1984 Presidential campaign, Walter Mondale asked: "What do we want our kids to do? Sweep up around the Japanese computers?"[56] Michigan Senator Donald Riegle is understandably concerned by Japan's inroads into his state's automobile industry, resulting in high unemployment. But he does not help matters by suggesting that, "The continuing Japanese attack on our basic industries is another Pearl Harbor. The time has come to close America's door to the flood of Japanese imported products."

Several factors that traditionally would have improved America's trade balance with Japan are not preventing a bad situation from becoming worse. As of this writing, the American dollar has weakened against the Japanese yen by about one-half since March 1985.[57] In America, many previously-inexpensive Japanese goods have drawn equivalent in price to domestic products. Major Japanese exporting companies, such as Mazda, Toray, and Hitachi have suffered declines in profits by fifteen to twenty per cent.[58] Imports of automobiles from Japan have been limited by "voluntary" quotas.

Further, the Japanese advantage in labor costs is declining. Japanese businesses do pay lower wages than American companies. But recent increases in wages for skilled labor in Japan together with wage rollbacks by American companies have markedly reduced the pay differential, especially in manufacturing jobs.[59] The average wage in Japan is now higher than for nations in the European Common Market.[60]

Despite these factors, the trade gap with Japan remains high. The blame is frequently placed on alleged unfair economic and trading practices. The Japanese government does, in fact, reduce the importation of foreign goods by instituting levies, restrictions, and a mountain of red tape. One of the reasons the Japanese public must pay high prices for food is the severity of import duties and restrictions. Beef imported to Japan is about four times more expensive than domestic beef, citrus fruits three times more expensive. If the widely used staple, rice, were allowed to be imported, the price would be half that of the domestic product.[61]

But official government trade restrictions have decreased markedly in the last decade and, overall, are not much greater than our own.[62] Other, less overt barriers to the Japanese market have a stronger effect. The Japanese are bountiful producers but stingy consumers. The government encourages its citizens to save more and consume less by giving meager retirement benefits and by taxing savings at a low rate. Moreover, because of the power of business organizations and the weakness of labor unions, corporate profits have risen much more quickly than wages, leaving working people with less money to spend on consumer goods and allowing the companies more cash for automation and research and development.[63]

The Japanese government declines to spend much money subsidizing housing, transportation, pollution abatement, sanitation, or parks, which would increase imports and syphon off money now invested in the production of exports. Also, the Japanese, by nature, are conservative spenders on such basic items as housing, heat, air conditioning, and cars. For all these reasons, the Japanese can be said to "work hard so others may live well."[64]

Imports are further reduced by the citizenry's prejudice against foreigners and a hierarchical economic system that works against foreign companies. Government bureaucrats frequently do what they can to impede imports. For example, when Tokyo's American club imported forty paddle-tennis rackets, a customs officer demanded to know why Japanese rackets had not been purchased.

Told that no such rackets were manufactured in Japan, the officer held up the shipment for over a month despite the absence of any legal justification for doing so.[65] In 1983, Johnson and Johnson attempted to sell medical imaging devices in Japan for $2 million each. The ministry of health stalled for eighteen months until Toshiba had introduced similar machines.[66] Regulations aimed at American-made portable computers, car telephones, telephone pagers, and two-way radios until recently limited their importation.

Japanese business is dominated by six major confederations of companies and a dozen smaller groups with interlocking boards of directors. These alliances show favoritism to their member companies and thereby make foreign entry into the Japanese market more difficult. Foreign companies were prevented from holding seats on the Tokyo stock exchange until 1985.[67]

The ability of American companies to attract qualified Japanese managers is reduced by the view that working for foreigners is demeaning. Hiring talented college graduates is made more difficult by the strong connections that exist between Japanese companies and prestigious universities. Professors serve as recruiting agents, steering their students to favored companies year after year.

Sales of imported consumer products are inhibited by a bloated distribution system with a multi-layered old-boy network of middle men who are much more inclined to accept products from companies that are Japanese rather than American. Imports of equipment are similarly limited by tight relationships between Japanese equipment manufacturers and purchasers. Unless an American company forms a partnership with a Japanese organization, the development of business relationships can take a number of years.

Despite these difficulties, foreign companies with a good product that are willing to work hard for a number of years before showing a profit can do quite well. It is often overlooked that Japan is the second largest importer of American goods, after Canada. Japan imports $22 billion in American products annually, including large quantities of American farm products and raw materials such as beef, citrus fruit, cotton, tobacco, corn, grain, coal and lumber. More than half of the imports from the U.S. are manufactured products, with large sales of such diverse items as data-processing equipment, razor blades, and disposable diapers.[68]

Overall, however, the American balance of trade with Japan is highly unfavorable. Japanese manufacturers in key industries concentrate on exports because of low domestic demand. In addition, capturing a high share of the world market is considered patriotic and produces more prestige for a company and its managers than high profits. The success of Japanese exports is made possible by a long-term outlook that promotes a willingness to work hard to achieve high-quality products at a competitive price.

Japanese managers' interest in moderate, sustained growth is advanced by the influence of investment banks that own a major share of most large companies or serve as their principle lenders. The banks are more concerned with stability and steady economic gain than maximizing short-term profits. Thus, the Nippon Electric Company was able to continue investing heavily in the development of computer chips for thirteen years before the research produced a profit.[69] Incentive stock options, which promote an emphasis on short-term profits among American managers, are seldom provided in Japan.[70]

American business also displays less concern with national welfare than the Japanese. In contrast to the long-term planning of Japanese businesses, American companies frequently maximize short-term profits by skimping on research and equipment. America's economic competitiveness thereby suffers.

More and more large American companies are identifying themselves as "multi-nationals," denying their responsibility for acting in this nation's best interest. In Japan, such an outlook would be subjected to devastating social ostracism and a clamp down by the companies' lenders, the investment banks. If American managers are rewarded for milking short-term profits from a company, their counterparts in Japan are rewarded for the sustained effort in research and development that will help that nation's future. Hard work directed toward increasing market share, more than quick profits, is admired in Japan.

In order to increase their share of the world market and drive competitors out of business, many Japanese companies have dumped products in America and Europe at prices lower than in Japan. The casual American shopper in Japan finds radios, cameras, VCRs and other Japanese manufactured goods much more expensive than in many American discount stores.[71] The Japanese sell small-sized color television sets in the U.S. at about one fourth the price in the home country.[72] Major Japanese companies are often willing to sustain a loss on overseas sales of a line of products until smaller foreign companies drop out of competition.

Not all such dumping reflects a malicious intent. Competing Japanese manufacturers usually expand their production capacity aggressively and saturate the market. Poor planning has been responsible for ships, household appliances, and computer components sold at a loss.[73] In their eagerness for high profits, some Japanese companies have unwisely exported their own technology. Huge shipyards built by a Japanese company in Brazil and Singapore greatly damaged the Japanese ship-building industry.

Investments in steel and textile mills and electronics factories in countries like Korea, Taiwan, and Hong Kong came back to haunt the Japanese with products sold at prices lower than their own.[74] Japan's Mitsubishi Company owns a fifteen percent share in the Korean Hyundai Motors Company and supplied crucial technology responsible for the Hyundai Excel, a low priced compact that has hurt the sales of Japanese cars overseas.[75] But overall, the general emphasis by Japanese business on market share rather than short-term profit has been quite beneficial to the country's economy.

Whenever the American government complains to Japan about government policies that discourage domestic spending, about barriers to the import of American goods, and about the dumping of Japanese products abroad, the Japanese offer their sympathies. They do not wish to offend. The self-effacing, ambiguous use of language in speech and writing is a fundamental component of Japanese culture.[76] The Japanese would not wish their trading partners to lose face. Frankness is characteristic of Americans but unacceptable among the Japanese:

> In contrast to the West, where it is the sender's responsibility to produce a coherent, clear, and intelligible message, in Japan it is the receiver's responsibility to make sense of the message. For a Japanese to express himself or herself too clearly is impolite. It shows deficient empathy. . . . Such an attitude helps avoid confrontation,

an adaptation well suited to a people destined to live for generations in a restricted area without much room for movement.[77]

Of course, the Japanese also recognize the political advantage of soothing an angry America. Year after year, they promise to stimulate imports. "We agree with you that there is a problem," they say. "We feel terrible about it. We are trying to do better. But you must remember we are a society that operates by consensus. We cannot import American farm products because our farmers will not agree. We are trying to import more manufactured goods, and to succeed we must gain the nation's approval. To try to move faster would create political chaos. You would not want a resurgence of anti-foreign nationalism, would you? We have acceded to your requests for an increase in the size of our military budget, despite domestic opposition. We are continually trying to reverse the inequities of which you speak. Have patience. You will see real progress."

The Japanese understand America better than most Americans understand Japan. The Japanese know that America has traditionally championed free trade. They know that much of the American buying public and the import businesses in the coastal states prosper from the flood of Japanese goods, creating opposition to import restrictions. They know that American exporters lobby heavily against such restrictions because of a fear of retaliation. The Japanese know that they have reduced protectionist pressures by their agreement to limit the export of automobiles to the United States and by agreements for the sale of Japanese-produced cars by the American auto makers.

The Japanese are beginning to mask the true dimensions of the trade deficit by building plants in the U.S., the products of which are not counted in the balance sheet. Some companies owned wholly or partly by American firms have large sales in Japan, including IBM, Coca-Cola, and McDonald's.[78] But the Japanese are rapidly catching up by building factories in the U.S. The Japanese ably circumvent import restrictions and create economic dependency in the southern U.S. by building car factories there, drawing from a pool a of non-union, poorly paid labor.[79]

The first Japanese car manufactured in America was turned out

116

in September 1986, and such production should greatly increase Japan's future share of the American car market. By contributing to competition, Japanese factories built in America reduce prices to consumers. Local employment is also helped. But the drain of profits to Japan removes funds that, if spent in America, would stimulate our economy.

Japan's investment in American factories is a clever move. Since many Americans are employed in such factories, the economic costs to the United States are less obvious than with imported goods. Moreover, because American industrial production is decaying, state officials find it politically expedient to reduce unemployment by encouraging such investment. Employment in many states is becoming increasingly dependent on Japanese investments. State politicians fear that import restrictions may cause the Japanese to retaliate by cutting back on future investments. The Japanese also spend $20 million a year on lobbying and public relations, buying the influence of those with high-level government connections.[80]

The Japanese understand the discontinuity in American foreign policy from one Presidential administration to the next. The Japanese play a game of economic hide and seek with each new American presidential administration. The President seeks redress of economic grievances to which the Japanese respond with soothing-but-vague promises and foot dragging. The game lasts four or eight years depending on whether the President is elected to a second term. Then the game starts over again with the incoming presidential administration.

Each new President wants to make a fresh start, to handle the "Japanese problem" in a more effective way than his predecessor. They recognize that no new President would want to subject his administration to harsh criticism for instituting major import restrictions until every area of discussion had been exhausted. And because no President wishes to admit failure in foreign policy, the Japanese can count on Administration officials to exaggerate the practical importance of symbolic gestures toward free trade.

A case in point is the Japanese export of computer chips (semiconductors) to the U.S., accounting for a very small percentage of the trade deficit. In order to drive out competition, the Japanese dumped computer chips in Japan, America, and Europe at very low prices. An internal memorandum of the Hitachi Company ordered the sales force to sell chips ten percent below the price of American companies, no matter what the cost. So the Administration in July of 1986 obtained an agreement guaranteeing that sales of American chips within Japan would increase from 8.2 percent today to more than 20 percent by 1991. Further, the Japanese government stated it would clamp down on future dumping of chips exported to America and Europe.[81]

But the agreement excluded the more powerful chips that are expected to dominate future trade. Moreover, the restriction on dumping required the good faith of a Japanese government that has continually promised much more than it delivered.

Administration officials saw to it that the agreement got plenty of publicity through television and press interviews. The White House claimed that the agreement was a major victory in the trade war when in reality it was only a palliative. At best, the bargain could have a very minor effect on the trade balance. The Japanese had simply continued their practice of stalling one President until a new one is elected.

When Americans respond with open anger at the unkept promises and evasiveness of the Japanese on the issue of trade deficits, the Japanese regard us as crude barbarians. Such demands violate the imperative of Japanese culture that "demands should not be made that the other person would feel uncomfortable meeting or be unable to carry out."[82]

Why aren't the Japanese grateful to the United States for treating them well following the second world war? Why don't they treat us more fairly now? There are a variety of reasons that allow the Japanese to feel perfectly justified in promoting exports while discouraging imports:

- The Japanese public blames the second world war on the militarists who were subsequently stripped of power and disgraced. The Japanese people feel they were simply following orders so that the absence of harsh treatment by America is not viewed as an especially great favor.
- The conservative politicians and industrialists who returned to

power after the war were in many cases hindered in their plans by MacArthur. They owe nothing to America.

- America contributed rather little financially to Japan's economic recovery immediately following the second world war. Japan's economy was helped much more by supplying the American military during the Korean war for which the Japanese can reasonably argue they owe us nothing.
- The Japanese believe that they are rising to their natural place in the economic hierarchy. They view Americans as a genetically inferior mongrelized people who are too morally lax to withstand the temptation to laziness that comes with material prosperity.

In addition, for the Japanese to admit that they are still indebted to the United States forty years after the war would create a great loss of face. The Japanese have been socialized to be made highly uncomfortable by the receipt of favors. They divide obligations into two distinct categories. *Gimu* refers to limitless repayments of obligations that have been passively incurred, including duty to one's family, country, and work. A person is born with such obligations, and must continue to respect them all through life. There is a Japanese expression that "One never pays one ten-thousandth of *gimu.*"[83] *Gimu* provides a strong moral obligation to carry out one's job carefully and well.

The Japanese culture accepts *gimu* as the natural order. But the Japanese dislike accepting major favors that will trap them in what they call *giri*. This refers to obligations actively incurred and which have specified limits such as duties to the extended family, admission of failure, and avenging an insult. The amount of a debt of *giri* can grow with time if left unrepaid and reach an enormous level. For the Japanese to now admit *giri* for our generosity after the second world war would, with interest, produce an intolerably great debt. To decline to pay such a debt would produce a devastating embarrassment and loss of face.[84]

Giri to one's ingroup is reinforced by *ninjo*, a feeling of empathy which extends very little to foreigners.[85] The Japanese feel shame and guilt primarily for transgressions committed against the in-

119

group, not foreigners.[86] How much more pleasant to view Japan's trade advantage over America as the natural order rather than worrying about repaying a great debt.

All of this is not to say that we would have done better to humiliate the Japanese, rather than to aid their economy, after the war. The Japanese do not admit their *giri* to the United States. But an economic war is better than a new war of weapons, which might have resulted if America increased the loss of face that the Japanese felt in defeat. We must be firm in our current attempts to correct the inequities of trade with Japan. But we must take care not to humiliate the Japanese, lest they turn from economic competition to military competition.

The current Japanese invasion of TV sets, VCRs, and automobiles is not without its benefits to the consumer. And if the Japanese condemn our "moral laxness," it is well worth considering whether we, ourselves, are responsible for much of our economic difficulties. The Japanese are engaged in unfair trade practices, but so is the United States. Consider the dumping of goods in foreign countries at below-market prices. Secretary of State George Shultz denounced President Reagan's decision to subsidize the sale of four million metric tons of wheat to the Soviet Union, saying "I don't think it's good for the United States to develop a system of protectionism. . . . Subsidies are a form of protection, just as much as a quota or a tariff."[87]

Textile imports into the U.S. are restricted by an international agreement, renewed for five years in 1986, which expanded import controls to popular fibers such as linen and silk blends.[88] American steel companies are protected to some extent by a trigger price mechanism for imports.[89] Limits on sugar importation in 1985 pushed prices so far above the world level that "it would have been cheaper to extract sugar from Canadian pancake mix and Israeli frozen pizza than to produce it from domestic sugar cane."[90]

Even if all trade with Japan would stop today, the United States would still import far more goods from other countries than it exports. Condemnations of Japan as the sole culprit ring a bit hollow when one realizes that our country's second biggest trading deficit is with Canada, a nation willing to import our goods. America's trade imbalance with Canada has deteriorated, as it has with free-market West Germany.

Canada, West Germany, Korea, Taiwan, and Hong Kong are among the diverse set of industrious nations that are prospering as America fails. Should America blame all these other countries? More to the point is Pogo's refrain: "We have found the enemy and they are us."

The answer is not protectionist tariffs. Reports by the staff of the Federal Trade Commission indicate that for each job saved through import restrictions on steel, textiles, and autos, the cost to the rest of the economy is several times that worker's salary. In other words, our domestic economy would benefit by paying these workers double their salary not to work.[91] Federal Trade Commission Chairman Daniel Oliver has noted that "Consumers already pay $50 billion a year to protect the jobs of comparatively few."[92]

Tariffs imposed on countries that trade freely with us beget retaliation. Thus, Canada imposed its own restrictions on imports from the United States when the U.S. government put high tariffs on cedar shakes and shingles.[93] Restrictive trade practices are costly to both sides because they limit each nation from exporting the items it manufactures most efficiently.

In March 1987, the Reagan administration desperately searched for ways to overcome its public image of impotence resulting from the Iran-Contra scandal. Seeking to portray himself as a tough, effective leader, Reagan retaliated against the alleged failure by Japan to live up to its eight-month old agreement to stop dumping computer chips. Restrictive import quotas amounting to 100 percent of a product's price were announced not on chips, but such items as motors, pumps, air conditioners, computers, small TV sets, video tapes, and pocket calculators.[94] The excuse for not responding directly with levies on chips was that this product was important to the national economy. In other words, the Japanese must be punished for the help they have been giving our economy by selling chips at low prices.

If, in fact, the Japanese were violating their agreement on chips, the reasonable reaction would have been levies on chips themselves. Punishing Japanese companies not engaged in dumping will turn Japanese public opinion against a more reasonable accommodation with the U.S. The Reagan administration put political expediency above its avowed dedication to free trade.

We cannot expect the Japanese to view a tough stance in trade negotiations as anything but sour grapes unless we put our own house in order. The decline in the value of the dollar has made our exports more competitive. But the deficit continues to accumulate. We must face the fact that the single most important reason why we continue to do poorly against the Japanese is the inferior quality of our manufactured goods.

The Japanese have done a remarkable job of taking American scientific and technological breakthroughs and adapting them for the mass production of high-quality products. They ship these goods back to the United States to a public eager to buy a car or VCR or TV set that will not fall apart in ten months. The poor quality of American goods also damages exports. Even though America excels in the innovation to produce new and powerful semiconductors, we manufacture them with a defect rate significantly greater than do the Japanese.[95]

Claims that America may effectively meet the Japanese economic challenge by holding the line on workers' wages and by importing a few visible aspects of Japanese management techniques miss some underlying motivational reasons for the Japanese success. Japanese parents, educators, and employers inculcate a strong work ethic in new generations by continually rewarding industriousness, teaching the importance of hard work, and serving as role models by practicing what they preach.

In America, the traditional sources of strong work values have disappeared. Individuals reared in affluence have not developed strong work values to transmit to children. Schools are prevented from inculcating a strong work ethic by a society that values freedom over positive social values and confuses the teaching of values with the promotion of sectarian religion. The great narcotic television promotes laziness and self-indulgence that interferes with the persistence necessary to pursue long-term goals. American business promotes managers for producing quick profits at the expense of sustained growth and fails to reward hourly workers for increased effort.

Japanese feel a strong racial identity in which each individual contributes to the well-being of the group. The Japanese are oriented toward conformity and therefore extremely susceptible to social pressure to work hard. Moreover, because the Japanese identify themselves as a superior "race," all school children are assumed capable of a high level of achievement. Failure is attributed to lack of effort rather than low aptitude. The Japanese national government spends large sums of money to provide egalitarian opportunities for all students so that few can blame society for lack of achievement.

The Japanese success story demonstrates the importance to a nation's economic and moral strength of its citizens' commitment to persistent work and concern for the entire nation's well-being. Yet, others features of the Japanese system would be antithetical to any progressive, egalitarian society. For all the emphasis that the Japanese place on industriousness and the ability to develop Western discoveries into high-quality technology, conformist pressures put them at a disadvantage when it comes to the creativity and individuality that foster scientific discovery and social progress.[96] One Japanese senior executive noted that careers are made by learning to keep one's mouth shut.[97] When asked for their opinion or personal preference, Japanese often respond with the expression "Do you mean me?," conveying a hesitance to set oneself apart from the group.[98]

Conformity to the group and to hierarchical authority hinder creative disagreement. The Japanese are more fearful than we of overstepping their authority by investigating a new concept in science or technology. They feel that failure is an aggression against authority and are frightened by novel situations that cannot be handled by rote skills.[99] In a carefully conducted study of work values of employees in fifty nations, Americans ranked first on individualism and eleventh on tolerance for uncertainty, whereas the Japanese scored forty-fourth on both measures.[100]

Japanese men react to conformist pressures at work by regularly going on after-hours alcoholic binges. Most marriages are arranged for economic and social convenience and are devoid of emotional intimacy between the husband and his wife or children. Housekeeping and the raising of children provide the only acceptable career open to most women. Japanese workers now earn as much as their American counterparts but, because of anti-consumer government policies, live in substandard housing with limited access to basic amenities.

The problem facing Americans is to restore strong work values and the public's concern with the nation's economic welfare without embracing conformity or jingoism. Individualism without self-discipline produces little of lasting value. Achievement depends upon hard, persistent labor. America needs to emphasize the creativity and innovation which is our great advantage over cultures that stifle dissent. We must also recapture our traditional ability to transform discoveries, American and foreign, into practical technology. Above all, we must return to our traditional ethic of vigorous work.

It is now clear that the Japanese will not yield to cries for help from a nation that appears inferior. The Japanese respect strength, not weakness. The real test for America, which we are now failing, is whether we can have abundance and hard work before the absence of hard work destroys our abundance.

CHAPTER 6

America's Industrious
Minority

10:00 P.M., 26 August. My colleague Alex Compton and his wife
Joanne arrive home in Delaware from a two-week vacation on the
West Coast. They visited relatives in Los Angeles and then in
Castle Rock, Washington, and then spent five days with Joanne's
mother in Vancouver, British Columbia.

8:00 A.M., 27 August. Alex is in his office at the Psychology
Department of the University of Delaware, writing a book. The
place is dead because the professors are taking a final rest before
the onslaught of students at the start of the Fall semester.

10:00 A.M., the same day. Taking a break from his writing, Alex
walks into the Psychology Department office to pick up his mail.
Two Department secretaries, Judy and Pat, ask Alex how he enjoyed his trip. Without thinking, Alex replies, "The trip was O.K.,
but I'm really glad to get back to work." They chuckle at what they
think is Alex's little joke. Pat says, "I'm *sure* you're happy to get
back to work, aren't you?" Alex smiles, hoping they will believe
he really was joking.

But Alex is not off the hook yet. "How was Vancouver?" Pat
asks. Now he's ready. Best to give an ambiguous response that will

provide just enough information to stop them from pressing for more details. "Really fun, but travelling is always hectic," Alex replies. Quickly, before Pat or Judy can follow up with another question, Alex asks them, "How are things around here?" The topic of conversation changes. That did the trick. No more chances for Pat and Judy to find out what Alex really did on his vacation. A smart fanatic knows better than to be too forthcoming.

How could Alex admit to his secretaries, colleagues, and friends that he actually was glad to get back to real work? How could they understand that he particularly enjoyed the six-hour plane trips in each direction because he was able to complete so much work on the book he was writing? What would they think if he told them that when he took a brief break from work during the flight westbound to glance at the latest issue of *Time*, he was overjoyed to find an article on economic conditions that was relevant to his book and which he proceeded to abstract? What would they think if he told them that he spent the majority of his days in Vancouver working?

Alex hoped Joanne would not reveal to any but his trusted friends, whose jibes he was used to, that the most memorable parts of the trip involved visiting book stores in Los Angeles, Vancouver, and Longview, Washington. Carefully perusing the biography and business sections of these stores, he was enthralled by some wonderful new source books.

Alex found Vancouver to his taste. While his wife and mother-in-law visited, he was able to spend three of the five days reading and writing. But don't think Alex was all work and no play. On the trip he told himself, "This is a vacation. Enjoy yourself so you'll be more efficient when you get back home." So he ate supper out with his wife and mother-in-law *every night* at fancy restaurants. Moreover, on the fifth and last day at Vancouver, he quit working at *noon* and accompanied them on a visit to the Vancouver zoo. Three and one-half days of solid work, good food, capped by a relaxing break at the zoo. Yes, Vancouver was Alex's idea of a good vacation.

Before and after Vancouver there were visits with other relatives, which were pleasant. Alex didn't feel guilty about these visits since there was plenty of time for work at odd hours. When Alex tallied the amount of work accomplished during the trip, he found that he'd read and abstracted six books and gotten some writing done on his own book. All in all, Alex concluded, it was a pleasurable and restful vacation. He felt invigorated, ready to get back to *serious* work.

4:00 P.M., 18 November. Alex discovers a piece of information in the University's school newspaper that had eluded his perusal of the New York Times for three weeks. He tells his wife the wonderful news: the new federal law abolishing the mandatory retirement age for most employees applies to college professors. He will no longer be required by the University to retire at age 70, some 27 years from now.

Why do Alex and many others continue to persevere toward distant and difficult goals? Why do they push ahead against all odds, sometimes in effective ways and sometimes when the more intelligent course would be to turn to more profitable endeavors? This chapter is about why some of us try very hard while others try hardly at all.

Nineteenth century Americans were socialized to value three intertwined components of the personal work ethic: a moral duty as a worthwhile person to work hard; a willingness to exert high effort to achieve material well-being; and a pride of accomplishment in performing a job well. The value most Americans placed on work declined as a result of the lessened relationship between effort and reward, the fractionation of jobs that reduced pride of accomplishment, and the promotion of leisure and self-indulgence by manufacturers, advertisers, and the entertainment industry. Recent generations have been less willing than in the past to persevere for desired material gains and less inclined to take pride in accomplishments at work or to see any inherent morality in labor.

For most Americans, the personal work ethic has shrivelled to a simple belief that one must pay his own way. It used to be that having no job was frowned upon, even for rich people. Employment is valued by most Americans for economic benefits and avoiding the embarrassment of public assistance, not for any inherent value attributed to work. Yet, strong work values continue to influence many people whose self-identity involves diligent work. Many subcultures—groups of individuals with common beliefs and values—inculcate their members with industriousness in opposition to the national culture that stresses leisure and sensuality. In addition, there are many individuals whose strong work values, often imbued by parents, far surpass those with a similar cultural heritage.

A strong work ethic has clear and distinct effects on behavior. College students, identified as having a strong work ethic on the basis of questionnaire responses, were found to work harder than other students on simple repetitive tasks. They also earned better grades in college courses and, when required to come to an experiment as part of a class assignment so we might study them, they were more likely to show up than were low work-ethic students.

High work-ethic students more than low work-ethic students have been discovered to attribute success or failure to the adequacy of their own efforts or abilities rather than to luck or fate. They were also more likely to state that they favored pay on the basis of effort or ability over equal pay for all or pay on the basis of chance factors. Furthermore, when given the opportunity to allocate pay between themselves and other students who had competed with them on a task, high work-ethic individuals were more likely than low work-ethic individuals to refrain from rewarding themselves when their own success appeared due to luck. On the basis of such findings, organizational psychologist Jerald Greenberg concluded that high work-ethic individuals believe that reward should be commensurate with achievement based on ability or skill. In contrast, he argued that low work-ethic individuals' "apparent aversion toward recognition of individual achievement is consistent with their being able to get something for nothing!"[1]

The effects of a strong work ethic do not stop with a person's retirement in old age. Retirees with a high work ethic tended to express greater satisfaction with various aspects of retirement such as daily activities, finances, social relationships, and health when they felt their daily activities were useful. In contrast, retirees with a low work ethic expressed *less* satisfaction with various aspects of retirement when they felt their daily activities were useful.[2] Apparently, low work-ethic individuals look forward to a retirement in which they can get away from utilitarian activities and are disappointed if they find retirement too similar to work. High work-ethic people, in contrast, prefer to perform useful activities even when retired.

One ethnic group known for great diligence are the Asian-Americans. Americans of Asian extraction demonstrate much better performance in elementary school, high school, and college, on the average, than American students of European ancestry. They score higher on college entrance exams, and graduate in far greater numbers from prestigious colleges such as Harvard, Princeton, Berkeley, Brown, MIT, and Caltech than would be expected from their proportion in the general population. In 1986, the top five winners of the Westinghouse Science Talent Search were Asian-Americans.[3]

Until recently, the academic and economic success of Asian-Americans were easy to ignore because they constituted a low percentage of America's population. Asian immigration to America was severely restricted by prejudicial federal legislation, and Americans of Asian extraction constituted only a small proportion of this nation's population. However, in 1965 the regulations were made more equitable by allowing an annual immigration of up to 20,000 from each foreign nation. In addition to this total, foreign relatives of Americans gained easier access. Large numbers of Asians took advantage of the freer policy, with the result that the number of Americans of Asian extraction jumped from 1.4 million in 1970 to 3.5 million in 1980, and is expected to increase to 6.5 million by 1990.[4]

The stereotype that Asians enter this country uneducated and very poor is generally true of refugees from rural areas, but many other Asian immigrants arrive well educated. During the past two decades, nations such as Korea, India, Taiwan and the Philippines have produced far more college graduates than can be absorbed into their economies. The greater availability of jobs and higher pay in the United States has created a "brain drain" similar to the influx of European scientists and professionals following the second world war.

More than a third of the Asian immigrants have a college degree, which is about twice the proportion of white adult Americans. Many Asian immigrants have advanced degrees in scientific and professional fields. There are, in fact, more Philippine medical doctors in the U.S. than black doctors.[5]

The half-million Americans of Indian extraction have the highest median family income of any Asian-American group. Indian-Americans do well in business not because there is any general Indian cultural value that stresses hard work, but because they have a high level of technical education and a strong personal work ethic that would stand out either in India or America. They desire, contrary to the general values of their culture, to find a society in which ambition and strong work values pay off. Asian-Americans from Japan, Korea, Japan, and Vietnam grew up in societies that stressed the Confucian ethical code of hard work, discipline, family loyalty, and respect for education.[6]

Whether their strong work values stem from the Confucian culture or family tradition, most Asian-American students work harder than students of European ancestry. The superior school performance of Asian-American students cannot be attributed simply to an advantage of having well-educated or wealthy parents. Asian-Americans get better grades, on the average, than students of European ancestry at all levels of parental education and economic status.[7]

The Asian-Americans' strong emphasis on industriousness is similar to dominant work values of Americans decades ago. John Brademas, the president of New York University observed, "When I look at our Asian-American students, I am certain that much of their success is due to Confucianism. And the more I see of Confucianism in action, the more I think it is the mirror image of the Protestant Ethic."[8]

Asian immigrants place educational achievement and hard work at the top of their list of values.[9] Their children do so well in school because they study harder than other students. A nationwide survey of high school sophomores found that almost half the Asian-Americans spent five or more hours a week on homework compared to less than one-third of the students of European extraction. Half the Asian-American students were never absent from school, compared to only a quarter of these other students.[10]

Journalist Fox Butterfield tells of a ten-year-old Vietnamese-American student named Alan Ngoc who is not permitted to watch television on week nights. If Alan plays with toys when he should be doing homework, his mother throws them away. She says:

"Helping my son do well in school is a sacred duty; you want your family to do well; I'm not like Americans who believe in freedom, freedom to let their kids do whatever they want."[11] Such strictness might be thought to produce either rebelliousness or sullen submission. But, as we shall see, children with strong emotional bonds to parents often adopt the parents' attitudes toward work.

Asian-Americans find their values challenged by a dominant American culture that promotes leisure and sensuality. Successive generations of Asian-Americans tend to become less diligent as they adopt American life-styles and values. For example, Chinese-Americans born in the United States have lower educational aspirations for their children than parents born overseas.[12] Nevertheless, the hard work and resultant high achievement by most Asian-Americans in school and on the job shows that strong work values held by subcultures can persist in opposition to the national culture. Asian-American parents, influenced by their Confucian values, effectively train their children to be industrious in opposition to the larger American culture that promotes ambition without fortitude.

While industriousness is often most apparent in immigrant groups, some American institutions continue to shape strong work values. Pride of accomplishment in the form of professionalism remains strong in a number of jobs that require specialized training. Professionalism refers to a commitment to high standards of training and performance in a given occupation. For many jobs requiring a high level of skill involving years of advanced education or training, respected teachers and colleagues serve as role models. Standards of excellence become internalized, and the individual's self-respect comes to depend on high achievement.

One example of workers for whom pride of accomplishment continues to be especially important is the machinists who make the precision instruments, molds, and parts necessary for industrial mass production. Proficiency as a machinist demands great skill acquired slowly over a number of years. Machinists take pride in their workmanship upon which the quality of manufactured goods greatly depends.

In one large shop that manufactures parts used in the maintenance and repair of equipment for a domestic airline, the skilled machine crew rebelled against their new role as assistants to a computerized machine that pressed metal sheets into desired shapes. The machinists obtained copies of the instructions used for the computer programing. They learned these programing instructions and, using their knowledge derived from years of experience as machinists, began to manufacture parts *more quickly* by writing their own programs.[13]

The way in which professional standards create pride of accomplishment is illustrated by the dedication of many teachers. Betty Robbins is a special education teacher whose students are learning disabled. Betty's dedication to her job results from a commitment to excellence instilled by college instructors in education courses and by teachers who directed her classroom training. A stated devotion to the best interests of one's students can be a hollow platitude, but the inculcation of professional values does motivate many teachers, as well as other employees, to strive continually to do a better job.

After Betty graduated from college in 1960, she joined the Peace Corps out of a mixture of idealism and desire for adventure. Assigned to Liberia, she wanted to teach inland where the people lived primitively without education or health care. Instead, she and other team members found themselves assigned, without choice, to an affluent private school in a coastal community. The teachers were to work in a finishing school for rich kids who were not quite smart enough to go directly to private colleges in Switzerland and England. Most of the youths' parents belonged to the ruling class, the descendants of American slaves who had been returned to found Liberia.

Despairing of any opportunity to help the poor, some of the Peace Corps teachers did a lackadaisical job. But Betty gave her best effort. Betty's concept of professionalism held that every student deserved the teacher's commitment to help them learn, even students from rich families who needed her help least. Betty's training to become a teacher had instilled in her a dedication that was central to her self-esteem.

After spending two years in Liberia, Betty returned to America and began teaching special education students. In her new job,

Betty found that the administrators liked her work, and she had access to an expert teacher who could give her advice about special education. But Betty did not believe she knew enough about learning disabilities to do a good job for her students. Betty's concept of professionalism drew her back to school to get a master's degree in order to become a better teacher.

Although Betty derives considerable satisfaction from helping students, her commitment to professional values is an even stronger motivating force. Like many teachers, Betty believes that accepting a teaching job requires a person to give all one's skill and effort. This commitment resulted from the inculcation of professional values by instructors in education classes and by teachers who supervised her classroom training. Professionalism can be a strong force driving an individual to work with diligence and fortitude.

But the question remains as to why some individuals studying to become teachers are, like Betty, receptive to professional values whereas others are not. Since our national culture no longer stresses the importance of industriousness, little positive influence on industriousness is usually exerted by most teachers, clergy, or employers. Under such conditions, parents play a crucial role in the transmission of positive work values, making their children more ready to adopt strong professional standards.

Betty was raised on a farm where it was understood that each family member would tackle chores vigorously. Her mother, whose husband died in his early 40s, frequently communicated to Betty and her two sisters the belief that if a person failed to do her best in a job, she was "a chiseler." Mother's adage that "Its just as easy to do a job right as to do it wrong" is one Betty reiterates. She recalls:

> As a child I had certain responsibilities and I just did them. There was lots of affirmation for doing your chores. When you did something, you were told what a good job you did and you were told that a lot. My parents would often say good things about my hard work to others when I was present. You were never told that you did a bad job. It was that your job wasn't done yet. Then you would be sent back to finish it.

Betty's description of her upbringing is consistent with the findings of a study by psychologist David Cherrington, who interviewed fifty employees rated as outstanding by their immediate supervisors. Almost all these workers recalled a warm family life during their upbringing and an emphasis by parents on the importance of industriousness.[14] The strengthening of positive work values by parents' example, encouragement, and reward made these employees more concerned than others with the quality of their work. The strong emotional attachment of these individuals to their parents made them receptive to parental values, including industriousness.

It is instructive to listen to the stories of people who developed a strong personal work ethic, despite being reared in the mainstream of American society amidst the increasing laziness of recent generations. Most of the hard-working individuals we will consider grew up reading elementary and high school texts that no longer stressed the value of hard work and that were filled with simplified language and concepts designed to be understood by the less able students. Most had teachers who slowed the pace of instruction to accommodate the poorer performers, had school friends who spent little time on homework, and attended churches that emphasized faith and good works over hard work. Most were subjected to thousands of hours of radio or television advertising and entertainment, as well as movies, that presented leisure and sensual satisfaction as the basic components of a good life. We will see that in almost every case, positive reward for high effort by loving parents was the crucial ingredient for overcoming the national culture's disdain for positive work values.

The oldest paragon of industriousness to be considered, a newspaper editor, reached early adulthood just as the carefree 1920s began to promote fun and gaiety over industriousness.

Gertrude Murphy Lowell is the eighty-five-year-old founder and current editor of the *Delaware Senior Citizen*, a monthly newspaper directed at the elderly and circulated throughout the state of Delaware. Because her staff is small, she spends a good deal of her time on odd jobs, working from eight in the morning until four in the afternoon on weekdays and part-time on Saturdays and Sundays. Before she started the newspaper ten years ago, Gertrude was well known to state legislators as a knowledgeable and effective lobbyist on behalf of the rights of the elderly. As time at the newspaper permits, she continues to work as an advocate for the elderly. For example, Gertrude complained to a charitable foundation that it was not spending money for the elderly, one of its functions specified in the will of Alfred I. DuPont. The head of the foundation responded by telling her, "When I need advice, I'll ask for it." So Gertrude complained to the state attorney general who took the case to court and won.

Gertrude's strong work values were inculcated by her parents. Gertrude's father was manager of the Academy of Music in New York City, later managed a race track, and was placed in charge of the first skyscraper in Brooklyn. He took civic responsibility seriously. He saw a need for improved public transportation in New York city and helped lobby the New York state legislature to provide funds for extending the subway through Brooklyn. He expected top school performance from each of his eight children, the youngest of whom was Gertrude:

> My father was very good to us. But what he expected was perfection (laughs). He'd go over our report cards and he'd check every little thing. You didn't argue with him. But he was good to us kids. He would always help with homework. If you didn't understand something, you could ask him. He always had the patience to explain things to us. We would ask him a question. We would get an answer, and we then had to tell him what he said.

Gertrude was made to feel uncomfortable when idle: We were all very independent children. I learned that if you want something, do it yourself. Go out and do it, don't wait for some one else to do it. As a child, I'd be sitting down and someone would see me sitting and say, "What's the matter? Can't you find anything to do?"

Gertrude was working as secretary to the vice president of a large insurance company in New York City when the Great Depression hit. She was disturbed by seeing loyal employees thrown out of work after many years of service. Gertrude became politically active on behalf of the poor by organizing support for proposed New Deal economic legislation.

The company that employed Gertrude's husband went bankrupt, and he died of a heart attack while still in his 40s. She was widowed with two children, the younger of whom was only two years old. Taught throughout her youth to work energetically to solve any problem, Gertrude quit her job and obtained employment with the Post Office at night so she could care for her infant son during the day. She worked from 11:00 P.M. to 7:00 A.M., would return home for a nap with the young child, and then get up to take care of him and do the housework.

Gertrude spent little time bemoaning her exhaustion from working all night and caring for her child through the day. She noticed ads in the newspaper by servicemen looking for rooms to rent. With the money Gertrude earned working in the post office, she put a down payment on a large brownstone house and took in boarders. The income was sufficient for her to quit the postal job.

Gertrude later moved to Delaware and went to work for a non-profit agency that provides counseling and a variety of services for the elderly. Acting with initiative and vigor, she developed an employment program for people over sixty. She also decided to become a lobbyist for the elderly and regularly went to the state capital where she helped push through favorable legislation.

Gertrude saw a strong need for more news coverage of information important to the elderly, especially benefits that they were entitled to under federal laws. At age seventy-five, Gertrude gave a stump speech in a public square during the noon hour, knowing she would draw the attention of businessmen from the surrounding office buildings who were on their lunch break. A judge was favorably impressed and helped arrange $5,000 to finance a news publication for senior citizens.

Gertrude contacted the largest Delaware newspaper and asked if she could contribute a page devoted to the elderly. Turned down, she started her own monthly newspaper. Each day that the paper came out, she would work from 8:00 A.M. to 6:00 P.M. with one of her sons distributing it from the top to the bottom of the state at senior centers, churches, newsstands, and supermarkets. The paper gradually grew in popularity over the past ten years. Today, each issue runs thirty-six pages in length and has a circulation of 18,000. The paper generates enough funds from ads and subscriptions to be self-sustaining.

Gertrude works without pay as editor for the sheer pleasure of performing the socially useful work. Now eighty-five years old, she remains busy at the paper and has not had a vacation in the past ten years. Gertrude says she works so hard because she enjoys it, because she believes the work is socially valuable, and because she feels guilty doing nothing:

> I've never considered work hard if you enjoy it. I keep going because it has to be done. I always have a guilty feeling if I sit down and do nothing. I just can't sit there and do nothing. I always kept busy, all my life. If I didn't work hard I wouldn't be happy. If I took on a job, I stayed with it. I never gave up until I accomplished it. I inherited that, I think, from my father.
>
> To me, the newspaper is important, and I enjoy it. People don't know how to get things done. We learned it at home. When I get tired, I want to finish what I'm doing. I want to finish. Get it out of the way.

Gertrude Lowell's persistence would be extraordinary in a person twenty or thirty years of age, let alone someone in her mid eighties. Consistent high effort has become as natural to her as breathing. As with our special education teacher, Betty, Gertrude's positive work attitudes can be traced to her parents' emphasis on hard work. Gertrude's industriousness was acquired from the example set by her parents and older brothers and sisters and from the approval her parents gave her for diligence in school work.

The approval Gertrude received from parents and siblings for diligent work was matched by guilt instilled in her if she sat around doing nothing. Gertrude's assertiveness and careful consideration of the most effective ways to meet her objectives were learned by observing a father who used politics productively on behalf of the community. He always stressed the importance of civic responsibility, serving as a role model when he helped get the subway extended through Brooklyn. Gertrude was shaped by the Depression to believe that government has an important role to play in helping the disadvantaged. Gertrude's strong work ethic complemented her social activism when she established the *Delaware Senior Citizen*.

Gertrude Lowell's creative industriousness is America's answer to the conformist perseverance prevalent in Japanese society. She is an exemplary case of what can be achieved by a combination of courage, ingenuity, and diligence.

When I began teaching at the University of Delaware, I was thirty-six years old and considered myself in good physical condition. But my strength was pushed to the limit to carry the heavy projectors that were supplied to show films to our classes.

One day, as I approached the building in which I teach, I noticed a man who looked not much older than I (but, I later discovered, is actually nineteen years older) step to the rear of a van, and lift one projector in *each* hand with such ease that he appeared to be dealing with empty boxes. He then carried the two film projectors to the building, walking quickly enough to pass most of the people who were approaching the building in front of him. Curious about this speed demon, I carefully observed his comings and goings.

Over the next seven years as I got older and slower, William Emory continued to work just as fast. What was also unusual about Bill was that having once met a person, he never seemed to forget that person's name. Furthermore, in the brief time between setting down the equipment and heading back to the truck, he chatted with such genuine friendliness and warmth that a person had to grit his teeth to stay in a foul mood. There you have Bill Emory. When he was promoted to the job of dispatcher, I asked him why he worked so hard during his years as a delivery man.

If you're working for somebody, you give them a day's work. I've always tried to give a good day's work. My father was basically the same way. He was a linotype operator, working for different newspapers. He did night work. He started at seven o'clock but he left home at 5:30 A.M. He wanted to get in and have a little session with the boys before he started work. When my father started work he was all business. He'd just sit at that linotype machine for how many hours it took him to complete his work. He always told me that if you work for somebody, give 'em a full day's work. So I guess I can say I got it from Dad.

I respected my father. Loving him as I did, I tried to do something to make him proud of me. Some people, if they can get out of something, they're going to do it. I've worked hard so that he would have been proud of me.

Accepting the attitudes toward work of a father he loved, Bill's industriousness as a child became habitual. With five brothers and sisters, there was little spare money. When Bill wanted extra cash he was encouraged to go out and earn it. As a teenager, Bill had a paper route, and on weekends he set up pins in a bowling alley. During summer vacations, he worked all day in a nursery and contributed much of his salary to the family's finances. Holding down several jobs during his school years made Bill accustomed to hard work to achieve the comforts of life. His father's emphasis on giving one's best on the job made industriousness seem natural to Bill and created his positive attitude toward work.

Bill says of his job at the University:

> I've always worked very hard and fast. I don't know if you call it nervous energy or what. When I first came here I was surprised at the pace people set. Nobody seemed to be in a hurry. I can't sit still very long. If I sit still I fall asleep. I plan on continuing to work as long as I still feel good. If I feel good 'til sixty-five or sixty-eight I'll still be here.
>
> I'm sure a lot of people look forward to retirement. Some people can relax a little better than others. I look forward to it in a sense; but not in another sense. I like to play golf but I can do that only three or four times a week. I'd like to travel. I've been to forty-six states and would like to visit the rest of them. But I don't think I could sit still long enough to retire.

As with newspaper editor Gertrude Lowell and special education teacher Betty Robbins, Bill Emory's parents inculcated him with the belief that an individual should work hard on any task he undertakes, including responsibilities on the job. Bill loved and respected his father so that the man's approval of conscientious work strengthened the boy's work values. Bill modeled his industriousness after the meticulousness his dad showed as a linotypist. Bill also took to heart his father's expressed belief that an employee owes his boss "a full day's work." Bill fully believes that leading a morally upright life, including hard work, is an act of love to the memory of his father. Bill's persistence also stems from his labor as a child to help support his family and earn spending money. Bill grew accustomed to hard work to achieve material well-being. Diligence, rewarded over many years, became a habit that he brings to any new task.

Since his graduation from the University of Pennsylvania School of Business four years ago, Ron Woodmansee has worked with twenty-four other insurance agents in a skyscraper located in Philadelphia's business district. Although all the agents are employed by the same large insurance company, each operates as an independent contractor. The agents receive commissions on the policies they sell and are free to handle insurance underwritten by other companies. Each agent decides the kind of insurance in which to specialize and the type of client to pursue. Ron sells life and disability insurance to corporations and to individuals who generally fall in the top five percent income bracket. His self-assurance and knowledgeability make him seem older than his twenty-six years.

It takes most insurance agents several years before they start making a sizable income. Overhead costs are high, including secretarial help, computer expenses for mailings and printing contracts, rent, utilities, telephone, and mail. New agents are tempted to take a job working as an agency employee at a fixed salary. Overhead costs are then paid by the agency but one's income is fixed. Ron, however, believes, "If I sacrifice now, I'll make out later on. It's like the sports' adage, 'Short-term pain, long-term gain.' "

Ron is an indefatigable worker who held multiple jobs as a boy, passed professional exams while still in college, and trod many unbeaten paths looking for clients while getting started in the insurance business. The long hours Ron spends pursuing prospective clients is reflected in the great number of small policies he writes. Despite being relatively new in the business, Ron led the office last year in the number of policies sold. Ron is willing to expend a great deal of time pursuing a prospective customer.

Efficiency is frequently on Ron's mind. He has a continual concern with making the best use of his time; that is, making the time he spends pay financially. He is driven to use his work hours effectively:

> Why waste time? Time is money. Walking and driving are mundane and unproductive. Do them as fast as you can. You don't want to walk behind me on the street cause I'm awfully fast. I try to travel during hours that are off-times for business, before eight or during the noon hour. Sometimes I'm impatient with people who tend to be a little wordy. I ask them to get to the bottom line. It might turn people off but that's the way I am. I'm busy. I've got 8,000 things running through my mind at once.

Ron thinks carefully and clearly not only about efficient scheduling, but also about the most profitable mix of insurance policies and financial investments to sell, the best mix of clients, and how to obtain an introduction to those clients. During his first two years as an agent, Ron worked sixty hours a week, not counting travel time to and from clients, and he refused to take a vacation. In his first year he made 2,000 knock-on-door, "cold" calls on corporations, wandering through huge industrial parks that contain as many as forty or fifty companies. He spent evenings visiting individual clients. By now Ron has acquired some 300 clients and spends much more of his time selling additional insurance to old customers.

Ron grew up in the small Rhode Island towns of Exeter and Hope Valley, where the proverbial Protestant Work Ethic was still strong. As our other paragons of industriousness, Ron emphasizes the influence of his parents' strong work values and their reward of his high effort:

> My parents have always been an example, a positive influence to be very hard working. They made me a hard worker more by example than anything else. The whole mentality in southern Rhode Island is that you work hard. You save your money. You're not extravagant. You're very thrifty. My grandfather's always been the

same way. He worked in the mill all his life and he also did odd jobs. It all trickles down.

My father has always been a very hard worker. I think that's been a big influence. When I was a kid, I remember he was out working every night. And I said to him one time, "Don't you like to spend time with us?" And he felt bad about that. But that's how it felt to us kids. He was always working. He was involved as a politician, state legislator, town council president. Always working.

Look at my mother today. She works full time. Even when we were kids she worked full time. She'd come home, have dinner on the table for us and not sit down until eleven o'clock at night. She's a perfectionist. My father's a perfectionist. The two of those people together. . . . There's no way I can get around it. To this day I'll come home to visit on weekends. She'll be working all day, have dinner on the table, do a few jobs around the house at night, and be cleaning up afterwards. She won't sit down from the time; she gets up at six or seven o'clock in the morning and goes until eleven o'clock at night.

Ron's father owns an insurance agency. As a matter of general principle Ron was required to earn his own spending money. By age eleven he was working part time on his uncle's garbage route, hauling trash. He says he began "real work" at age fourteen. Ron would take three, sometimes four jobs during the summer for a total of eighty or ninety hours a week. He would work on a summer recreation job as a supervisor, hire out as a painter, and cut wood on weekends. Sometimes he umpired and kept score for baseball Little League during the day. Then he would go harvest sod at night.

The importance of education was emphasized to Ron beginning in his first years of schooling. Privileges such as playing in Little League depended on maintaining high grades. His father was strict; Ron believes too strict. But his father was careful to spell out appropriate behaviors to help Ron avoid punishment, and he made it clear that he loved the boy and that the strictness came because he cared for him.

As with our newspaper editor, dispatcher, and special education teacher, Ron's work values were greatly influenced by industrious parents who served as role models and teachers. Ron's love for his parents made their encouragement of his hard work a powerful reward that strengthened his work values. He found it easy to be open and frank with his parents and never had major fights with them.

Ron nevertheless has an ambivalence about overworking. His father's dedication to his job left little time for the family and, Ron believes, contributed to a heart attack at age forty-five. Recently married, Ron looks forward to spending more time with his own future children than his father spent with him.

Ron is enthusiastic about his job and feels he is providing a service to the community. But his strong persistence comes from openly materialistic motives; his work is a way to make a good deal of money to afford a nice house and comfortable life style. Unlike our newspaper editor or special education teacher but more like Bill Emory, the dispatcher, Ron's job seems not to hold much intrinsic interest in itself.

Future-oriented endurance is central to Ron's self-esteem. But his work values are balanced by the desire to enjoy the fruits of his labor. He is willing to work hard while he is young but unlike Bill Emory, our dispatcher, he looks forward to retirement. Recently married and a bit wistful about the lack of time his father spent with him, Ron talks about spending ample time with his future children. Mindful of his father's heart attack at an early age, Ron does not want to be trapped into a life of all work and no play.

Sandra Roca obtained straight A's both in high school and college, where she is now a senior. She is majoring in special education, preparing for a job teaching mentally retarded children. Sandy works very hard to maintain high grades. She regulates her own study by great fortitude and uses tricks to keep herself working. For example, she sometimes makes the receipt of a reward or the release from discomfort contingent on completing her homework. If hungry, Sandy may place food in front of herself and refuse to eat until she has learned enough new material. One evening recently, Sandy got a cramp in her neck and refused to move until her study was complete.

Getting a "B" on a test is a signal to Sandy that she has been lax. She then overstudies for the next test because she knows "the reason I didn't do well is that I didn't try hard enough. Even if I think I tried hard enough. I tell myself, "Obviously Sandy you didn't try hard enough because you didn't do well."

Sandy enrolled in an advanced psychology course, designed to help students learn research methods by taking part in the planning and execution of an experiment. There were six students, all of whom except Sandy were psychology majors and had completed several psychology courses. Even though she had taken only an introductory psychology course, Sandy was accepted because of her excellent grades.

In the first research meeting Sandy volunteered astute suggestions and criticisms. With genuine modesty, she would frequently preface her comments with the statement, "Now, I don't know anything about psychology," and then offer an alternative explanation to the instructor's concerning basic human motives. Sandy's interpretations were sometimes as plausible as his, sometimes more plausible, and sometimes ingenious. It was not just her creativity that was unusual, but also her willingness from the beginning to challenge the instructor's ideas.

When the students were asked to write down their research suggestions in advance of a meeting to encourage them to think concretely about specific issues, her work was invariably the most detailed and complete. When they performed the actual experiment, there was no one who worked more diligently than Sandy to make sure that the plans were carried out precisely.

In contrast to the other individuals described in this chapter, Sandy's industriousness did not result from reward for high effort throughout childhood by loving parents. On the contrary, Sandy's parents discouraged her hard work. Sandy is an exception to the rule that industriousness must be learned from parents. Her story demonstrates the greater truth that although parental encouragement of strong work values is influential, strong rewards for industriousness from other sources can have a major impact.

Sandy was a premature baby and suffered severe asthma attacks about once a week until age fourteen. Doctors and teachers told Sandy's parents that she had subnormal intelligence, was incapable of performing as well as the average child, and should not be

144

pushed. Being careful not to raise Sandy's expectations beyond her abilities, her parents often told her that she was slower than other children and should be satisfied if she got Cs.

Beginning with kindergarten, Sandy was placed in classes designed for slow learners. Sandy was infuriated by the belief of doctors, teachers, and parents that she was inferior mentally and physically to other children. She worked extra hard just to prove everyone wrong. After being placed in slower classes for the first several grades, Sandy showed enough progress as a result of hard work to be placed into a regular class.

Having been given easy material to learn for several years, Sandy found normal school work extremely difficult:

> I would be up in my room crying and throwing my book against the wall because it was too hard. But I never admitted that the work was too difficult, because I just wanted to stay in that better section.

Sandy struggled persistently to catch up and later surpass others both in course work and athletics. Her efforts were rewarded. Long hours of study throughout her schooling resulted in an outstanding record of academic achievement. The positive results of this sustained effort improved her self-image, and she developed the habit of redoubling her efforts whenever a barrier was placed in her path.

Sandy was told that because of her asthma she could not become a cheerleader or take part in sports. Sandy did become a cheerleader by getting in shape through strenuous exercise and by literally screaming at her parents until they gave in. Being told she was incapable of any task made Sandy want to take on the task all the more:

> When I wanted something, I just never gave up, ever. Especially if I thought my parents were holding me back because I couldn't handle it. Everybody always said, "Look at little Sandy with the skinny arms. She's so weak." In high school in my senior year they had a competition to see who was the most physically fit. I did 364 push-ups, girls' push-ups, not guys' push-ups. But I was dying. I said there is no way I am giving up. I did push-ups all through my

gym class, and I had to stay out of my English class because I was still doing push-ups. I was just jello the next day.

I always knew what I wanted. If I knew there was some way to get something, I wouldn't give up until I got it. I remember when I was applying here at the University and they told me that I couldn't get any scholarships or financial aid because my father made too much money. They said just forget about scholarships. I said, no way! I'm not going to forget about scholarships. Otherwise I'll run up a big debt which I'll have to repay when I graduate. I must have applied for fifty or seventy-five scholarships. I kept applying, figuring there has got to be someone who wants to give me some money. So I wound up getting five thousand dollars a year.

Sandy's successful rebellion against doctors, teachers, and parents, all of whom believed she was inferior intellectually and physically, encouraged her to be stubborn for poor reasons as well as good. Today, Sandy writes with her right hand bent over like a left hander. While a student in Catholic elementary school the nuns told Sandy to keep her wrist straight when she wrote. Sandy refused to cooperate because she wanted her cursive writing to be straight up and down rather than slanted. The nuns strapped her arm to long rulers to make Sandy keep her wrist straight. But as soon as Sandy got out of grade school she went back to writing as she did before.

Rebelling against others' view of her as physically inferior, Sandy went through years of long, difficult practice to became an accomplished gymnast. But she could not do a complete backbend because two of the vertebrae in her back are fused. Having proven the experts wrong concerning her physical and mental capacities, Sandy insisted she could make her back more flexible regardless of what the doctors said. For years she worked unsuccessfully to accomplish the feat.

Once, practicing for a meet Sandy wanted to perfect a double back flip on the parallel bars. She had been told never to practice anything so dangerous without someone around to help break a fall. No one was in the gym that day to help Sandy but she was not going to be limited by any rule that seemed to question her ability. So Sandy tried the difficult flip and fell, tearing ligaments in her thumb and destroying her ability as a gymnast. With the strength gone in her thumb she worked for months in a futile attempt to regain her former skills.

Sandy's struggles made her sympathetic to all those who must persevere to cope with physical or mental deficiencies. She remembers:

> When I was younger I would always see mentally retarded kids. Everyone would say: "Aw, look at that. Isn't that a shame." I'd say: "No, that's not a shame. Don't you admire those kids? Look at them. They're out there in the store wheeling themselves around. I don't feel sorry for that person. I admire that person." So I always thought these people have so much potential. They're willing to work and try so hard to do something simple. I admired them so much I wanted to learn more about them. So I was interested in them while in grade school and all through high school. I remember my seventh grade teacher asking us to write down what we want to be when we grow up. I remember writing: "A teacher for the people who go around in wheelchairs."

In contrast to Sandy Roca, the other industrious individuals we considered—the newspaper editor, dispatcher, special education teacher, and insurance agent—had parents who continually gave them approval for high effort and who served as effective role models by practicing what they preached. Sandy Roca's circumstances were different. Her industriousness stems from a stubborn refusal to accept the belief by doctors, teachers, and parents that she was mentally and physically inferior to others.

Being told repeatedly that she was inferior and then succeeding by hard work increased Sandy's persistence, made her sympathetic toward those with physical impairments, and created a disrespect for conventional viewpoints. When Sandy's ability is challenged, she focuses all her energies on the task at hand. A grade of "B" on a test is attributed to laziness. Scolding herself, she works harder. As an affirmation of her self-worth, success on a difficult task has become rewarding in itself.

The evidence reviewed in this chapter points to simple and direct conclusions. Most of the industrious individuals we considered developed strong work values because they received approval for high effort from their parents throughout childhood, heard parents repeatedly express the belief that hard work was a central part of a decent and worthwhile life, and observed parents practicing what they preached by their own high effort. Our hard workers wanted to emulate their parents' work habits and were greatly influenced by parental reward for diligence because of a strong emotional bond. They had a desire, as our dispatcher Bill Emory put it, to act in a way that would have made their parents proud.

Like the stories of individual hard workers, we saw that Asian-American students are, as a group, highly diligent in their school work because of the strong work values inculcated by parents. We noted that the great majority of fifty top-rated employees, interviewed by Psychologist David Cherrington, recalled a childhood in which parents emphasized the importance of hard work and in which there was a strong emotional bond between child and parent. This emotional attachment makes children more willing to accept parental values, including positive attitudes toward work.

Most American parents fail to inculcate their children with a commitment to industriousness because their own work values, influenced by the general culture, are weak. Recent generations of Americans have developed an ethic of self-indulgence at a cost to work values. Among parents who do possess a strong work ethic, many are hesitant to inculcate their own values in children because of the popular contemporary view that children should be allowed to find their own way.

Other parents' attempts to encourage their children's industriousness fail because there is no strong emotional attachment that would lead the children to emulate their parents' positive attitudes toward work. When a child grows up in a culture that promotes leisure in contradiction to parental work values, acceptance of the parents' attitudes depends on the existence of a strong positive emotional bond.

Parents who raise industrious children often pass on the values of a subculture that has resisted the dominant American emphasis on pleasure-seeking. Asian-American parents' industriousness frequently arises from the Confucian culture of their homelands. Asian-Americans actively indoctrinate their children with a strong

148

personal work ethic because they identify the child's progress as central to the family's well-being. Our industrious special-education teacher's strong work attitudes were instilled by parents whose values were shaped by the surrounding community of industrious farmers and by the reward for hard work provided by farm life. Our insurance agent's parents were raised in small new England towns where the work ethic remained strong.

Sandy Roca's remarkable success overcoming her childhood disabilities shows that industriousness can be learned outside the home. Unfortunately, schooling and jobs in contemporary America have rarely been the source of strong work values. But as we will see in the next chapter, effective techniques do exist for teaching industriousness at school and on the job. One positive example is the teaching of professionalism to strengthen work values by instilling pride of accomplishment. Groups such as machinists and teachers are encouraged to work hard for their clients by years of specialized training that causes them to relate self-esteem to first-rate performance.

In all the cases we have examined, repeated reward for high effort trained strong work values. In the next chapter we will examine recent research that explains in more detail how this learning process operates.

CHAPTER 7

Learned Industriousness

A Greek myth tells of Heracles being approached by a stately and dignified woman dressed in white and with a look of truth in her eyes. She said, "Young sir, I know your parents and your breeding, and how you have been educated and brought up; which makes me hope that you will be a good workman of noble deeds. I will not deceive you with promises of pleasant things, but I will tell you the truth. Nothing that is really good can be got without labor and hardship, for so the gods have ordained. If you wish to enjoy the fruits of the earth, you must plough and sow, and reap and mow. . . ." Heracles asked, "And what is your name?" She answered, "My name is Virtue."

W. H. D. Rouse

Bill, a ten-year-old learning-disabled student, frowns at the page of math problems in front of him. Pushing the math book aside, he grinds the his pencil point into the desk top. Bill strolls toward the pencil sharpener, taking time to look out the window at students taking recess. At another desk, a another learning-disabled student, Joe, stares intently at a math problem. After a few seconds he writes down the answer, checks his work and, without looking up, moves on to the next problem. Working quickly and carefully, Joe solves problem after problem.

Alice, a depressed psychiatric patient, sits glassy eyed, methodically rocking back and forth. The set of file cards she has been asked to sort lays untouched on the table in front of her. An attendant stops by to ask Alice if she is going to sort the cards. Still rocking, Alice slowly says, "I don't want to do anything." In the adjacent room, Alice's ward mate, Sara, methodically sorts a similar set of cards. When the attendant drops by, Sara volunteers, "I've got almost got these cards finished. How about giving me some more?"

In the preceding examples, the two learning-disabled students received an equal number of points toward their test grades for every math problem solved, and the two depressed mental patients obtained equivalent verbal approval for every pack of cards sorted. Even though the two members of each pair obtained similar benefits for good performance, one individual exerted far greater effort.

A similar difference in performance would have been demonstrated for each pair using a variety of tasks. Because of prior experience, one member of the pair was industrious and the other lackadaisical. The principle of learning involved is simple but powerful: repeated reward of high effort increases an individual's general industriousness; conversely, habitual reward of low effort increases general indolence.

In the preceding chapters we examined how an individual's industriousness or indolence is shaped by parents, teachers, employers, and the media. In the present chapter we examine this learning process in more detail. Our understanding of learned industriousness comes from a combination of experiments with animals and humans.

Carefully controlled research with animals increases our confidence that the learned-industriousness principle just described is not restricted to a person's particular culture or desire to please the investigator. The human research allows us to assess the practical implications of the animal findings and to study development of industriousness in cognitive tasks. The animal and human studies thus complement each other, forming a clear and consistent picture concerning how individuals become industrious or indolent.

In 1967, a team of investigators at Roanoke College in Virginia demonstrated the first learned-industriousness effect with animals. Rewarding high effort for one task increased rats' subsequent effort in an entirely different task. One group of rats received food for each trip down a narrow wooden runway. Another group was required to make fifteen trips for each food reward. Next, the learned industriousness of both groups was observed with an entirely different behavior, pressing a lever.

At first, every lever press was rewarded. Both groups pressed at a high rate. Next, the experimenters made the going tough by disconnecting the lever from the feeder, eliminating the reward for pressing. The rats previously rewarded for each runway trip now went on strike, refusing to press the lever. In contrast, the rats that had been accustomed to making fifteen runway trips for each food reward continued to press the lever frequently. Requiring high effort in one situation had produced a generalized readiness to work hard in an entirely different situation.[1]

These results raise the intriguing possibility that requiring high effort to achieve reward in any one task will increase the individual's subsequent industriousness in all other tasks. If there were such a generalized effect of reward, the findings might have profound implications for understanding how humans become generally lethargic or industrious.

At the time these findings were reported there seemed to be no clear explanation for them. The results failed to fit any current theory concerning how animals learn, and psychologists ignored the data. It would be nine years before a similar result was reported by three investigators at the University of Texas: rats' speed of running in a straight alley following termination of reward was greater if the animals had previously pressed a lever fifteen times for each food presentation instead of being rewarded for each lever press. Required high effort involving one task had again increased the effort exerted in an entirely different task.[2]

The results were again ignored. One of the Texas investigators, Abram Amsel, was a preeminent experimental psychologist. But the findings still seemed odd, not explainable by standard views of how animals learn. Six years later, my students and I found a similar effect and became intrigued by the implications for human industriousness.

How can we explain the finding with rats that increased effort in one or more tasks raises subsequent performance in other tasks? In the rat experiment just described, the high-effort group initially received food for the completion of every fifteenth lever press, as compared to a low-effort group that was rewarded for each lever press. Subsequently both groups had to traverse a runway for food reward. Although the new runway task was considerably different from the previous lever-press activity, the degree of effort required in lever pressing had a major effect on subsequent performance. The group initially rewarded for a large number of lever presses had evidently learned something about hard work that went beyond the specific training tasks. These rats had learned a general trait of industriousness.

I suggest that individuals can learn about the energy expenditure necessary for reward independently of the particular task involved. The occurrence of reward following high energy expenditure would reduce the aversiveness of hard work in a variety of subsequent tasks. Therefore, the degree of effort repeatedly rewarded would contribute to a general trait of indolence or industriousness. Reward for high effort on various tasks during early life would make a rat or human generally more willing to work hard to achieve goals.[3]

Using rats and later humans, my research team further investigated the causes of an individual's general willingness to work hard to obtain reward. The previous research had found that the rat's general willingness to work on a task after elimination of reward depended on prior effort training. Such training, we reasoned, should also produce differences in performance in tasks where hard work pays off with reward. We required two groups of rats to go back and forth in a runway in order to receive food. One group was rewarded with food for each round-trip whereas a second group had to make five round-trips to receive food. Next, all the rats pressed a lever for periodic food reward. The rats that had made five round-trips for each food pellet later pressed the lever more frequently for the food reward than the rats that had made one round-trip. Reward for high effort in one task had increased the rat's subsequent willingness to work hard for reward on an entirely different task.[4]

Fine for rats, but what about people? Do humans learn to be indolent or industrious in the same manner as rats, that is, by repeated reward for low or high effort? Differences in learned industriousness could help explain why some people are willing to work harder than others in pursuing equally desired goals. Will a student study hard enough to earn "As" rather than "Bs"? Will a dentist work six days a week, rather than five, to earn additional income? Will a middle-level manager in an insurance company work nights to earn a promotion?

Part of the answer may lay in the individual's past history of rewards for low or high effort. A person who repeatedly receives valued rewards for high effort in a variety of tasks would develop a greater industriousness than another individual who always achieved his or her goals easily.

The industriousness of many college students shows substantial room for improvement. Is it possible to increase the industriousness of college students by rewarding them for increased effort? One group of college students was given simple anagrams (scrambled letters that can be ordered to form words), a second group was given complex anagrams, and a third group did not receive any training with anagrams. We reasoned that the group solving the complex anagrams would be rewarded for the greater degree of cognitive effort. Success on the difficult task should reduce the aversiveness of high cognitive effort and thus lead to a greater willingness to persist on new difficult tasks.

All the students next performed a perceptual task requiring the identification of differences between cartoon drawings. For half the students, the differences between the cartoon drawings were subtle and difficult to discriminate. For the remaining students the differences between the cartoon drawings were nonexistent, making success impossible. The students who had previously solved the complex anagrams worked harder than the other students on the perceptual task. They identified more differences between the cartoons on the solvable perceptual task and they spent more time trying to find differences on the unsolvable perceptual task. Rewarded high effort had increased the generalized persistence of college students on difficult tasks.[5]

Because students study a variety of academic subjects concurrently, the combined effects of many courses may influence general academic diligence. My colleague Fred Masterson and I gave college students training tasks involving anagrams, mathematics, perceptual identifications, or the combination of all three of these. Half the students received easy tasks and the remaining students received difficult tasks. For example, the dificult math task involved adding pairs of printed seven-digit numbers whereas the simple math task employed two-digit numbers. The students who received all three tasks were given fewer problems in each task than the students who received only a single task. In this way, all students received the same total number of problems so that the effects of task variety could be determined. To examine the generalized effects of this training, each student was next asked to write a short essay. Students who had worked on a combination of all three high-effort tasks wrote essays of greater length and quality than the essays written by those who worked on only one high effort-task. These results indicate that a small amount of effort training in each of several different tasks is more effective in increasing industriousness than a large amount of training concentrated in a single task.

Consider the two students discussed in previous chapters who experienced early success in a variety of school work as a result of very different amounts of effort. Bill Larson scored extremely high on tests of academic aptitude. In elementary and high school he was able to achieve excellent grades with minimal study. Bill compared his ease of outperforming other students to a race in which everyone else had only one leg. Bill would let the other students study hard for a test while he did little study. Then, as Bill saw it, the other students would struggle toward the finish line as he breezed past them with minimal study.

Bill had such an easy time at school that he was greatly amused at the praise his superior performance brought from his parents and teachers. After Bill got into a difficult college program he flunked out. His prior education had been too easy. Low effort had been rewarded repeatedly in a variety of classes until, by comparison, studying hard was extremely unpleasant.

Throughout this nation, bright students like Bill Larson succeed in high school with minimal effort. Such students are frequently admitted into advanced university programs designed to attract high school seniors who score exceptionally well on college placement exams. Entry into an advanced college program causes some of them to fail quickly and drop out of college. These students have been rewarded for low academic effort all their lives and find high effort on school tasks too unpleasant to withstand.

Many less gifted students have to work hard in elementary and high school to achieve success and thereby develop strong work values that allow them to thrive in college. Sandy Roca was often sick as a child because of her premature birth. She was told by doctors, teachers, and parents not to expect to do well in school. She rebelled against the view that she was intellectually or physically inferior and worked harder than her classmates. Sandy was rewarded for sustained effort by gradual improvements in school achievement until she acquired both the skill and industriousness to become an outstanding student in high school and college.

Continued high effort had lost most of its unpleasantness for Sandy. It was precisely because Sandy had to work harder than others to keep up in school work, and was rewarded for greater effort, that she developed her extraordinary diligence. Rewarded high effort in early schooling reduces the aversiveness of hard work and helps students persist in their studies.

Rewarding various kinds of high effort may contribute to an individual's industriousness. The number of times a task has to be performed, for example the number of round-trips by a rat in a runway or the number of book reports a student must write for a particular grade, is only one method for increasing effort. We reasoned that the rat's industriousness should be increased not only by requiring it to make a large number of lever presses for reward, but also by raising the force that the rat must exert on the lever.

One group of rats was rewarded with food for exerting a force of five grams against a lever, which the rats could accomplish with a weak tap. The force required for another group was gradually increased to seventy grams, which the rats accomplished only with great difficulty. Each rat was next placed in a runway in which round-trips were periodically rewarded with food. The rats that had previously been required to exert high force on the lever ran quickly back and forth in the runway and paused only briefly between trips. In contrast, the rats that had been required merely to tap the lever plugged along slowly in the runway and took long breaks between runs.

This evidence that various kinds of rewarded effort increase industriousness has implications for the old truism that a healthy body makes a healthy mind.[6] Perhaps training the body to work hard increases cognitive industriousness. Psychologists Lee Boyagian and Jack Nation at Texas A & M University found that increasing the force that college students had to exert against a pad raised the subsequent speed with which the students solved anagrams. Rewards for greater physical effort had indeed increased subsequent cognitive effort.[7]

Of course, hard physical exercise is not a necessary part of training for increased industriousness on cognitive tasks. Tasks that require high cognitive effort are probably more effective than physical exercise for increasing cognitive industriousness, because learned effort probably generalizes more to similar tasks than to dissimilar tasks. Reward for hard physical exercise may reduce the aversiveness of other kinds of physical labor more than it lessens the unpleasantness of difficult cognitive tasks. Nevertheless, it seems reasonable that the self-discipline involved in strenuous physical exercise programs could increase subsequent cognitive industriousness. The stress on physical fitness in this country is a countervailing force against the general culture's encouragement of self-indulgence.

The development of industriousness is also favored by the strong work values taught by a minority of American parents, teachers, and employers. However, individuals more commonly are trained to be indolent. Nowhere are the results of rewarding inaction more apparent than among many depressed mental patients and learning-disable children. Reward for low effort helps explain how lethargy develops and how it can be combated by rewarding greater effort.

Psychiatric patients diagnosed as depressed are typically less active and respond with less vigor than most other mental patients at the time of hospital admission. The institutionalized depressed patient may perform such behaviors as grooming and dressing sporadically. Some depressed patients do not eat unless urged to do so or unless partly hand fed. Some must have their morning dressing routine finished by another person and, unless coaxed, fail to go to bed in the evening. Many are unresponsive during psychotherapy.

The depressed patient's general lack of responsiveness may be maintained, in part, by reward for low effort. In many mental hospitals the patients are treated as if they are young children. Since staff members find that letting depressed patients vegetate is much less trouble than encouraging greater activity, lethargy may be inadvertently rewarded and thus maintained.

Patients frequently are given little to do all day. Mental hospital administrators often deal with patients' complaints of boredom by giving the group a television set. A survey of directors and staff of seventeen New York state psychiatric centers, covering eighty percent of New York State's inpatient population, indicated that of television watching was a "pervasive and time-consuming" activity. According to the report:

> Most respondents [directors and staff] in all centers agreed that TV enabled them to better care for patients, specifying that its presence freed them to do other things, quieted the patients when they were upset, and stimulated obedient, helpful behavior in patients. Most respondents agreed that heavy viewers were . . . less troublesome than the average patient.[8]

Television was valuable, the hospital directors and staff claimed, because it kept a large number of patients sufficiently entertained or at least distracted to enable staff members to focus their attention on patients who required more attention. Many respondents indicated that television, by concentrating patients in one area, facilitated keeping track of where patients were and what they were doing.

On the other hand, some respondents believed that television viewing kept patients from taking part in more-constructive, planned therapeutic activities and diminished opportunities for social interactions.[9] An attempt to incorporate television watching into therapy using discussion of the watched programs was used in wards representing only one percent of the patient population. Clearly, in the overwhelming majority of the cases, television was being employed as a mild sedative. Even those staff members who believed that television had a detrimental effect on the patients' recovery reported using TV as a baby sitter.

It is understandable that administrators and staff would value television for giving the patients something to do and keeping them out of mischief. But as we saw in Chapter 4, television watching teaches indolence. Thus, television adds to the negative effects of mental and physical inactivity in the mental hospital ward.

We investigated whether rewarding depressed patients for high effort on the ward would increase their industriousness. We had the ward attendant repeatedly ask patients to help him with cleanup and maintenance tasks that were normally his responsibility. Each patient was thanked by the attendant for completing such tasks as putting away phonograph records, cleaning counters in the day room, making coffee, assisting in getting materials out for recreational therapy, and so forth. Some patients were asked to help on several consecutive tasks. Other patients were asked for only a small amount to help each time. And some patients were treated as usual on the ward.

Next, on four separate occasions a staff psychologist asked the patients in all three groups for help sorting computer cards. Patients treated as usual or rewarded for low effort on the ward quickly gave up on the card-sorting task. In contrast, the group rewarded for high effort on the ward persisted much longer. Rewarded high effort had transferred across tasks. These results suggest that depressed patients' general lack of industriousness is maintained, at least in part, by the usual conditions of reward for low effort on the psychiatric ward.[10]

Being rewarded for laziness on the psychiatric ward may lessen the effectiveness of therapy for mental patients. Donald Woods and Jack Nation of Texas A & M University have written of the importance of teaching the depressed patient persistence in working with the psychotherapist to correct maladaptive behaviors and in the application of newly learned ways of dealing with the outside world.[11] Unfortunately, the treatment of the mentally ill in this regard has changed little from half a century ago when the mental health movement was founded to fight for better treatment of patients. Brutality has largely disappeared from mental hospitals. Drug therapies and psychological treatments have greatly improved. But the encouragement of patients' laziness by long hours of inactivity spent in the psychiatric ward has shown little change.

The low academic persistence of most learning-disabled children may similarly be maintained by reward for low effort. Many children with learning disabilities are unable to keep up with class-mates. These students often become convinced that they are incapable of successful school work and simply stop trying. Placed in a special education class, they may be given tasks that are so unchallenging and simple that success brings no gain in indus-triousness. Without special training, the learning-disabled child may fail to develop the persistence required for academic success.

We investigated whether the low persistence among children in special education classes results from rewarded low effort. Learn-ing-disabled preadolescent school children were rewarded for low effort or for gradually increasing effort in reading and spelling. In each group, accurate spelling and reading earned points that could be exchanged for such prizes as toys, candy, comic books, and playtime. We drilled the children individually on spelling words and reading words for an average of twice a week for twelve weeks. Children in the low-effort group were rewarded with a point each time they correctly spelled or read one or two assigned words. For the high-effort group, the number of words that had to be learned in order to receive a point was gradually increased until four or five words were required. Some children in the high-effort group initially grumbled about the increasing effort requirement, but the difficulty of obtaining points was increased slowly enough so that these children adjusted to the task.

Several days following the last drill session, the teacher gave the class assignments in mathematics and handwriting. In both cases, the group previously rewarded for high effort in spelling and read-ing spent more time working than the group previously rewarded for low effort. The high-effort trained children solved more math problems and wrote more words correctly than the other children. Rewarding a gradual increase of effort in one academic subject had raised the learning-disabled students' subsequent persistence in other academic subjects.[12]

Learning disabled students are helped neither by trivial tasks that teach indolence nor by attempts to convince them they are as academically talented as others. Betty Robbins, the teacher of learning-disabled children who was discussed in the preceding chapter, tells her students realistically that they are slower than most others on academic tasks and that they must try harder than the others to succeed. By slowly increasing the difficulty of the tasks she assigns, Robbins shows them that hard work brings eventual success. Robbins instills a high degree of industriousness and pride of accomplishment, which the children generalize to new academic tasks.

Reward for high effort should not be confused with providing impossibly difficult tasks. Continual high effort without success weakens an individual's industriousness. When a person works hard and repeatedly fails, high effort is paired with the absence of reward. Under such circumstances, hard work can become highly unpleasant. Little resilience may be left for new situations in which one's path to a goal is blocked.

In order to examine the detrimental effects of unrewarded effort, we arranged for one group of college students to fail following high effort and compared their later performance with another group that had succeeded as a result of high effort. The success group received difficult but solvable anagrams. The failure group was given anagrams having solution words (e.g., kylix, malae, padus) that were unknown to the students.

Next, both groups worked on a perceptual task that involved finding differences between cartoon drawings. Unknown to the students, the two drawings of each pair were identical, making success impossible. The group previously rewarded for high effort spent a great deal of time working on the unsolvable perceptual task. The group that previously failed with high effort at first attacked the unsolvable perceptual task vigorously. They appeared to want to make up for their prior poor showing. But initial failure on the new task quickly dissipated their effort. They quickly gave up on the remaining unsolvable drawings. Failure for high effort involving one task had reduced these students' subsequent resilience in the face of failure.

Many of the students who had failed on both tasks looked devastated. Although it was unlikely that such a brief failure experience would have a lasting effect, we wanted to spare the students the unpleasantness of dwelling on their failure for even a short time. So we wound up the experiment with a series of solvable cartoon drawings that allowed all the students to experience considerable success. Later, we explained the experiment, including the deception, to all the participants.[13] Industriousness is best learned by reward for gradually increasing effort. Through such training an individual learns to tolerate initial failure. A reservoir of persistence is developed to deal with tasks in which success depends on sustained high effort.

Rewarding children for steadily increasing effort can have important effects on their behavior later in life. Regardless of children's success at school, teachers and parents generally consider them too immature and inexperienced to make decisions important for their future. By adolescence, however, most American youngsters are allowed an increasing role in charting their lives, such as deciding whether to take vocational courses or prepare for a college education. This lessening of observation and control by parents also allows teenagers considerable latitude about obeying taboos concerning alcohol consumption, drugs, premarital sexual intercourse, etc. Teenagers' decisions that will have lasting consequences may depend, in part, on whether they have been rewarded in the past for low or high effort.

The term *impulsiveness* is usually used to refer to acts that are uncalculated, the result of sudden urges or desires. Individuals are said to have the trait of impulsiveness if such acts occur often enough to interfere with important long-range goals. Impulsive behavior is a societal concern when the results are viewed as damaging to the individual or to the larger community, as in the cases of dropping out of school, drug addiction, and unwanted pregnancies. Conversely, delayed gratification or *self-control* involves resisting temptation. Self-control can be thought of as the individual's choice to undergo the discomfort necessary for achieving the larger of alternate goals. For example, staying in school, avoiding drugs, and practicing sexual abstinence or birth control involve self-control.

The essence of self-control, choosing to undergo the discomfort necessary to achieve reward, can be studied in the rat. A history of reward for high effort has been found to make difficult tasks less unpleasant. Therefore, an individual repeatedly rewarded for high effort should subsequently show greater self-control.

Our first study concerned the effects of rewarded high effort on the subsequent choice between a large reward requiring high effort versus a small reward requiring low effort. In order to test the effect of rewarded high effort on later self-control, we first gave rats food for making round-trips in a runway. One group was rewarded for each round-trip and a second group for every fifth round-trip. Next, the rats were repeatedly required to choose which of two boxes to enter. If they entered one box, say the left one, they stayed until they earned a small amount of food by lightly tapping a lever. If they entered the right box, they stayed until they earned a large amount of food by exerting high force on the lever.

Self-control, choosing the hard-work compartment to obtain the larger reward, was more frequent by rats that had been rewarded previously for five round-trips in the runway than by rats that had been rewarded for each round-trip. Thus, rewarded high effort involving one task (running in an alley) increased rats' later self-control involving an entirely different task (choosing the heavier of two levers for the larger reward). The rats required to work hard had acquired greater self-control.[14]

We designed an experiment with children to find out whether, as with rats, effort training would increase subsequent self-control. Second- and third-grade students were given repeated opportunities to choose between the tedious task of copying nonsense words for three cents versus receiving two cents without working. Most of the children were ambivalent about the choice. They wanted the extra money but they found the copying task quite tedious. So they compromised. The children chose to copy an average of six of their ten choices.

During the next several days, some of the children were paid for exerting high effort in several tasks, including object counting, picture memory, and shape matching. Other children were paid for low effort in these tasks, and still others had no training at all. Finally, the children were again tested for self-control in the original copying task. The children who had received high-effort training showed the greatest self-control. They increased their choice of copying for the larger reward, whereas the other two groups showed no change from their earlier self-control. These results indicate that rewarded high effort increases children's self-control.[15]

Although self-control often involves the choice of greater work for larger reward, the toleration of other kinds of discomfort is frequently involved. For example, prospective teachers often have the opportunity to work in a public school for greater pay than in a private school, but at a cost of greater emotional tension. Public schools, unlike private schools, cannot refuse to enroll unruly children. The prospective teacher's degree of tolerance for stress might influence the decision concerning where to teach.

Reward for high energy expenditure should raise the individual's subsequent readiness to work for small gains of reward. Thus, the decrease of a reward's value occasioned by adding discomfort should be better withstood by individuals previously rewarded for high effort. In that case, an individual who has received rewards for completing difficult tasks would become more willing to choose a large reward that requires tolerating stress over a small reward that does not involve stress.

To investigate the effects of rewarded high effort on subsequent self-control involving stress, we first gave rats food for each round-trip or for every fifth round-trip in a runway. Next, the rats were required to choose repeatedly between an empty compartment and another compartment in which they could press a lever for food at the cost of an occasional weak electric shock. Rats that had made five round-trips in the runway for each piece of food later showed a much greater preference for the combination of food and shock than did the rats that had been rewarded for each round-trip. These results indicate that rewarded high effort increases subsequent self-control involving the toleration of stress.[16]

We can see that reward for high effort has very general effects on self-control. Following reward for high effort, an individual becomes more willing to pursue a large reward that involves a difficult task or a stressful situation. Repeated reward for high effort during childhood could affect subsequent decisions having major consequences, such as whether to attend college. Such training could also influence lesser decisions that have substantial cumulative impact, such as daily choices between leisure versus study or work.

There is one kind of self-control, however, that may not be influenced much by effort training: the capacity to tolerate long delays to obtain large rewards. For example, leaving money in an investment to accumulate the amount needed for an expensive purchase would require a greater wait than withdrawing the money frequently to make inexpensive purchases. Such self-control, involving the toleration of delay, may depend upon one's past history of learning to wait for rewards.

We paid second- and third-grade students for low effort or for high effort on a variety of tasks over several days. Half the children of each group were paid as soon as a task was completed whereas the other half were required to wait sixty seconds before being paid. Next, we measured self-control involving delay by giving the children the repeated opportunity to choose between receiving two cents immediately or three cents hours later at the end of the school day. The children who had been made to wait for their rewards were subsequently more willing to choose a large-delayed reward over a small-immediate reward.

Requiring high effort on the preliminary tasks had no effect on such self-control involving delay. And requiring children to wait for reward in the initial tasks had no effect on later self-control involving working hard. These results suggest that self-control involving delay and self-control involving effort are independent traits that have different causes. Learning to work hard for reward on a variety of tasks will not increase an individual's tolerance of delays, and getting used to delays of reward will not increase a person's tolerance of high effort. Both traits must be trained separately.[17]

Some remarkably industrious individuals lack the training that produces the capacity to wait. They insist on attacking tasks vigorously even when delay would be the wiser decision. For example, the Antarctic explorer Earnest Shackleton showed remarkable endurance in journeys across the Antarctic ice cap, but on repeated occasions he greatly increased the risks involved in the journey because he did not have the patience to wait before sailing until all the required equipment was obtained. Shackleton was willing to work but not wait. During the second world war, General Patton used his tanks brilliantly to pierce weak points in enemy lines and he showed dogged persistence by driving deep into the enemy's territory. He thereby isolated the enemy's front line units and disrupted their lines of communication and supply. But, Patton's inability to wait for his own lines of communication and supply to be established often resulted in coming so close to running out of ammunition and fuel that he had to give up much of the territory he had won. Both Shackleton and Patton were paragons of industriousness but did not have the capacity to wait when such was the wiser course of action.

When children are promised toys, movies, candy, or any of a great variety of enjoyable items that require a wait, they would naturally prefer the treat immediately. In many families, the child discovers that rewards can be quickly obtained by whining until parents give in. Such complaining requires little effort on the child's part but is often sufficiently annoying so that parents surrender and give the child the desired item immediately. A child never taught to wait for rewards may carry to school and later life the burden of an underdeveloped capacity to delay gratification.

Several years ago, the Kenner Toys Company inadvertently contributed in a small way to the acquisition of self-control involving delay for many thousands of children. The President of the Company, Bernard Loomis, read an item in the *Hollywood Reporter* about a new science fiction movie being produced with the title *Star Wars*. Loomis became interested and obtained the right to manufacture Star-Wars toys that he planned to begin selling a little over a year after the movie came out. The movie appeared shortly before Christmas and was a smash hit. It was too late to speed production in order to have the toys ready by Christmas. So Loomis hit on the ingenious solution of selling certificates promising to deliver *Star Wars* toys at a later date.[18]

Thousands of children received one instance of learning to wait for reward that probably contributed a bit to their general capacity to delay gratification. Parents should take a cue from Kenner toys, teaching their children delay of gratification by accustoming them to wait for desired toys and other rewards.

The generalized effects of rewarded high effort on self-control have important implications for situations in which an individual may choose between pursuing a goal by the sustained performance of a socially sanctioned behavior or by a less-difficult shortcut that violates conventional morality, such as cheating, lying, or stealing. A strong desire to succeed does not always increase task persistence. In fact, students who scored high on a questionnaire measure of achievement motivation cheated more than others.[19] The psychologist who performed this study argued that achievement-oriented individuals are more concerned with ends than means, and he questioned whether training programs designed to instill high achievement motivation are in the best interests of society.

Learned industriousness resulting from repeated reward of high effort might result in a stronger task orientation that reduces a person's tendency to achieve his goals dishonestly. Distraction of attention from temptation by keeping busy is a well-known method of impulse control.[20] By concentrating on working for a desired goal, rather than dwelling on the goal itself, a person may be less inclined to resort to dishonest shortcuts.

My colleague Fred Masterson and I carried out an experiment with college students to test whether rewarded high effort increases an individual's subsequent resistance to cheating. The students in one group were required to solve difficult mathematics problems and perceptual identifications. A second group received easier versions of these problems, and a third group had no effort training at all. Next, all the students were asked to work on a series of anagrams that preliminary research revealed were almost impossible to solve in the short time alloted for each word. A few easy anagrams were included to make all the anagrams seem solvable.

In order to convince the students that they could get away with cheating, they were told that speaking out loud interfered with the task and that they should try to solve the anagrams without speaking. When the time was up for figuring out an anagram, they would be shown the correct answer. They were simply to place a plus on the answer sheet if they previously figured out the answer they were shown. They were to put a zero if they had not figured out the correct answer. It seemed easy to the students to cheat because they never actually had to supply an answer, simply to claim the solution after it was shown to them.

Most of the students did cheat. However, the students who had previously been required to solve difficult anagrams cheated less than the others. Rewarded high effort on preliminary tasks reduced the number of anagrams that students falsely claimed to solve.[21] Rewarded high effort by teachers, parents, and employers may reduce the dishonesty sometimes engendered by strong achieve-ment motivation.

In our experiments on learned industriousness, we have trained people over periods of time ranging from a few minutes to several months. The obtained positive effects on task persistence, self-control, and honesty are consistent with recollections concerning childhood training by the industrious individuals discussed in Chapter 6. But more experiments are needed that directly study the effects of *long-term* training with reward for low effort or high effort.

Because rats reach adulthood within three months after birth, it is easier with rats than humans to study the effects of long-term effort training during youth. We tested whether reward for high effort during youth would make rats more industrious when they must later earn their keep by serving in experiments. Researchers have usually considered the choice of the method of maintenance feeding during a rat's youth too unimportant to mention, let alone justify. Yet it is possible that the effort involved in obtaining food and other rewards at home systematically influences the rat's effort in various tasks on the job.

In most laboratories that employ rats, daily feedings consist of large food pellets placed either on the floor of the home cage or in a hopper attached to the outside of the home cage's wire-mesh front wall. The use of the hopper requires rats to gnaw the food pellets through the wire mesh. Rats that eat from the hopper work harder than rats given their meals on the cage floor and so may develop a greater industriousness.

My colleague Fred Masterson and I trained young rats to run down a runway for food reward. For the next month we fed half the rats with the hopper method and the remaining rats with the floor method. Then all the rats were returned to the runway where they received reward for a few trials, followed by trials without reward. The hopper-fed rats continually ran faster than the floor-fed rats.

Having to work hard at home during their youth had caused rats to be subsequently more persistent on the job. These results are consistent with the view that repeated reward for high effort decreases the aversiveness of difficult tasks and thereby makes the individual more industriousness in all its behaviors.[22]

Unlike the controlled upbringing of rats, we cannot directly observe a person's life-long history of learning to work hard or to be lazy. But the development of a strong or weak personal work ethic that arises from rewarded high effort during youth can be inferred by questionnaires that measure the desire to perform work of high quality and to keep active and busy on the job. In a study that required college students to attempt to decode anagrams having solution words unknown to the students, I found that three-fourths of the students cheated when they thought they would not be caught. However, the students who had a strong personal work ethic, as previously measured by questionnaire, spent twice as long as the low work-ethic students trying to solve the task honestly before resorting to cheating.

The resistance to cheating among low work-ethic students was found to be changeable. Providing the low work-ethic students with preliminary success in difficult mathematics and perceptual-identification tasks reduced their cheating.[23] The similar way in which a strong work ethic and rewarded high effort increase persistence and reduce cheating suggests that reward for high effort strengthens the personal work ethic.

Our examination of research evidence shows the powerful effects of rewarded high effort on subsequent industriousness. Carefully controlled experiments with rats, depressed psychiatric patients, learning-disabled and ordinary children, and college students all found that rewarded high effort produced a generalized increase in industriousness that transferred to new tasks. These findings are consistent with the life stories of industrious individuals, described in the preceding chapter, each of whom received repeated reward for high effort during childhood. Psychologist David Cherrington's previously described interviews with outstanding employees similarly indicated the importance rewarded high effort in the development of a strong work ethic. These converging lines of evidence indicate that reward for high effort provides a behavioral technology for teaching industriousness.

Careful planning of effort training is required regardless of the intended recipient. Parents, teachers, and employers should take care to use rewards that have been observed to be effective. In research with learning-disabled children, we utilized a "token economy" that allowed children to earn a toy of their choice for high effort on academic tasks. Since the children were allowed to select from a considerable variety of toys, each child found some personally appealing toys for which they were willing to work.

Some of these children were motivated to work hard for additional reasons. Many learning-disabled kids are pleased simply by seeing their own progress, including the receipt of higher grades in subject areas in which they have previously failed. Others value the praise they receive from parents or teachers for improved performance. The token economy supplements the ego-boosting value and social rewards for success on difficult academic tasks.

In our study of depressed mental patients, we had originally planned to use a monetary reward. But we found these individuals so deprived of attention and approval that simply being thanked for their assistance by the ward attendant served as a potent motivator. In many of our studies with college students, successfully completing a difficult cognitive task and demonstrating one's prowess to others served as effective rewards. Social approval and ego-boosting success are valuable rewards for most students and employees and can be used effectively to train industriousness.

It should also be recognized that providing success without effort kills industriousness. In our research we have repeatedly found that rewarded low effort fails to improve performance on subsequent tasks. Required high effort appears to be an important ingredient in teaching individuals to be more industrious.

Rewarding students or employees for high effort should not be confused with setting impossibly difficult goals. Repeated failure for high effort causes people to become more brittle on subsequent difficult tasks, giving up quickly even when sustained performance might bring success. Teachers, parents, and employers should take care not to require impossibly difficult performance. Required effort should be increased gradually enough to insure frequent success.

CHAPTER 8
Marathonists

The only happiness a brave man ever troubled himself with asking much about was happiness enough to get his work done. It is, after all, the one unhappiness of a man, that he cannot work; that he cannot get his destiny as a man fulfilled.

Thomas Carlisle

A careful study of the lives of hard working individuals suggests three different styles of industriousness. A person who works durably toward long-term goals will be called a *marathonist*. A marathonist who pursues a goal continues until success is achieved or until convinced by clear evidence that there is very little chance of attaining the goal. Other industrious persons are *sprinters*, working toward their objectives with spurts of intense physical or mental effort. Although a person can be both a sprinter and marathonist, most sprinters rise to the occasion only when great effort is required for a brief period and fail on projects requiring high perseverance. The third style of industriousness is shown by *explorers* who continually search for ways to reach their goals more efficiently. Before beginning to work toward an objective, the explorer meticulously checks the advantages and drawbacks of various approaches. After selecting a particular plan, the explorer remains attentive to new information that may require a change in tactics.

According to the view of learned industriousness presented in the preceding chapter, the durability, intensity, and flexibility of effort provide similar but distinguishable kinds of experience. The style of industriousness that a person may develop depends on the kind of effort that is most often rewarded. Repeated reward for endurance creates a marathonist; continued success for intense physical or mental activity produces a sprinter; continual reward for carefully investigating and adopting more efficient means to attaining goals spawns an explorer.

In this chapter and the two that follow, we will examine the styles of industriousness possessed by American heroes and villains whose brilliance, bravery, or luck were not enough to earn them a place in history. Only by becoming marathonists, sprinters, or explorers were they able to succeed. These examples will illustrate how parents, teachers, and employers train the three styles of industriousness.

Two epic marathonists, Henry Ford and George Patton, were born during the latter half of the nineteenth century into an American culture that placed strong emphasis on hard work for achieving materialistic success. During that era, parents showed children by reward and their own example that persisting on difficult tasks was how an upstanding person became successful. Teachers, clergy, and the writers of textbooks and popular magazines preached the gospel of getting ahead by great fortitude.

As most Americans of his era, Henry Ford was raised on a successful family farm where nature's lesson was that high effort yielded bountiful returns. Henry's grandfather, William, left Ireland in 1846 during the Great Potato Famine, immigrating to America with only £2 of borrowed money in his pocket. But he had relatives in the new country willing to help him get started farming near the small frontier town of Dearborn, Michigan.

William Ford found the Michigan countryside covered with thick forests that provided lumber and fuel. The soil was fertile, producing abundant harvests of wheat. In the winter, when the land could not be worked, William laid in a store of the plentiful deer and wild turkey, and he fished the well-stocked streams.

When William married Mary Litogot, the adopted daughter of a neighbor, he built a large house for his new wife and his inlaws on the Litogot land and began farming.[1] Hard work paid rich dividends on the ninety acre farm, and the family prospered:

William Ford grew wheat and hay, tended horses and sheep and cows and pigs, cut wood, pruned his apple and peach orchards, carpentered for pay, smoked his bacon, salted his pork, dug and filled his vegetable pits for the winter, tapped his maples for sugar, made and repaired his own tools, built and painted his own walls, . . . tanned skins, and went by the ancient ethics of farming that to plow a crooked furrow was a disgrace. Mary Ford cooked, washed, churned, made candles and soap, knitted, preserved, and gardened.[2]

The Ford homestead's rooms were large and well-furnished, and the family was prosperous enough to purchase a fancy organ used for group sings in the parlor.[3] The Fords recognized that their affluence depended on long hours spent laboring in the fields. The bountiful harvests that rewarded sustained labor and the lesson of perseverance ingrained by parents helped fashion Henry a strong marathonist.

Young Henry walked a mile and a half to his one-room elementary school in Dearborn. There were no complaints about the length of the trip; after all, the neighbor children walked a similar distance. At school Henry was instructed from McGuffy readers with stories of boys growing up to be economically successful through hard work and righteous morality.

Most farm families accepted without question the necessity of great physical endurance to obtain necessities and a few comforts of life. Children learned the importance of industriousness by seeing the fruits of the family's labor. Henry's mother reinforced this imperative with aphorisms about the importance of hard work.

Henry idolized his mother, adopting her values as his own. By the time she died when Henry was twelve years old, Mary had inculcated him with an ideology of self-reliance and perseverance:

Fun we had plenty of it, but [Mother] was forever reminding us that life cannot be all fun. "You must earn the right to play," she used to say to me. One of her favorite sayings used to be, "The best fun follows a duty done."[4] . . . She taught me that disagreeable jobs call for courage and patience and self-discipline, and she taught me also that "I don't want to" gets a fellow nowhere. . . .

My mother used to say, when I grumbled about it, "Life will give you many unpleasant tasks. . . . Your duty will be hard and disagreeable and painful to you at times, but you must do it. You may have pity on others, but you must not pity yourself."[5]

The memory of his beloved mother's lessons concerning diligence was a powerful force in Henry's life. As with most of today's minority of industrious people, a strong emotional bond between parent and child led to the acceptance of the parents' strong work values.

The dawning machine age captured Henry's imagination. Wilderness still surrounded Dearborn. But only eight miles distant, the city of Detroit was becoming an industrial center. The rapid growth of smokestack factories was quickly decimating Detroit's trees.

In 1876, a large Exposition of new machinery was held in Philadelphia in honor of the nation's hundredth anniversary. Most of the country's population lived on farms. It was a long trip to a railroad terminal, let alone Philadelphia. Most farmers had little money or time to spend on such frivolity. But the nation always loved an excuse for a celebration. William Ford and some neighbors joined forty-five million others who went to Philadelphia for the festivities.

The travelers brought back the news of an enormous steam engine, two stories high, that generated power equivalent to 1600 horses. They reported seeing craftsmen operate a band saw, which was to introduce decorative flourish to American housing. They had observed the operation of the British inventions of the Maudsley lathe, the milling machine, and the planer.[6] They had watched a steam-driven elevator that was to make skyscrapers possible. William Ford likely regaled son Henry with descriptions of these technological marvels.

As a child, Henry was always tinkering with equipment. When new toys were brought home, someone was likely to yell: "Don't let Henry see them! He'll take them apart!"[7] Henry did his chores conscientiously but preferred toying with machinery to plowing or other farm tasks.

Industrialization had yet to alter the way farmers worked their fields. Farm equipment was little changed in a past hundred years, and cultivating the land still required the brute strength of man and horse. The same year his mother died, young Henry watched in awe as a thresher traveled down a country road under its own power, propelled by a steam engine.[8] Henry was frequently to be found reading technical magazines that told about the new automatic machinery.

The possibility of creating new machines to conquer nature dominated Henry's interest. At age sixteen, he left the farm to look for a job working with machinery in Detroit. For a time, he worked in a foundry and machine shop. Castings made of brass or iron were finished into a variety of items, including fire hydrants, valves for water pipes, and steam whistles. To be ready for any new job, there were more pieces of large equipment in the foundry than the number of craftsmen who worked there.

Henry labored a typical schedule of six days a week, ten hours a day. But his salary as a journeyman would not cover food and lodging. To make ends meet, he worked six hours a night fixing clocks and watches for a jeweler. He had learned watch repair on his own by tinkering. The jeweler kept Henry hidden from customers who might doubt the skill of a youngster.

Henry did not mind the long hours spent on the two jobs because he was accustomed to the combination of farm chores and school. Moreover, the opportunity to work with machinery was a powerful reward that reduced the discomfort of the long hours. Henry's two jobs continued to lessen the aversiveness of durable effort, making him a stronger marathonist. Looking back on these years, Henry said, "No work is ever hard. . . . The man who has the largest capacity for work and thought is the man who is bound to succeed."[9]

Henry dutifully went back to his father's farm each Fall to help with the harvesting. The new motors that drove the farm machinery were finicky. When new equipment broke down, there was often no one in the neighborhood who could fix it. One farmer who was intimidated by his malfunctioning Westinghouse portable steam engine heard of Henry's talents as a mechanic. He asked Henry for help.

Henry fixed the steam engine and went to work for the farmer, driving the contraption to other local farms whose owners paid for his help bringing in the harvest. The engine had attachments for threshing clover, hauling loads, cutting corn stalks, grinding feed, and sawing wood.[10] Henry recalled: "I became immensely fond of the machine . . . and [its] complete and expert master. I have never been better satisfied with myself than I was when I guided it over the rough country roads of the time."[11]

Henry's perseverance and innovativeness would have made him a marathonist in any of a variety of vocations, but tinkering with machinery was his main interest. He became a demonstrator and repairman for the Westinghouse Company in an era when the novelty and utility of farm machinery brought mechanics considerable respect. Each winter, once the snows halted farming and equipment repair, Henry fiddled with machinery in his small machine shop which he had equipped with a forge, upright drill, and hand lathe.

Henry's good looks, respected skills, and diligence made him appealing to the local girls. He married a farmer's daughter and built a house in a thickly wooded section on his father's land. Henry wanted not to cultivate the land, but conquer it. He set up a saw mill and in a frenzy of decimation he proceeded to strip the land of trees, selling all the lumber in Detroit. He brought down more than 200,000 feet of wood each year for five years.[12]

Henry recognized that the self-propelled Westinghouse steam engines he repaired had the drawbacks of delivering limited power and requiring frequent feedings of wood as fuel. On a trip to Detroit, he observed the fuel-efficient, internal combustion engine that operated on gasoline. It occurred to him as to dozens of other self-styled engineers that the internal combustion engine could be used to propel a vehicle. With that in mind, when each winter's snows prevented Henry's systematic destruction of the forest, he experimented with internal combustion engines in his small machine shop:

> When I was not cutting timber I was working on the gas engines —learning what they were and how they acted. I read everything I could find, but the greatest knowledge came from the work. A gas engine is a mysterious sort of thing—it will not always go the way it should. You can imagine how those first engines acted.[13]

To find out more about the electricity that fired the gas engine, Henry obtained the job of mechanical engineer working on the Edison Illuminating Company's generators in Detroit. He used a hay wagon to transport his wife and their furniture to the city. At age twenty-eight, Henry worked the night shift from 6:00 P.M. to 6:00 A.M. He excelled at quick repairs that kept the unreliable equipment running. That was just the what the manager needed, and Henry became the Edison Company's chief engineer.

Most workers would have dreaded a job that required being on call twenty-four hours a day. But for Henry there was a most agreeable side benefit. He could come and go as he pleased and had many free hours to read about engines and try his hand at building them. Henry used extra space in the power station as his own workshop. His excitement about new machinery was infecting the imagination of other Edison mechanics who spent their own time helping with Henry's pet projects.

Henry and three other Edison employees began building a prototype gas-driven car in a shed in the back of the Ford's rented house. Up to this time, many of Henry's attempts to build self-propelled machines had failed, including a steam locomotive designed for the road that ran only twenty feet before it died, and another model that never moved at all.[14] Henry did not consider such outcomes necessarily bad; he saw that only by trial and error could he gain the knowledge that would ultimately bring success.[15]

Modest successes in the construction of engines, requiring months of work, continued to shape Henry's resilience as a marathonist. For five years, Henry's small group of mechanics built engines and tried interconnecting them to the wheel shaft of a horse buggy. Finally, in 1896, the self-propelled carriage was ready. Henry and his helpers had to smash down the walls around the shed's door because they had failed to consider that the buggy was bigger than the entrance. Henry's buggy was soon running reliably under its own power. His first customer would write him two years later that the engine worked flawlessly.[16]

Henry was not the first to build a gas-driven car. In the early 1890's there were at least 300 tinkerers who saw the promise of the internal combustion engine and were working on their own car designs.[17] But Henry worked tirelessly. And unlike other successful designers who built heavy, expensive cars to be sold to a wealthy elite, Henry concentrated on a car that common people could afford. This led him to build small, inexpensive models that were both rugged and light, reducing fuel use and engine wear.

In 1899, when Henry was thirty-six years old, he formed the Detroit Automobile Company with the backing of prominent investors. However, lack of manufacturing experience hindered him from moving beyond prototypes to regular production.[18] Besides, he was having too much fun tinkering to concentrate on production. Henry nonchalantly drained the investors of their money, and within a year the company went bankrupt.

Most early attempts to manufacture cars ended, as Henry's, in failure. But start-up costs were low, and the smart money held that some mechanic was going to succeed very soon and earn investors an enormous profit. The novelty of sustained speed excited investors as well as the general public. The best way for a prospective car manufacturer to get financing was to show the car's worthiness by winning a race. Henry entered his car in a race against the world record holder before 8,000 spectators, and he won.

New financial backing was easily obtained. Henry repeatedly assured the investors that he was gearing up for production when, in fact, he was simply building another racer. His disgusted backers eventually forced Henry out of the company, but he took his car plans with him. Henry completed his new car and again beat the competition in a race.

For the third time, Henry obtained financing by solemnly promising to concentrate on production. He and his fellow engineers solved the production problems, and the new Model A soon began outselling hot cakes. Henry's backers told him it was time to concentrate on producing more-expensive models aimed at the luxury market. But Henry would not budge from his dedication to building the common man's car.

Henry took enormous pleasure from using inventive skills to overcome the technical problems that stood in the way of an inexpensive but reliable automobile. Money was important to him mainly for the opportunity to follow his creative instincts. In the Ford Company's first years, he saw the automobile as a way to help the common people. He wanted his simply-designed, sturdy car to provide the public with cheap, reliable transportation which would be a boon to their lives. And he wanted his workers paid well and treated decently.

Model A sales multiplied and soon made Henry rich. In his early forties, Henry had enough money to live lavishly without ever working again. But wealth corrupted neither the intensity nor durability of an industriousness that had been ingrained in Henry's early childhood. He had become a marathonist by the close relation between sustained labor and reward that he had experienced as a boy growing up on a successful farm, by adopting his beloved mother's belief in the value of diligent work, by success for persevering in his workshop and at a variety of jobs, and by his unquestioned acceptance of an American culture that assumed durable effort was the norm rather than the exception. He therefore worked year after year to make his cars sturdier and more reliable and to build new and more efficient factories.

Marathonists such as Ford are not satisfied by initial success. Marathonists are so little discomforted by sustained effort that achieving one long-term goal creates another. Henry's team now began work on the Model T which incorporated light, tough Vanadian steel from France, a streamlined engine, a better transmission, and a variety of other mechanical improvements. Henry worked day and night for a year with his engineers on every one of the Model T's technological improvements. Once, caught up in experimentation on a better starter, he worked forty-two hours without let up. [19]

Henry retained his vision of a light, rugged everyman's car. He recalled:

In 1909, I announced one morning, without any previous warning, that in the future we were only going to build one model, that the model was going to be the Model T, and that the chassis would be exactly the same for all cars, and I remarked: "Any customer can have a car painted any color that he wants so long as it is black." [20]

The model T was a triumphant success. From 1908 to its last production year in 1928, some fifteen million were sold. Henry maximized sales rather than profits, cutting the price of the car over the years from its initial $950 to its final $290.[21]

Repeated reward for innovation made Henry an explorer, as well as a Marathonist, which channeled his great perseverance into a continual search for new ways to achieve his objectives more efficiently. He had gotten a job at the Edison Lighting Company to learn about electricity. He built race cars to interest investors. When one set of investors quit on him, he found others. When the new investors became disenchanted, he found a third set. Henry had the wisdom never to view an experimental engine's failure as his failure. He understood that trial and error were necessary to improve engine design.

In the first few years of the Ford Company, Henry had welcomed technological innovations from people both within and outside the company and was eager to try out new ideas. Henry was happy to accept useful ideas from any source, whether Vanadian steel from French inventors or design improvements as suggested by his engineers. Henry created the moving assembly line in which each worker stood at a fixed location performing a single task as car components passed by. The lines converged to allow the large pieces to be fitted together.

But the rewards for listening to the advice of others were overwhelmed by the ego-inflating flattery of sycophants. He began to believe the stories of the Company's public relation's department that he was personally responsible for all the Company's innovations. As sales continued to surpass all expectations, he became egotistical and rejected any car improvement in which he had not played a major role. Henry also became increasingly adamant about deciding all of the company's policy questions himself.

The assembly line was soon adopted by a great variety of industries and led to an abundance of reliable, inexpensive products. But the fractionation of jobs and repeated increases in the speed of the line in Henry's plants and others reduced the workers' pride of accomplishment and created a bitter antagonism between labor and management. In addition to poor working conditions, employees had to suffer layoffs during the introduction of new equipment and downturns in the economy.

By the end of 1913, employee turnover at Ford reached a colossal

380 percent, meaning that the average employee worked only three months before quitting or being laid off.[22] As manufacturers of other products turned to mass production, their turnover rates also increased dramatically. In order to strengthen employee commitment and reduce turnover, Henry used the enormous profits generated by the assembly line to double the wage for workers who stayed longer than six months. The unprecedented five-dollar-a-day wage captured the public's imagination and angered many industrialists who favored keeping employees lean and hungry.

Henry stated that raising pay was wise economically because workers would reciprocate the beneficial treatment with loyalty and hard work. However, he continued to speed up the assembly line so that any time taken off for lunch, rest, or toilet made it difficult for a man to catch up. Many a Ford worker spent almost all his free time sleeping.

Henry made the high wage contingent on maintaining a good home life, as defined by Henry. To that end, and to get rid of union sympathizers, employees were continually investigated at home and on the job by inspectors from a created "Sociological Department." Company spies were everywhere inside Henry's factories. Henry was content to allow Harry Bennett and his squad of armed goons to use fists and clubs to beat union sympathizers into submission.

Henry's son Edsel became the figure-head president of the company in 1918 at age twenty-five when Henry was fifty-five. Edsel loved his father and had been an important part of Henry's satisfying home life. Henry could have used his son's love to inculcate Edsel with his own strong work values. Instead, Henry often humiliated Edsel by rescinding engineering improvements or policies designed to improve employee relations. Henry claimed he was highly critical of his son to strengthen him, to create backbone by goading Edsel. But by making success impossible, Henry punished Edsel's diligence and assertiveness. This treatment weakened rather than strengthened Edsel's work values.

When the Depression struck, the patriarch announced it came about because "the average man won't really do a day's work unless he is caught and cannot get out of it. There is plenty of work to do if people would do it." A few weeks later, Henry closed his plant and threw 75,000 people out of work.[23] In 1933, several thousand unemployed men, whose families had little food or other necessities, marched toward the Ford plant demanding jobs. The company responded with machine gun fire, killing four and wounding many others.[24]

Ford employees continued to receive poor treatment until the second world war. Only after his wife Clara threatened to leave him and after Edsel displayed an unusual show of firmness did Henry agree to let his workers vote on union representation. Out of touch with the feelings of his employees, Henry was astonished when the union was approved by overwhelming vote. He continued to grasp the reins of the company even as he grew old and infirm. When Henry was in his eighties and too senile to understand what was going on about him, Edsel and Clara finally rescued the company from his misguided leadership.

Henry Ford's great endurance and initiative, directed toward the manufacture of reliable and inexpensive automobiles, brought the fruits of capitalism to the average American. He helped create the clear-minded public philosophy that capitalist economies can succeed only by fostering mass markets. Following this principle, Ford constantly sought to provide a reliable product at a low price and to give his workers wages high enough for them to afford a diversity of consumer products.

The slowly accumulating rewards for great effort that Henry experienced in youth and the inculcation of strong work values by loving parents created an indefatigable persistence. Before achieving great financial success, Henry was eclectic and open-minded in his pursuit of engineering and manufacturing ideas. But he always wanted the last say in what was to be done; to follow his own vision. As his power grew, he could be more openly dictatorial, no longer needing to please anyone else.

Does reward for enduring effort necessarily result in unreasoning egotism? Our prior examination of less-famous Americans having high perseverance suggests not. Many of these individuals are simply dedicated to their jobs. It is the failure of parents, teachers, and peers fail to instill egalitarian precepts that makes a marathonist like Ford view success as confirmation of personal, familial, or racial superiority. When children are actively taught that they come from a superior ancestry, success through high effort confirms and strengthens snobbery. A case in point is General George Patton Jr.

George's father graduated with honors from the Virginia Military Institute in 1877, despite having to finance his education by janitorial work and tutoring classmates. The Army had declined in size following the Civil War, and opportunities for a military promotion were limited. So George Patton Senior turned away from a soldier's life and become a highly successful Southern California lawyer with a rich clientele. [25]

George Junior was raised on his father's ranch. The boy's step-grandfather, a Confederate cavalryman during the Civil War, and the elder's cronies captivated George with war stories. The boy listened to the legendary Confederate Raider John Mosby portray battle as noble and exciting. The two engaged in numerous mock combats, with George on his horse posing as General Lee. [26]

George was taught that a man's success is strongly influenced by the quality of his blood line. The child exulted in the knowledge that his father's side of the family had an ancestry of acclaimed soldiers, and he hoped to achieve military greatness. [27] But George's pride in his military forebears was mixed with a fear of his own inferiority. The problem was that George had great difficulty learning to read. He often saw words upside down or backwards, now recognized as a symptom of a common reading disorder called dyslexia.

Knowledge of dyslexia and teaching methods designed to help such individuals were not available at the time. George's parents wanted their son well-educated, and they had the good sense to encourage him patiently and kindly to persevere in overcoming his disability. Learning to read well would require many years of intense concentration and persistence.

George's reading deficiency made school work more difficult than for other children, and he became accustomed to working harder to achieve academic success. George's parents encouraged him to regard small improvements in reading ability as successes. Reward for sustained effort gradually forged George into a strong marathonist whose durability would later allow him to tolerate painfully slow advances during his army career.

George's favorite subject was history. George Senior read the young boy stories of mythical figures and great military leaders throughout world history.[28] George came to believe that history turned on the personal qualities of preeminent leaders. His glorification of warriors and battle, together with pride in his lineage, led inexorably to a military career.

At age eighteen, while waiting for a scarce opening for admission to West Point, George enrolled in the Virginia Military Institute. Reading remained an agonizingly difficult task for him, and he was depressed at being unable to understand posted handwritten orders. As always, George Senior encouraged fortitude, writing that George should practice reading different kinds of handwriting, deciphering each letter in every word until he understood the message.[29] George's dogged study produced excellent grades and scholastic recognition. This reward for durable effort helped fashion Patton's great resilience.

George was admitted to West Point after his father and prominent friends lobbied a U.S. Senator from California. George was highly motivated to succeed at West Point, but his dyslexia made this difficult. He concentrated intently on assigned texts, working slowly and methodically. Unhappy with his slow progress, George wrote his father that there was "no one in my class who so hates to be last or who tries so hard to be first and utterly fails," and that it was "exasperating to see a lot of fools who don't care beat you out when you work so hard."[30]

Despite great effort, George had to repeat his first year of course work. However, George's perseverance paid off with much better marks during his second school year. Moreover, his military bearing, discipline, and respectful treatment of teachers earned him the leadership rank of adjutant of the cadets.

By the time George graduated from West Point, his long struggle to overcome dyslexia was largely successful and had "instilled in him the need for sustained application and hard work, together with the driving will to overcome every obstacle hindering his march toward his goals. He understood that he had to work harder than others, but he was confident that devotion to duty paid off and led to victory."[31]

George's dyslexia had been a continual problem from his early

schooling to his graduation from West Point. In school others succeeded more easily than he, and George was often the butt of
ridicule by other students for his slowness. If his parents had simply
accepted his failure at school as an indication of inferiority, George
would probably have concluded that he represented an aberration
in the family's esteemed bloodline. But George's parents expressed
confidence in him, encouraged him to work harder than others and
taught him that endurance would bring ultimate success. George's
sustained effort was rewarded by slow improvements in reading
ability, creating the resilience that he would employ in pursuing
his military career.

George's goal was not simply to be famous, but to *earn* fame by
exploits in battle. He hungered for the glory of leading thousands
of men to vanquish the enemy. For George, bravery in battle was
a lineage that went beyond his ancestors to the greatest military
heroes of modern and ancient history. The opportunity to lead
armies required high military rank. But promotion was slow because Congress refused to fund a large standing army in peace
time. Moreover, his father had few influential contacts in the military. It would take George seven years to reach the inauspicious
rank of first lieutenant.

George believed that diligence, bravery, and skill would help
him get promoted. But also required, Patton felt, was the cultivation of a proper image and the ingratiation of senior officers.[32]
After being stationed for a couple of years near Chicago, George
appears to have used the influence of prominent friends of his family
or his wife's to be transferred to Fort Myer, Virginia. George
wanted this posting so that he might capture the attention of the
Chief of Staff and other senior officers stationed at the base.

The officer corps was dominated by upper-class gentlemen attentive to young men who showed their leadership capability by
the "quality" of their family line, their military bearing, and their
skill in upper-crust sports.[33] George therefore became a vigorous
exponent of the blue-blooded sports—polo, steeple chase, fox-
hunting, skeet-shooting, tennis, squash, and handball—the mastery of which he hoped would draw the attention of his superiors.[34]
Entering the Olympic Games at Stockholm, George pressed himself so hard that he passed out from exhaustion in two different

events—at the end of the 300 meter swim and at the finish line of the 4,000 meter cross country run. His performance was the best showing of any regular U. S. army officer.[35]

George would later insist on a link between physical endurance and unwavering perseverance toward important goals:

> The enthusiasm which permits the toil and promises the achieve-ment is simply an all-absorbing preoccupation in the profession elected. Endurance . . . is linked with self-confidence. Mentally it is the ability to subvert the means to the end, to hitch the wagon to a star and to attain it. Physically, it presupposes sufficient en-thusiasms to force on nature, no matter how reluctant, the obligation of constant bodily fitness through exercise. The expanding waist line means the contracting heart line both in length and vigor.[36]

George's success did depend on remarkable endurance shaped by reward for sustained effort in school and in the military. But George was also an adept explorer, searching for short cuts to a successful military career. He wrote to his father about additional advantages of upper-class sports:

> What I am now doing looks like play to you but in my business it is the best sort of advertising. It makes people talk and that is a sign they are noticing. . . . The notice of others has been the start of many successful men.[37]

George ran many a horse race to try to capture the elitists' attention, but his performance was unexceptional. George did strike pay dirt when he took up the study and practice of fencing. He wrote a paper advocating the use of the straight sword by the cavalry, which was passed up the ranks with glowing approval. George was encouraged to enlarge upon this thesis for publication. Accepted for the prestigious *Army and Navy Journal*, his design became known as the Patton sword. The Secretary of War had 20,000 of them manufactured.

George was learning the fine art of military politics, adding the flexibility of the explorer to great perseverance. An article in the *Cavalry Journal* on the history of saber fighting continued to strengthen Patton's reputation among the higher officers.[38] The use of the horse and the Patton sword in mock battles delighted the officer corps. Consistent with the adage that armies always prepare to fight the previous war, the army brass would continue to emphasize the use of cavalry after it was rendered useless in the first world war by the car, tank, and machine gun. Even after the German blitzkrieg of Poland in 1939, the Army was still holding cavalry maneuvers.[39]

George was assigned to General John Pershing's expedition in Mexico. The general was supposed to destroy Pancho Villa's troops who were conducting forays across the American border. Pershing's wife died while the General was in Texas. The general became strongly attracted to George's sister Nita who came to visit George briefly, and stayed much longer. George encouraged the romance. His use of his sister to further his own career was rewarded by an appointment as a personal aide to Pershing.[40]

George accomplished all the assignments Pershing gave him quickly and competently. He earned his promotion to first lieutenant, learned about the coordination of dispersed fighting units, and adopted Pershing's attention to detail and emphasis on discipline.[41] George's goal, expressed in letters to his wife, remained fame.[42]

George continued to probe for ways to quicken his rise to power. He was a snob and understood the kind of image that would stir the army's caste of top officers. He persistently used his understanding of elite dress, manners, and sport to impress military leaders. He had exploited family connections to get posted to Fort Myer where the Army's select officers were stationed. His fencing and treatises on saber fighting might have had little to do with modern warfare, but they achieved the objective of impressing the army clique. These successes strengthened Patton's emphasis on political manipulation to advance his career.

George worked cleverly to ingratiate himself with others who might be useful in the future. The strategic use of his sister as romantic bait helped get him appointed as an aide to General Pershing in the Mexican campaign. His attention to Pershing's personal comfort and ways to ease the commander's administrative burden got George a preferred command in the first world war.

He spotted Eisenhower early on as a comer. He loaned Ike war college notes, helping Ike to graduate first in his class.

George was intensely jealous of younger men than he, including Ike, who rose above him in rank and power. But to Ike and others he similarly resented, Patton showed the greatest respect and courtesy. George's investment in Ike paid off with the command of an Army in France during the second world war. Ike's indebtedness may also have contributed to his refusal to sack George for slapping shell-shocked patients and calling them slackers and cowards.

George showed endurance and flexibility by his continual search for better ways to win military battles. He bought a library of books on history and warfare, read them cover to cover, and thought carefully about their application to modern warfare. Patton was a chess master of battle, employing brilliant variations of ancient stratagems. He studied the latest weapons and was wise enough to understand during the first world war that the tank would become the modern cavalry.

General Pershing was appointed the commander in chief of American forces sent to France in World War I. The general left for France while engaged to be married to Nita.[43] In France, Pershing gave George the choice between commanding a battalion of infantry or serving in the tank corps.[44] The allies had made inefficient use of tanks up until then. But ever the alert explorer, George noted the excitement the novel weapon had received in the press and saw great opportunities for publicity.[45] He was also intrigued by the use of tanks as a possible way to break the stalemate on the Western front. So George accepted the responsibility of training and commanding two tank battalions.

This was quite a job since the Army had thus far a total of only two tanks.[46] George was the only person at the training center who even knew how to drive a tank.[47] He had to learn everything about tanks, figure out the type of tanks to procure, decide how they would be employed, and train all the men in his command. He attended British and French tank schools and, in order to observe tanks in action, he went as an observer on all allied military operations that involved tanks.[48]

George was an effective leader. He established strict discipline, trained his men to operate tanks proficiently, and developed tank tactics by trial and error. He also worked hard to ensure his men had the best available housing and that they received nourishing meals.

In battle, George displayed the unbridled aggressiveness for which he would subsequently become famous. He insisted on accompanying his troops in battle, always encouraging rapid movement and literally pushing those who dawdled. George hit one reluctant solder over the head with a shovel who then started advancing quickly.

Seriously wounded in the Meuse-Argonne offensive, George bled profusely from a wound in his side. As medics were taking him away in the ambulance, he yelled for the driver to take him to headquarters to report on the fighting. Only then would he agree to be driven to the hospital.[49]

George prayed earnestly to God for military medals. His ability to imbue his men with discipline and spirit did impress senior officers. His superior leadership, rather than his prayers, brought George the decorations he coveted.[50] George was promoted to the rank of colonel. But the war was over before he could fully demonstrate his leadership skills.

Personal advancement had not come easily for George. He became a strong marathonist because throughout his youth he was rewarded for durable effort. George's struggle to conquer dyslexia and obtain military promotions taught him to work diligently and flexibly to achieve success and gave him the resilience to tolerate periods of failure.

Back in the United States, George's rank reverted back to captain. A warrior trapped by peace and fearing he would never get back into battle, George would wait eighteen years before he again was appointed a colonel. Trained in youth to persist in bettering his abilities, George kept himself in good physical condition by his continued participation in sports, and he searched for ways to better himself as a soldier. He studied dutifully, graduating with high marks from all of the army's command level service schools.[51] George also experimented with tanks and various other new kinds of equipment.[52]

But even George's perseverance had its limits. In 1935, he reached his fiftieth birthday. George despaired his ever having the opportunity to achieve greatness through battle. He began drinking heavily, treated his wife cruelly, and had adulterous affairs.[53]

The threat of war in Europe revived George's spirit and self-control. In 1940, he was given command of an armored division and made a brigadier general. He shaped new draftees into a physically tough, well-disciplined fighting unit and imbued them with a jaunty esprit de corps. For this, he was promoted to major general. Letters of congratulation poured in from many army officers. He wrote back, thanking one letter writer after another for being the *single* person most responsible for his success.[54]

George enjoyed his flamboyant image, but also understood that symbolic acts of bravery and paternalistic devotion to one's troops inspired the loyalty and aggressiveness that won battles.[55] He noted, "It then appears that the leader must be an actor and such is the fact. But [he is] is unconvincing unless he lives his part."[56] George did not want his men to take wild chances, but he did want them to fight vigorously and take calculated risks for the greater glory of army and country. He told his troops:

> When the great day of battle comes, remember your training, and remember, above all, that speed and vigor of attack are the sure roads to success. And you must succeed, for to retreat is as cowardly as it is fatal. Americans do not surrender.[57]

George was a remarkable combination of marathonist and sprinter. He would concentrate all of his physical and mental vigor toward a goal, as when he fainted from exhaustion twice at the Olympic Games. In battle, he would drive himself for days virtually without sleep. He traveled with his troops as often as possible to inspire them, to maintain discipline, to make sure his orders were carried out quickly and carefully, and to render timid and indecisive officers and soldiers more afraid of his wrath than attacking the enemy.

In Tunisia, George was given command of an inexperienced and undisciplined ragtag corps of American troops who had been poorly led and badly defeated in battle. Within ten days he had cajoled, pushed, and kicked the men into a disciplined, effective fighting unit.[58] In battle, George was always in motion, visiting as many units as possible and prodding his troops to fight aggressively.

From his first military action as a commander of the Seventh Army in Africa to his final drive across France and Germany, George moved with the front line into battle. He displayed the military innovation and ruthlessness that made him a superb tactician and increased the self-assurance and aggressiveness of his troops.

George believed foremost in exploiting the enemy's weakness with swift, unremitting force. He would focus his tank attacks to puncture a weak spot in the fabric of the enemy's defense. His tanks would dash through the opening and continue advancing as quickly as possible, disrupting enemy lines of supply and communication, and isolating their front-line units. George would often continue advancing until his own troops were threatened by outdistancing their logistical support, leaving them with dangerously low supplies of fuel and ammunition. No other army in history captured as much territory as quickly as Patton's armored divisions.

George disparaged critics who called his actions wild or who said he disregarded the welfare of his men:

> From time to time there will be some complaints that we are pushing our people too hard. I don't give a good goddamn about such complaints. I believe in the old and sound rule that an ounce of sweat will save a gallon of blood. The harder *we* push, the more Germans we will kill. The more Germans we kill, the fewer of our men will be killed. Pushing means fewer casualties.[59]

George had great confidence in himself, saying he was "the best damn butt-kicker in the whole United States Army."[60] If his egotism brought criticism from politicians and the press, George knew his swagger and personal bravery would inspire his troops to greater aggressiveness. He wanted his men to enjoy killing the enemy, and to acquire the traits of "Self-confidence; Enthusiasm; Abnegation of Self; Loyalty; and Courage".[61]

George's brilliant tactics, nerve, and aggressiveness saved tens of thousands of lives by ending the war more quickly. He showed the power of a marathonist's undivided attention to an ideal, even if that ideal involved efficient murder. George's enjoyment of battle had little to do with dislike of the enemy; he would have been happy combating any enemy of his nation that put up a good enough fight to increase his pride in victory.

After the war in Europe ended, General MacArthur blocked George's request to fight in Asia. MacArthur knew better than to compromise his own place in history by allowing so talented a competitor into the Far East. The Russian menace in Europe did little to excite George's enthusiasm because he knew that America would not soon be willing to fight another war. Having achieved fame through battle, there was nothing left to give life meaning. Not even a visit to the United States that included 100,000 people cheering him in the Los Angeles Collosseum could reduce his unhappiness for long.

George was a superior politician but not without blind spots. He failed to realize that violence toward shell-shock victims or his known anti-semitism would make him a public relations risk and slow his promotions. At the end of the second world war, Patton's pro-Nazi speeches, designed to build Germany into a bastion against Communism, were not well received. George was willing to say what he believed because he knew he had fought his last war.

After returning to Germany from his trip home, George sullenly wrote his wife, "I think I was never so tired and stiff as I was yesterday."[62] Shortly thereafter, he was in an automobile accident and was taken to the hospital paralyzed from the neck down. He died a few days later.

As with Henry Ford, George Patton's personal failings must be differentiated from his endurance as a marathonist. George's mind-set, which allowed exploitation of his sister for personal gain, was fostered by his parents' own use of carefully planned manipulation of those who could help Patton's career. His snobbery resulted from his parents' emphasis on the superiority of his bloodline. However, George's dissatisfaction with anticipated retirement is typical of marathonists. Their satisfaction depends on the opportunity to pursue useful goals whether on the job or during retirement.[63]

Growing up in the last half of the nineteenth century, Ford and Patton shared the basic American belief that persistent hard labor was a small price to pay for achieving long-term goals. As we have seen with the minority of contemporary Americans who are industrious, parents who are loved by their children play a key role in shaping work values. Ford's mother explicitly proclaimed the benefits of unceasing labor. Her lessons were cemented by rewards for enduring effort on the family's successful farm and later by Ford's slow success as an engineer. Less given to homilies than Ford's parents, Patton's mother and father strengthened his persistence with encouragement as he struggled throughout childhood to overcome dyslexia. Patton's slow rise to power in the army, coming as a result of enduring effort, continued to shape his great perseverance.

We see far fewer marathonists in the general population today than a half century ago. No longer does the popular culture encourage parents to inculcate their children with strong work values. It is Japan's Confucian culture, rather than the forgotten Protestant work ethic, that now produces generation after generation of marathonists. Young Americans today who partially escape the nation's emphasis on leisure and self-indulgence are more likely to be found in the ranks of sprinters or explorers than marathonists. They have found success in school or business with brief spurts of effort or cleverness, but they show little persistence.

CHAPTER 9

Sprinters

By the 1920s, most Americans' work ethic had been weakened as a result of the excesses of the factory system and the promotion of leisure goods and sensual satisfaction. Parents, teachers, clergy, and textbook writers were less concerned than in the past with inculcating industriousness in the nation's youth. Families that owned farms or small businesses were still likely to rear marathonists because of the strong connection between durable effort and rewards. But because large companies had replaced most family-owned businesses and farms, marathonists were a dying breed.

The decreasing number of marathonists has meant that less perseverance than before is necessary to be considered a diligent employee. In place of marathonists, sprinters who exert brief surges of effort at critical times are considered hard working. These individuals have been rewarded repeatedly for tolerating the discomfort of intense effort for short periods as the need arises. The two sprinters whose backgrounds we will examine displayed considerable vigor at crucial times in their careers but lacked the durability that parents and the national culture previously molded in a Henry Ford or George Patton.

* * *

Chuck Yeager was the test pilot who first broke the sound barrier and became the best known flyer since the Wright brothers.[1] Competitive but not ambitious in his youth, Chuck might well have wound up an expert mechanic like his father. If born a few years later, his limited formal education and lack of political guile would have prevented him from becoming an astronaut. But then, he would not have been interested in becoming a space pilot, a job that requires little flying skill and provides little of the excitement of testing jet planes.

Chuck began flying at just the right time and stumbled into just the right opportunities to become a pioneer of supersonic flight. Expert combat flying and test piloting required a combination of perceptual abilities, technical skills, and intense concentration— all of which Yeager possessed. Pushing experimental planes to the limit of their capability later provided irresistible challenge and excitement.

Born in 1923 in rural West Virginia, Chuck was taught to hunt squirrel and rabbit with a .22 rifle by the time he was six years old. Years of hunting small game gave Chuck the ability to concentrate intently for several hours at a time. He thus had a head start in his development as a sprinter.

Chuck learned to be self-reliant and strong-willed from the example his father set. Chuck was a highly competitive kid. He wanted to be the best whether swinging from a vine over the swimming hole or racing in bobsleds. But being best always involved shows of manliness, not self-denial or sustained effort.

Chuck's father was a fine mechanic who was always tinkering with generators and motors; he passed his skills down to his son. Chuck was taught to respect talent and ability but not the importance of diligent effort in pursuit of one's goals.

During the second world war, Chuck joined the Army Air Force and became an airplane mechanic. He became a pilot because he was impressed that they were not assigned K.P. or guard duty. Although diligent in sports, he sought to avoid the long-term drudgery that is better tolerated by a marathonist than a sprinter. As many young knights of the sky, Chuck found he loved the excitement and danger of the dogfight.[2] He wanted to be the best fighter pilot, second to none.

Chuck was shot down over France and brought by the French Resistance to the Pyrenees near the Spanish border. He and another airman tried to cross the border, which involved an exhausting climb over the mountains during which each step made them sink up to their knees in wet, heavy snow. Near total exhaustion, the two were happy to find an empty cabin. They set some clothing out to dry and promptly fell asleep.

The flyers awakened to a hail of German bullets coming through the front door. They leapt through the window on the opposite side of the house. Chuck heard his partner scream in pain and yanked him along. The two went spinning down a hill into a creek.

His partner's knee had been shattered by a soft-nosed bullet, and only a tendon was left connected to the foreleg. Chuck amputated the leg of his now unconscious companion and bandaged the stump as well as he could. He then hauled the tall, heavy man through deep snow across the mountains to Spain. His partner made it back alive.

Chuck became something of a hero for his Spanish adventure. He had displayed courage, quick thinking, and the ability to summon up a few days of intense physical effort. The capacity to concentrate intently in a dangerous situation and to respond effectively had its roots in Chuck's hunting experience. Chuck understood the positive effects of such concentration in helping him accomplish the escape and became a stronger sprinter.

There was a rule that no downed flier who escaped could be returned to the combat zone. Captured again, he might be tortured or killed. So Chuck was scheduled to be shipped back to the States. He fought the rule up the ranks until obtaining a personal meeting with General Eisenhower, who was curious about this obstinate airman. Ike made an exception to the rule for Chuck.

Because Chuck lacked the capacity for self-denial or the endurance of a marathonist, it was lucky for his career that Ike was helpful. If returned home, said Chuck, "I would probably have been mustered out and my flying career abruptly ended. But I wasn't consciously thinking about my future; I was just being stubborn about the present."[3]

Chuck's fine-grain eyesight helped make him a superior fighter pilot. Other fliers who worked with Chuck throughout his career claimed his extraordinary vision allowed him to catch sight of enemy planes before anyone else. Of perhaps greater significance for his success was the capacity, learned from hunting, to concentrate intently on scanning the skies for hours at a time. Such a high level of attention, allowing a pilot to spot an enemy plane at great distance, is very difficult to maintain for more than a few minutes at a time. The ability to summon up a few hours of intense concentration, the quality of a sprinter, was one key to Chuck's achievements.

Chuck's love for flying kept him honing his skills, carrying out more practice flights than virtually any other pilot. His combat flying was pugnacious but disciplined, and he showed good teamwork. Chuck was soon made a squadron flight leader, passing over others of greater experience and rank.

Because of his competitiveness, Chuck was at first frustrated that unlike many of the men he commanded, he was not an ace with five or more kills. Then one day on a run protecting bombers over Germany, Chuck spotted a group of M-109 fighters and led his group after them. He got behind a 109. But before he could begin firing, the German pilot panicked and turned and crashed into another M-109. Chuck had downed two German planes without firing a shot. Expert flying brought down three more planes, and Chuck achieved celebrity for becoming an ace in a single day.

As a flight officer, Chuck acted carefully and intelligently to protect his men and saved lives by responding effectively in crises. On another bomber escort mission over Germany, a fellow pilot's engine quit and the plane fell rapidly. Chuck radioed the pilot with careful step-by-step directions, leading him to check out every component of the instrument panel. As the plane fell below 5,000 feet, Chuck told the pilot to examine the fuel mixture, which turned out to be the problem. The pilot's life was saved.

Since Chuck was the most junior officer in his squadron, his position as squadron leader aroused resentment among higher-ranking officers who served under him. On one flying mission, an officer was lagging behind and refused Chuck's order to close up. Such arrogance endangered the whole group and threatened to undermine discipline. Chuck executed an enormous loop and came up behind the officer, who never saw him. Chuck fired a burst of bullets right over the miscreant's canopy, gaining a ready compliance with orders.

As the war drew to a close, Chuck thought little about long-term career plans. He hoped to be stationed at an air base with his best buddy so they could dog fight every day. By a stroke of luck he was stationed at Wright field where experimental jets were being tested. Chuck's 1,100 hours of flight time and knowledgeability in maintenance earned him the job of test pilot. Loving to fly, Chuck took up every type of plane he was allowed.

Chuck was capable of remarkable concentration while flying and could be counted on to act effectively in a crisis. Chuck said of his motivation: "I wasn't an ambitious kid, but I was competitive."[4] Outclassing others by brief periods of skill, courage, and concentration made Chuck an outstanding sprinter. He became a superlative test pilot because of his skill and intense concentration and because he understood the advantage of studying the details of how each plane operated.

With his knowledge of machinery he quickly gained a better understanding of engineering systems than the great majority of other test pilots. This made him more proficient, better able to test a plane to its limits and deal with emergencies.[5]

Chuck was given the task of puncturing the sound barrier with the X-1 rocket plane. It was known that as planes approached the speed of sound, buffeting became severe. A British test pilot's plane had disintegrated at eight-tenths the speed of sound, and many engineers believed that the sound barrier was an impenetrable wall. A private test pilot previously given the task of breaking the sound barrier in the X-1 feared for his life and demanded such exorbitant pay that he was dismissed.

Earning low military pay, Chuck nevertheless viewed the job as an exciting challenge. At nine-tenths the speed of sound, he found that the X-1 buffeted severely, and many of the controls malfunctioned. He was convinced that the plane's performance would improve at faster speed. However, shortly before he was to attempt a supersonic flight, Chuck broke two ribs in a horse riding accident and was unable to use his right arm. He kept this a secret so he would not be stopped from flying. With one usable arm, Chuck summoned up the nerve and concentration to be the first person to break the sound barrier. By doing so, Chuck risked his life. Such foolhardiness is common of sprinters. They are always anxious to be done with a job, lacking the patience of marathonists.

Chuck had developed into a magnificent sprinter, always able to beckon concentration and skill during times of danger, whether outsmarting an enemy pilot on his tail, talking down another flyer in trouble, rescuing a wounded fellow airman from pursuing Germans, or dealing with jammed controls of an experimental plane. All such perilous situations evoked his intense mental concentration, which saved lives including his own and enabled him to achieve remarkable feats with malfunctioning equipment.

He continued to test faster and faster planes for a few years, coming close to crashing on several occasions. He set a new world speed record in a rocket plane, which then proceeded to go out of control, spinning crazily and sending him smashing about the cockpit. The plane fell from 60,000 to 5,000 feet before Chuck was able to regain control and avoid crashing.

Now thirty years old, Chuck decided to stop risking his life test flying and he settled down to a career as an Air Force officer. Chuck was a stringent task master. The pilots who served under him set records for shooting accuracy, and his insistence on careful equipment maintenance produced an outstanding safety record. He was for a time the safety director of the Air Force.

But Chuck lacked the durable effort and political guile of a Patton or Eisenhower that were necessary to achieve high rank. He had achieved rapid success as a test pilot without acquiring the durability required to pursue long-term goals. He had not been shaped to persevere as had Patton who worked years for modest successes in school and during his military career. When greater responsibilities or further promotions seemed unlikely, Chuck took early retirement at age fifty-two. He was a bit disappointed that the scope of his duties never extended further and that he did not achieve higher rank.

Chuck loved the excitement of flying but also enjoyed the more mundane entertainments of hunting, fishing, and boozing. Unlike Patton who could not imagine a life outside the military, Yeager found pleasure in retirement.

James D. Watson is the discoverer of the chemical mechanism for the transmission of heredity. In 1953, when Jim was twenty-five years old and only three years after completing his graduate education, he joined collaborator Francis Crick in making a fundamental discovery concerning the genetic code. Watson and Crick identified the spacial arrangement of the molecules that transmit hereditary information (the double helix) and suggested the general mechanism by which the genetic material duplicates itself in order to pass on genetic information to each new body cell. With characteristic immodesty, although not entirely without justification, Watson called his finding "perhaps the most famous event in biology since Darwin's book."[6]

The discovery was not only a great theoretical achievement but would have important practical consequences. Techniques of "gene splicing," based on Watson and Crick's work, are currently being used to alter the genetic code of viruses and make them biological factories that manufacture drugs. Insulin can now be made without the impurities that taint supplies obtained from animals. The largest biotechnology company, Genentec, has begun distribution of a drug, produced by gene-splicing, that dissolves blood clots in heart-attack victims.

Viruses will be used in the future to manufacture other complex chemicals normally produced by the human body. There is also little doubt that gene splicing will be used to produce larger and heartier fruits and vegetables, more resistant to cold, heat, and insects. Cows that produce more milk and chickens that supply more meat also await us.

The discovery of the genetic code was made possible by the integration of Jim's American approach to genetics, involving the reproduction of viruses, with collaborator Francis Crick's British method of using X-ray crystallography to obtain photographs of genetic molecules. If not for Jim's brilliance and determination, the discovery would clearly have gone to other investigators also on the trail of the genetic code.

Although little is known of Jim's youth, it is clear that by the time he graduated from college he was infected with the American disease of ambition without perseverance. Jim was driven to some degree by his intrinsic interest in the science of heredity, but more by an intense desire for scientific prestige. No marathonist, he selected the problem of discovering the basic mechanism of heredity because the solution seemed obtainable in the near future and would lead to scientific fame.

Jim set himself the goal of winning the Nobel prize, to be acclaimed as a great scientist. Jim wrote that he imagined himself "becoming famous [rather] than maturing into a stifled academic who had never risked a thought."[7] Learning that two-time Nobel prize winner Linus Pauling made a crucial error in conceptualizing the gene structure and thus had not yet won the race to discover the vaunted secret of life, Watson and Crick drank a toast to Pauling's failure.[8]

Jim was a strong sprinter. When faced with a puzzling piece of new information, he would concentrate on the problem hour after hour trying to integrate the new finding with what was already known. But, as we shall see, he was not so persistent as to let his work interfere with his pursuit of romance or travel.

As a sprinter, Jim's interest was not easily sustained. The argument that studying a new topic would make him a better geneticist did not motivate him. He would tackle new studies vigorously only if they seemed likely to propel him toward understanding the genetic blueprint.

Jim restricted his knowledge of mathematics and chemistry to the minimum he felt he absolutely needed for his immediate research.[9] Rather than using a stay at a zoological station in Naples to learn from the resident biochemist, he proceeded to "daydream about discovering the secret of the gene."[10]

Because Jim paid attention only to information that seemed clearly relevant, he avoided taking notes at most scientific lectures. He claimed that, "If a subject interested me, I could usually recall what I needed."[11] But he did, in fact, miss important information. Worse, when he realized a lecture he had previously heard was relevant, he was liable to depend on details he had remembered incorrectly. For example, he wasted his own and Crick's time by

his confident, if mistaken, memory of an important molecular structure presented in a lecture.

Such cultivated ignorance gets in the way of good science because discovery often involves insights in which seemingly unrelated facts are integrated in a new manner. In the field of genetics
it was impossible to predict exactly what degree of sophistication
in mathematics and chemistry would be needed to understand and
synthesize different kinds of information in order to understand
the hereditary code.

Jim was ready to abandon a line of research whenever there was
evidence that a new approach was more useful. He nevertheless
shut out much useful information because its utility was not immediately apparent. Confining his study to the portions of genetics,
mathematics, and chemistry that seemed obviously relevant to a
problem was the sort of approach that hinders more often than
abets important new discoveries.

Jim's blinders slowed his discovery. But brilliance, luck, and
intense concentration did the trick. When he perceived some area
of scientific knowledge relevant to his goal, his nonchalance disappeared. He would concentrate all his efforts learning the subject
and trying to integrate the new information into what he already
knew about the mechanisms of heredity.

He got the idea that molecular pictures using X-ray crystallography might provide useful evidence. So he immediately dropped
his current research. At a risk to his funding by the National Research Council, Jim set off for Cambridge, England, which was the
best place to learn the techniques of crystallographic research.[12]
With the connivance of half a dozen British scientists, he fooled
his funding agency into believing he was studying the subject matter it was willing to accept.[13] Having done all this, he still did not
feel what he called a "real incentive" to tackle the new procedures
until their benefits seemed assured.

Erwin Chargoff, a prominent biochemist at Columbia University, seconded Watson's confession of ignorance: "I never met two
men [Watson and Crick] who knew so little—and aspired to so
much . . . They talked so much about 'pitch' that I remember I
wrote down afterwards, 'Two pitchmen in search of a helix.' "[14]
Chargoff overstated the point. Watson's lack of breadth was not

unusual for a new Ph.D. who had received specialized training. Moreover, the opprobrious epithet "pitchman" implies a lack of concern with discovering the truth. That is certainly not the case. But as a sprinter, Watson was after truths that would come quickly.

Watson and Crick tried to fit each new piece of information into what they already knew, letting the quest dominate their attention for weeks at a time. But although Jim worked intensely, he gave little evidence of the durability found in marathonists. According to Max Perutz, the head of the laboratory where Jim worked:

> People . . . say that all he did in Cambridge was play tennis and chase girls. But there was a serious point to that. I sometimes envied Jim. My own problem took thousands of hours of hard work, measurements, calculations. I often thought that there *must* be some way to cut through it—that there must be, if only I could see it, an elegant solution, which is what I admired. He found it partly because he never made the mistake of confusing hard work with hard thinking; he always refused to substitute the one for the other. Of course he had time for tennis and girls.[15]

We know from Jim's autobiography that he chose his particular problem precisely because it did not appear to involve thousands of hours of hard work. Nor was Jim so driven by his work that he failed to take a two-month vacation in Europe during the height of the DNA race.

As Jim came closer to the solution of the gene structure, his thoughts dwelled more and more on his impending personal triumph.[16] He now worked day and night toward his goal. Once the grand discovery was made, Jim was off to Paris for months of fun, with little work. He would let others pursue the many new questions that arose from the findings.

Regardless of what he now did, it was only a matter of time before the Nobel prize was awarded. Because one major discovery establishes a scientific reputation, Watson's place in history was set.

Success had come quickly following short spurts of effort, developing Jim into a sprinter but not a marathonist. His rapid ascent to fame failed to instill the resilience required for rigorous scientific research. Soon after his discovery, Jim wrote in a letter:

I have a rather strange feeling about our [molecular] structure. If it is correct, we should obviously follow it up at a rapid rate. On the other hand it will at the same time be difficult to avoid the desire to forget completely about [it] and to concentrate on other aspects of life. The latter mood dominated me completely in Paris, which as expected is by far the most enchanting city I shall ever know. [17]

The Nobel awards committee waited a long enough time to make sure the claimed discovery was valid, and bestowed the prize to all the researchers most closely involved. Watson was only thirty-four years old. He was like a burnt-out star, publishing only one more scientific paper during his subsequent career. Harvard was nevertheless happy to have Jim as a professor, in addition to which he has spent much of his time as an administrator of prestigious research laboratories. [18]

Jim Watson and Chuck Yeager grew up in an America that still valued ambition but not the endurance of hardship to achieve long-term goals. Parents and teachers failed to imbue Yeager and Watson with any great persistence. They became sprinters, although not marathonists, because their jobs rewarded them for rising to the occasion with brief periods of extraordinary concentration.

Yeager's career, like Watson's, was an anticlimax to dazzling initial achievement. Yeager acquired military fame in a fraction of the years it took General Patton. But Yeager was satisfied thereafter to retire early rather than fight his way up the career ladder. Still in his twenties, Watson's great scientific achievement gave him the opportunity for virtually unlimited research funding. He became instead primarily an administrator, for which his scientific genius was irrelevant. It was as though Watson had been given the key to unlock the secrets of life, took a brief look, and then decided he was not interested.

CHAPTER 10

Explorers

Explorers continually search for more effective ways to achieve objectives. Before starting work on a new task, explorers conscientiously gather and evaluate information concerning possible alternative approaches. Once started on a particular plan, they are attentive to changes in the situation or new information that may make a different approach more useful.

Many individuals develop a mixed style of industriousness, combining the attributes of an explorer with those of a marathonist or sprinter. George Patton was rewarded for endurance throughout his childhood as he slowly conquered dyslexia. Later, Patton's political manipulation successfully advanced his career and increased his capability as an explorer. Together, these experiences strengthened the durability and flexibility of Patton's industriousness.

America's glorification of achievement has always encouraged a concern with pursuing goals more effectively. Parents of most explorers are typically found to use reward and example to instill the habit of carefully evaluating alternative approaches to any objective. Consider a teacher of learning-disabled high school students, Betty Robbins, whose industriousness we discussed in a previous chapter. When as a child Betty had difficulty with chores or schoolwork, her parents used to advise, "There is more than one way to skin a cat," or "You must be doing something wrong, think about it." Betty was taught to react to setbacks by withdrawing long enough from the situation to improvise a new approach. By learning to consider carefully the relative effectiveness of alternative plans, Betty became a strong explorer. This training shows in Betty's teaching.

Betty instructs her students in improved study methods and better time management. She continually searches for better ways to teach a particular student:

> You have to have a clear goal that you're trying achieve with each child. And then you have to analyze the path to that goal, and you have to keep the kids on that path. When problems arise, you have to backtrack and analyze what didn't work. When you see a weakness that doesn't allow the student to get to the goal, you have to repair the skills that are missing. You use a variety of modes—visual, tactual, auditory—so that you touch on the way they learn best.

In contrast, college professor Alex Compton provides a good example of a durable but inflexible industriousness. Alex's father and mother believed that there was ultimate victory for anyone who worked long enough and hard enough at a task. They interpreted failure as a signal to work harder rather than thinking about what went wrong. Whenever Alex had difficulty in school or on the job, his parents counseled, "Stick with it, you'll succeed eventually." He became an intrepid marathonist but not an explorer. Alex learned to react to failure by redoubling his efforts on the same task rather than thinking about how to pursue his objectives in a more effective manner.

Alex's checkered education and career show the dangers of rewarding children for durable effort but not flexibility. He chose to study for his Ph.D. with a strong-willed professor named David Preminger who took great pride in his own research. Alex naively believed his mentor would react agreeably to an article he published proposing a modification of Preminger's theories.

When the article appeared, Preminger was very angry. He demanded that Alex confine his research to finding support for a mundane and unimportant aspect of Preminger's theories. Failing to consider adequately the implications of Preminger's attitude, Alex simply worked harder on the research that had angered Preminger in the first place. A perseverator rather than an explorer, Alex felt that if he increased his research efforts, the situation would somehow straighten itself out.

Alex continued on this path even when Preminger angrily stopped speaking to him. Finally, Preminger had Alex thrown out of graduate school. Had Alex been trained to step back and think carefully about blocked goals, he would have recognized that his perseveration could lead only to disaster and that the only sensible alternatives were either to carry out the research Preminger desired or to transfer to a different graduate school.

That unhappy experience was not enough to change a strongly ingrained style of perseveration. After obtaining his Ph.D. at a different graduate school, Alex's first job as a professor was at the State University of New York at Albany. He had great difficulty getting his research accepted in the most prestigious scientific journals; their exclusivity is what makes them prestigious. Each time a top journal rejected one of Alex's manuscripts, he would leave the manuscript unpublished and go back to the laboratory to obtain more evidence. Then Alex would re-write the manuscript to include both the old and new data and resubmit the work to the same journal. When this too failed, Alex would obtain still more data and repeat the process. Sometimes Alex would spend a year or two of work on a single topic for which he could show no published work.

Alex never withdrew from the fray to consider that the top journals were simply not interested in his line of research, no matter how carefully the work was done. With little published work during his seven years at Albany, Alex was denied tenure and had great difficulty finding another teaching position.

The explorer's flexible pursuit of goals does not presuppose that the goals are just. Of the two explorers this chapter considers in detail, one was an enterprising entrepreneur and the other a clever crook. But both learned to search continually for improved ways to achieve their objectives and thereby achieved great professional success.

*   *   *

Estée Lauder was born in Queens, New York, the daughter of Hungarian immigrants.[1] Her father operated a hay and feed store. She is secretive about her background, and little is known about her life before the Depression years when she began peddling her uncle's cosmetics. But by the 1930's, Estée had graduated from high school and was attempting to turn the sale of cosmetics into a lucrative business.

She would push her wares any time or place, always thinking of ways to attract new business. A resourceful explorer, Estée did not restrict herself standard business practices or conventional etiquette. She sometimes aggressively stopped strangers on the street to peddle her products.

Throughout her career Estée would make effective use of the social norm that doing someone a favor obligates that person to reciprocate.[2] She began by giving facials to prosperous women at Jewish resorts and beach clubs so that they would return the favor by purchasing her products.

Estée has jealously guarded the story of much of her youth and early business experience apparently because she is embarrassed by her Jewish heritage, her lower middle class origins, and her hawking of cosmetics to women whose social standing was as low as her own. But some idea of her early selling techniques can be gleaned from her instructions to sales representatives after her company became a success:

> When you stop talking, you've lost your customer. When you turn your back, you've lost her. Touch a face. Touch a hand. Say, "This is for you, this is what I want *you* to wear."[3]

During the 1940's and 50's, Estée traveled throughout the country trying to get specialty and department stores to accept her line of cosmetics. Along the way she would hawk her products to anyone encountered casually in a train or retail business. Once at her destination, Estée would make effective use of the norm of reciprocity by treating important buyers for department stores to extravagant dinners and sometimes making extravagant promises of stock in her company once it went public.

Once Estée got a fashionable store to take her merchandise, she concentrated on convincing the salespeople to push her product ahead of competitors' stock. Bribing cosmetics salesgirls with gifts of her products took no great imagination. But Estée also worked on salespeople in other departments. She would give salespeople working in Hats or Shoes a gift of her expensive cosmetics and ask that after purchases, customers be told that the Lauder counter had just the perfume or lipstick to complement what they had bought.[4]

Always looking for new ways to use the reciprocity principle and not having enough money for advertising campaigns, Estée innovated the technique of giving free samples in the billing envelopes that department stores sent to their charge customers. Estée herself later sent postcards with an imaginative appeal to snobbery and greed: "Madam, because you're one of our preferred customers, please stop by the Estee Lauder counter and present this card to get a free gift."[5]

Estée began making good money which somehow did not reach the uncle who supplied her products. The man died poor and left his wife no life insurance because he had been forced to cash in his policy. Assessing how to expand her business, Estée decided to avoid the lower-class cosmetics market that was dominated by major companies such as Revlon. She needed her own market niche and decided on the upscale clientele. To give her products prestige, Estée continually tried to obtain access to upper crust stores such as Saks, Bergdorf Goodman, and Bonwit Teller.[6]

Estée wanted, above all else, to be a cosmetics tycoon. To this end she spent much of her time cultivating store buyers, hiding her Jewishness so that prejudice would not reduce their willingness to accept her products or slow the social climbing that she used to obtain free publicity.

Over the years Estée became a close friend of A. L. van Ameringin, the Dutch-born head of a major flavor and fragrance company. She went to him looking for a fragrance that she could use in her line, and he made her a present of a pungent bath oil she named Youth-Dew.[7] Taken in the bath, Youth-Dew would stick to a person for twenty-four hours. Estée wore the fragrance everywhere, spraying friends, elevators, and department stores. Called "vulgar, cloying, brassy and nauseating"[8] by those who had more delicate sensory preferences, the American public loved it. Estée included the fragrance in her perfumes as well as bath oil, and its popularity made her company a major financial success. The Youth-Dew fragrance still accounts for annual sales of $150 million.[9]

Once Estée's cosmetics became popular, she allowed them to be sold only in selected stores. The financial value of the right to exclusive sales of Estee Lauder products in a given town gave the company the clout to demand effective sales promotions and merchandising. By 1960, Estée's company sales hit the million dollar mark and was successfully marketing medium-priced cosmetics as well as upscale products such as a skin cream costing $115 a pound. Estée was careful to shop in Paris several times a year for stylish clothing, as befitted the owner and symbol of a company that sold the dream of beauty.

Estée still did not have funds for massive advertising campaigns. But she had the explorer's knack of circumventing seemingly impenetrable obstacles. She hit upon the idea of promoting her products by promoting herself. In New York, Miami, and the south of France, Estée managed to befriend and appear in newspaper social-page pictures with such luminaries as the wife of the Aga Khan, the Duchess of Windsor, and the rich daughter-in-law of financier Jay Gould.

Estée persistently tried to insinuate herself into the Miami social hierarchy through a flexible mix of aggressiveness, flattery, financial favors for the less wealthy and gifts to the favorite charities of those who did not need her money. Flattery and gifts, Estée well knew, evoked the norm of reciprocity. Having lavishly entertained a celebrity or owner of a chain of upscale department stores or having helped with that person's favored charity, was it so much to ask that Estée be invited to the recipient's parties? Wasn't it only fair for the department store owner to agree to Estée's request to sell her products?

Unlike Henry Ford who kept his son from power until the old man was too senile to know the difference, Estée gave progressively increasing control to her two sons and took pride in their achievements. Estée's elder son Leonard came up with a sophisticated attack on the youth market. Using talented writers and photographers, the Clinique line of fragrance-free cosmetics were promoted as a healthy, "hypo-allergenic" way to maintain youthful looks.

At cosmetics counters, "consultants" who worked directly for Estee Lauder were clothed in white coats and used a "Clinique computer" to recommend products just right for the buyer's skin. The combined appeal of science and naturalness was a landmark in sales psychology and increased annual receipts by tens of millions of dollars.

The names Estée gives her products, Like Clinique, create the impression of medicines that will rejuvenate the skin:

I'm very good at naming. I named Age-Controlling Creme. Night Repair. Re-Nutriv. All the lipsticks. I named Youth-Dew, years, years ago. I think up names in the middle of the night. I call up my son, Leonard, and say, "Please have it registered immediately."[10]

Estée conveys by hint and implication the message that her products medically rejuvenate the skin, avoiding suits by the Federal Trade Commission that would result from more open claims. Estée stated in her book that one of the reasons she was able to sell her products at Saks is that her Creme Pack produced a "fine improvement" in the "unpleasantly scarred" skin of an assistant buyer.[11] Estee Lauder advertisements always focus on young, handsome women with a look of self-assurance. The essence of the cosmetics industry as proclaimed by Estée is that, "We were selling jars of hope."[12]

Today, the company is run by elder son Leonard. The firm has annual sales in the hundreds of million of dollars, dominating the high-priced cosmetics market, and ranking about fourth in the world for total cosmetics sales.[13] Seventy-five hundred "beauty advisers" work for commissions behind Estee Lauder counters in department stores all over the nation.[14]

Although the Lauder family can now afford extensive advertising, they remain masters of inexpensive publicity. Who else would have thrown a luncheon at the New York Helmsley Palace for the hundred of "The Most Handsome Men in New York"[15] Who else would have the cleverness and audacity to sponsor a polo match to which Prince Charles and Lady Di lent their names for charity?[16]

Estée is a highly flexible *explorer.* When she lacked money for advertising campaigns, she obtained free publicity by imposing herself on celebrities. She gained access to these celebrities by working charity functions. Estée circumvented barriers to prestigious department stores by hiring people with good connections, by wining, dinning and bribing store executives, and by treating fashion magazine editors with deference and facials to obtain favorable stories about her products.

Estée Lauder's inventiveness and originality were repeatedly reinforced by success. A social nobody who offered an unknown product, Estée used gifts to salespeople, buyers, celebrities, and customers to elicit reciprocity. To gain publicity for her line, she cultivated celebrities with indefatigable attention. Dashing to the side of a celebrity whose picture was about to be taken by a news photographer was worth thousands of dollars of advertising. She was scorned by many of the socially elite either because was Jewish or was pushy. But she was able to capture the friendship of some well known people, whose publicity value made them an excellent investment. Estée understood that her success depended as, she says, by finding "the route around the stone wall."

Estée is now in her 80's and still hustling. She appears at large sales meetings to encourage the team and at major promotional events to garner publicity. At department store publicity events, women cue up in long lines to have the latest scent sprayed on their hands by Estée herself. Sitting with a journalist, Estée sent an aide for a bottle of Night Repair. Estée said: "Restores damaged cells. Only a few drops, that's all you need. Sells for forty or fifty dollars. Saks can't keep it in stock." Estée pressed the bottle into the woman's hand, closed the woman's fingers over it, and said, "Put it in your pocketbook."[17]

Henry Hill was born in 1944 in Brooklyn, New York, to a father who came from Ireland and a mother from Sicily.[18] His father's job as an electrician earned just enough money to provide the necessities for a wife, four daughters, and three sons. At age eleven,

Henry wandered into a cab depot looking for an after-school job that would provide a little spending money.

The Euclid Avenue Taxicab and Limousine Service turned out to be the headquarters for Paul Vario, a prominent mafioso engaged in gambling, loan sharking, labor rackets, and extortion schemes. Henry was given the job of gofer, running out to purchase cigarettes and coffee, and delivering messages. Henry was impressed by his employer's lavish life style and the deference paid him by the community. Wanting to work his way into Vario's good graces, Henry carried out his tasks carefully and quickly.

Henry stopped going to school and began spending all his time at the cab depot. Discovering Henry was half Sicilian, Vario let him remain when racketeering schemes were discussed. By age twelve, Henry's ambition was to become a gangster.

Fascinated with the variety of unlawful ways Vario made money, Henry was overjoyed by the opportunity to begin taking part. Henry delivered betting slips, passed bogus money for counterfeiters, and used stolen credit cards for purchases. He steered high rollers to craps games and served as a lookout to warn of plainclothes police officers who would demand payoffs to allow a game to continue. Henry was given a no-show job on a construction project by a contractor willing to appease the Mafia. Henry did visit the work site regularly but only for the purpose of picking up workers' bets and loan-shark payments.

Clever crimes earned the respect of the mobsters. The reward of respect, excitement, and money strengthened Henry's explorer approach to crime.

Henry's father was aware of Paul Vario's reputation and occasionally yelled at Henry to quit the mobsters, but the issue was never forced. Once, Henry got a beating from his father because of a letter from school stating that the boy was truant most of the time. Henry was greatly impressed when, told to take a ride with several Vario henchmen, he watched his mailman kidnapped and told forcefully to deliver to Vario's cab station any letters from the school addressed to Henry's father.

The three Vario brothers were always discussing the pros and cons of prospective illegal schemes. They made effective role models for a boy learning to become an explorer in crime. There was always a premium placed on good ideas for making money illegally.

Because Henry was eager to please and learned quickly, Paul Vario's brother Vito had Henry help him in numerous criminal activities. At Christmas, Vito showed Henry how to drill holes into the trunks of fake Christmas trees and stuff them with loose branches to enhance their appearance. Vito also got Henry a job unloading deliveries at a fancy Italian food store in order to steal merchandise. Henry was making more money than he could spend and showed off his wealth to other neighborhood youths. He was gaining confidence and self-respect as a junior racketeer.

Having been taught the habit of continually thinking about illegal ways to make money, Henry was himself becoming a talented criminal explorer. Henry showed considerable creativity. He got cab drivers to buy him six-packs of beer so he could sell the liquor in school yards. He served as a fence for burglaries by juveniles of such items as radios and clothing. The direct relationship among Henry's innovativeness, the amount of money he made, and the respect afforded him by his new gangster family continued to strengthen his explorer outlook.

By the time Henry was a young adult he was a full-fledged member of the gang. He constantly searched for quick ways to make money. Henry would buy several hundred cartons of cigarettes at a time from wholesalers in North Carolina and sell them cheaply in New York by illegally failing to collect state tax. Henry got a bank employee to give him credit cards of people waiting to receive them. Henry would use the cards to purchase merchandise safely before the cards were reported missing. Henry also hired youngsters to steal cars, which he fenced.

The continuous action of planning and carrying out schemes sometimes took up the full working day. But Henry was no marathonist. The self-denial involved in working toward long term goals was rejected by Henry and his colleagues. Henry quickly spent his profits on liquor and women. He enjoyed the image of being a high roller and would lavishly spend all his cash as soon as he stole it.

By the time Henry was in his middle twenties his innovation had been rewarded by a great variety of lucrative crimes. An explorer always searching for more effective ways to steal, he now found the opportunity to obtain a large amount of U.S. currency from an Air France holding facility at the John F. Kennedy Airport. Henry had been stealing shipments of merchandise stored temporarily at the airport. Freight foremen and cargo handlers, who were on the take, tipped the Mafia concerning the type of goods available, where they were stored and how they were guarded. But cash was a better prize.

To make a duplicate of the key to the cash room, Henry and his partners had to obtain the original key from an honest guard. Henry failed to find the key after breaking into the guard's apartment when the fellow was off duty and away. Apparently, the guard took the key with him wherever he went.

So Henry developed an elaborate scheme in which one of the guard's co-workers, conspiring with the gang, would befriend the guard and introduce him to a girl friend who was actually a prostitute. The prostitute began having an affair with the guard and lured him to a health club. While the prostitute and the guard were together in the steam room, Henry went through the locker containing the guard's clothing and obtained the key. He made the duplicate key and replaced the original before the guard came back. The gang used the key to make off with half a million dollars, and Henry's reputation as a creative crook was firmly established among New York mobsters.

Henry's luck seemingly ran out when he received a ten-year sentence for extortion. The conviction came from beating up a bar owner who was recalcitrant about repaying a debt to a loan shark. Unfortunately for Henry, the bar owner's sister was a typist for the FBI. Trained as an explorer to analyze any situation for illegal gain, Henry got a job checking the fence on the prison farm, allowing him to smuggle in liquor and drugs to sell to the other inmates.

While in prison, he bribed a clergyman to request that Henry be given a three-day religious instruction weekend once every month. He spent these retreats with his wife, gambling and drinking. Henry was similarly able to use bribery to turn five-day rehabilitation furloughs, run by the Chamber of Commerce, into enjoyable vacations. Henry was released after only four years because he was considered a model prisoner.

In addition to his previous kinds of crime, Henry began selling guns to mobsters, and he bribed college basketball players to shave points. Henry made another big score at the airport as part of a gang that robbed a Lufthansa airlines vault of almost six million dollars in cash and jewels.

Henry was once more arrested, this time for selling narcotics. Now he really was in trouble because he had contravened Paul Vario's order that the gang stay away from selling drugs because of the high danger of getting caught. Moreover, one of the leaders of the Lufthansa burglary group was systematically killing his partners to keep their share of the money.

If convicted, Henry faced a sentence of twenty-five years to life in addition to four years for violating parole on his extortion conviction. His associates feared that in order to avoid imprisonment, Henry would tell the authorities all he knew about the Lufthansa theft and other crimes. Paul Vario tried to lure Henry to an isolated location in Florida where, Henry believed, he would be killed. So Henry agreed to testify against the other criminals in return for placement in the Federal Witness Program, which would provide him a new false identity and allow him to stay out of prison. Henry Hill now has a new identity and expensive home, purportedly earned from an honest business.

Estée Lauder and Henry Hill became explorers because they were repeatedly rewarded for innovation. Careful thought about alternative plans produced concrete results. Estée was a successful entrepreneur because she learned to think her way around implacable obstacles rather than continuing a fruitless head-on attack. The positive results of her inventiveness provided repeated reinforcement for thinking carefully about the most effective and efficient way to meet her objectives.

In contrast, our college professor Alex Compton was taught by parents that overcoming failure required pursuing one's current approach more vigorously, as opposed to thinking about more effective alternatives. Compton courted failure by believing that endurance itself would insure success; Lauder created her own success by continually re-evaluating the effectiveness of her current pursuit of a goal.

By example and demand, Estée inculcated her sons with the pragmatic philosophy of careful-planned innovation in product development, distribution, and advertising. More, Estée created a corporate culture, now headed by her eldest son, that accepted and promoted innovation as the normal course of business.

Unlike Estée Lauder's long-term outlook, Henry Hill simply wanted respect and money for today without worrying about tomorrow. Because there is an ocean of honest citizens to be robbed and cheated and because Henry had no ambition to become a crime lord, he had few worries about intruding on other criminals' turf. There was a market for his innovative ideas, providing he was willing to split the proceeds with his bosses and other mob chieftains into whose territory he would venture.

In the neighborhood where Henry grew up, successful mobsters had enormous prestige. The approval by criminals Henry admired was as important to him as the flow of money produced by his crimes. Henry's acquired ability to find an illegal scheme to fit any occasion and his careful planning of major robberies brought cash and respect. It was precisely because most criminals are not clever or innovative that Henry's talents were in such demand.

Judging by Henry Hill's criminality and Estée Lauder's dubious medical claims for her products, it might be thought that explorers are by nature more willing than most people to engage in immoral activities to reach their goals. But there is nothing inherently moral or immoral about innovation. Our teacher Betty Robbins is an explorer who continually searches for the technique that will best help a particular learning-disabled student. The influences of parents, teachers, peers, and the media are what shape the ethicality of explorer's methods and goals.

We have now considered how repeated reward for high effort shapes three styles of industriousness. Success for persistence produces marathonists, willing to expend durable effort in pursuit of their goals. Accomplishment for intense physical or mental effort creates sprinters, ready to deal with a problem with brief spurts of great energy. Achievement produced by the flexible pursuit of goals yields explorers, prepared to think carefully about alternative strategies. The next chapter will consider the application of our knowledge concerning learned industriousness to the revitalization of the American economy and the creation of more meaningful work.

CHAPTER 11

Teaching Americans to Try Harder

The only fruitful promise of which the life of any individual or any nation can be possessed, is a promise determined by an ideal. Such a promise is to be fulfilled, not by sanguine anticipations, not by a conservative imitation of past achievements, but by laborious, single-minded, clear-sighted, and fearless work.

Herbert Croly

Near the turn of the century, Herbert Croly observed that Americans had grown to expect continual economic progress. He was troubled not by this optimism but by the public's complacent assumption that material gains would continue to accumulate automatically. It is easy to slide downhill into the valley of fulfillment when economic conditions are good, wrote Croly, but when conditions were bad, it would be just as easy to slide into economic ruin.[1]

The Great Depression dealt blind optimism a temporary defeat. After the second world war, America's industries turned to peacetime production and the standard of living doubled in two decades. Individuals who grew up in the years of easy prosperity saw no need to teach children that self-denial and diligent work were necessary to obtain long-term goals. The decades of prosperity have reinstated the traditional popular fallacy that economic progress will continue without hard work.

Living high on borrowed money is the norm for private citizens and the federal government. Most Americans fail to consider that with no one paying the bills, the party cannot last much longer. The nation's standard of living will slide as the value of the dollar cheapens and more of our wealth is returned to the foreigners who have financed our debt and are buying up chunks of American business.

The deterioration of the personal work ethic is a major cause of America's lessened ability to compete economically with other nations. The failure by parents, educators, and employers to reward industriousness has produced poor work values and lackadaisical effort at school and job. The emphasis on entertainment and short-term pleasures as promoted by advertisers, the entertainment industry, and the human potential movement, makes Americans less willing to put aside today's enjoyment for future gain. The worship of wealth, combined with weakening work values, causes managers to strive for short-term profits. The quality of current products and services thereby suffers, and research and development languish.

The decline of Americans' work ethic in combination with the retention of strong desires for material success has negatively affected ethics in a variety of professions. We discussed two examples in the second chapter: the fabrication of data by scientists unable to sustain the long, careful work often required to gather scientific evidence, and the increasing frequency with which members of the armed forces and private employees working on top-secret projects pass military secrets to nations in the Soviet block. Dishonesty is tempting to individuals who cannot tolerate the sustained effort necessary to achieve the life styles they seek.

The decay of work values has implications that go beyond the deterioration in Americans' morality and standard of living. Without the sense of purpose provided by pride of achievement, many Americans have turned to the escapes of alcoholism and drug abuse. Deprived of the material wealth required to satisfy their consumption-oriented lives and the hope for future economic gain, Americans' dedication to capitalism will be challenged. Calls for trade protection against foreign competition will escalate into demands for slamming down an iron curtain to stop all imports. Demagogic politicians will be elected with calls to disown foreign allies who compete with us economically. Many who are ashamed of the nation's lost virility will view military force as an increasingly attractive option for settling international disputes.

Americans must recognize that the country's economic decline can be stopped only by persistent hard work. It took half a century for the nation to slide into its present state of indolence. The recovery of strong work values will be a slow and difficult process. Patience and an overarching sense of purpose will be needed as the country proceeds by trial and error. Americans ought not to embrace utopian solutions that will cause economic havoc if unsuccessful, but they should proceed cautiously with a readiness to put aside failed experiments and to capitalize on successful innovations.

The strong effects of rewarded high effort on work values is demonstrated by our analyses of the industriousness of past generations of Americans, the diligence of the Japanese, the lives of famous people who succeeded by great persistence, the minority of contemporary hard-working Americans, and the controlled experiments on learned industriousness. Americans in their roles as parents, educators, employers, media owners and programers, and legislators can help restore weakened work values.

Improving the nation's economic competitiveness does not require a revolution in work attitudes so much as a steady evolution that can be accomplished by sensible behaviors. Small increases in industriousness attained by large numbers of students and workers will have a demonstrable effect on the nation's welfare. When watching a baseball game, it is difficult to predict whether a team averaging a .275 proportion of hits at bat will beat a team averaging .250. But over the season, the cumulative effect of this relatively small advantage will significantly alter the number of games won.

Certain traits in the American character can be used to help restore economic vitality. Materialism is as strong as ever and will generate great effort once positive work values are strengthened. Patriotism and public approval or condemnation remain potent forces that can be used to encourage individuals to rise above simple greed. We should strive to change the nation's laws and attitudes so that each individual identifies the public's welfare as good for himself.

The greatest potential for restoring strong work values lays with parents. Our examination of the lives of ordinary industrious Americans, psychologist David Cherrington's previously discussed study of high-performing employees, and the success of Asian-American students show that parents can inculcate strong work values in their children even when the popular culture promotes leisure and self-indulgence.

To ignore whether a child works hard to complete his chores or homework nurtures the child's laziness. The American parent's role as a teacher of strong work values has declined because most parents themselves do not retain a strong work ethic to transmit to their children. Other parents who do have strong work values are hesitant to inculcate their beliefs in children because the laissez faire popular culture calls for children "to find their own way." Parental guidance is also discouraged by the popular idolization of the "vitality" of youth over the sagacity and skill of experience.

The entertainment media's sanctification of youth and the acceptance by parents of children's independence of conduct has created the world's first *juvenocracy*. Youngsters help themselves to generous portions of parents' financial resources in order to pursue the improvident hedonism promoted by advertisers and the entertainment media.

Reward for high effort is an effective tool that parents can use to strengthen a child's work ethic. Most adults with strong work values were frequently praised as children by their parents for high effort, were told of the importance of industriousness for a worthwhile life, and observed their parents practicing what they preached. Crucial to the child's acceptance of positive parental work values over the popular culture's glorification of indolence and sensuality is the existence of a strong emotional bond between child and parent. By establishing a loving relationship, parents' approval for high effort becomes a powerful reward that instills a strong personal work ethic.

Parents should distinguish between encouraging high effort versus establishing impossibly difficult goals. Some parents make the mistake of continually demanding school performance greater than the child can achieve. One sufferer recalled: "When I was second-highest on a test, my father scolded me for not trying hard enough. When I was first, he said the test was too easy."[2] Such impossibly difficult standards have consequences that are very different from rewarding high effort.

There are numerous carefully controlled scientific experiments demonstrating that repeated failure produces a generalized helplessness that lessens subsequent persistence on difficult tasks.[3] Parents who demand perfection from their children often think they are teaching them to persevere. But such training pairs hard work with the absence of reward. A child who values parental approval but fails repeatedly to meet inordinately high standards is likely to develop a distaste for persistent effort and, eventually, become as indolent as children spoiled by easily obtained rewards.

I attended elementary school and high school with a girl named Linda Wells whose parents demanded straight As on her report cards. Although Linda was bright and studied hard, the perfection demanded was beyond her capability. Linda was depressed by her inability to please her parents, and she reckoned herself a failure. Linda developed an emotional ambivalence about her parents and a hatred of school work. She quit school as soon as she was allowed.

Parents may punish their children's school efforts in more subtle ways than demanding perfection. Improved performance sometimes lags behind high effort, and children need recognition for hard work before achievement becomes apparent. Recall that one reason why General George Patton continued to labor throughout his youth to overcome his learning disorder was the patient encouragement of high effort by his parents.

Observant parents know when their children are working hard on a school subject and so can reward high effort even if success is slow in coming. By gradually increasing the degree of effort required for approval, the child will succeed on most occasions. If such a program is followed, occasional failures by the child will have little aversive effect because repeated reward for high effort increases the resilience for withstanding failure.

Parents who value the development of a strong personal work ethic in their children should consider limiting the use of the television set as a baby sitter. Watching a bit of mindless fluff does little damage; one does not have to be constantly engaged in uplifting activities. But the national average of four hours watched every day of the week is clearly detrimental.

We described how the *act* of watching television promotes mental passivity, flightiness of attention, and a hedonistic life style. The fast *pace* of programing involving frequent changes in scene and character similarly interferes with the development of the ability to persevere on difficult cognitive tasks. The *content* of advertising, beginning when children are too young to differentiate between commercials and programs, instills cravings for sensual pleasure that reduce the willingness to suffer present discomfort for future gain. Entertainment programming also teaches viewers that continual sensual gratification is the ideal, thereby reducing an individual's willingness to work hard at school or job. TV soap operas and nighttime series further discourage industriousness by degrading working-class and middle-class occupations.

Allowing the prolonged television viewing that encourages passivity and the pursuit of leisure in children is a costly evasion of parental responsibility. Even when adults and children watch together, the shows selected often have no redeeming value. In most families, parents and children often disagree concerning which television programs to watch together, and children win the argument almost half the time.[4]

Parents who wish to instill strong work values in their children should bite the bullet; beginning when children are young, parents should take an active role in limiting youngsters' total daily watching time and the proportion of that time involving programs most damaging to the work ethic. As David Owen noted: "If parents prevented their children from watching the shows, they wouldn't be on. Parents complain about the quality of the shows but don't prevent children from gluing themselves to the boob tube."[5] Work values will be strengthened by guiding their children's viewing away from shows that glorify sensualism, and toward shows that emphasize achievement and hard work.

What would children do with all the spare time created by a reduced access to television? They could be encouraged to spend more time on homework and chores and more time reading books, getting out of the house to see friends, and chatting with parents. Children might find they enjoy playing board games with parents as did previous generations. More time spent with parents will, in most cases, strengthen mutual attachment and make children more willing to adopt strong work values promoted by parents.

Teachers influence students' attitudes toward work by the values communicated in assigned readings, lectures, and discussions, by the use of grading practices that reward diligence or laziness, and by the personal example of preparing classes carefully or lackadaisically. The secularization of American education has produced a widespread reluctance to use schools to inculcate children with codes of conduct useful to society. Because religion is concerned with ethics and morality, the teaching of values has seemed counter to the American tradition of church-state separation. Moreover, the indoctrination of beliefs appears to contradict American empiricism and science which emphasize careful inquiry into the validity of concepts and theories.

But is it not in the best interest of a democracy to promote fundamental ethical beliefs that transcend partisan political concerns? There are, of course, great differences of opinion concerning which values should be promoted in school. Many conservatives favor the inculcation of beliefs in free-market capitalism, anticommunism, and patriotism. Many liberals support teaching the dangers of economic monopoly, the value of a more even distribution of wealth, and the importance of international cooperation.

Diligent goal-oriented work seems a fundamental component of the American ideal which, as honesty and freedom of speech and religion, should be explicitly promoted by the schools. The freedom and pluralism basic to a democracy must be supplemented by a commitment to industrious work if the nation is to thrive economically and culturally.

Schools could make an important contribution toward instilling positive work values. Japan's remarkable economic success shows the ability of educators, together with parents, to shape a strong work ethic. The school system could be used to promote industriousness without emulating the Japanese emphasis on conformity.

Like Americans, Israelis are independent-minded. But among Israelis living on the kibbutz, hard work is instilled as a fundamental cultural value. As one worker put it, "No one wants his kids to hear that his dad is a slacker—so we work hard."[6]

To present basic American ideals in a positive light does not mean shoving them down students' throats. Free discussion of varied viewpoints is itself a transcendent value. But to refrain from teaching the basic value of work invites the nation's economic decline.

The present method of teaching children nothing about the merits of work and allowing the entertainment media to instill leisure-oriented values has weakened traditional work ethic. Although the McGuffey Readers commonly used in schools half a century ago can be faulted for ignoring important social problems, they did have the value of promoting positive attitudes toward work through stories of young people whose diligent effort brought economic success. The traditional components of the personal work ethic— the moral value of industriousness, the willingness to work hard for material gain, and the pride of accomplishment in carrying out one's job with skill and care—might be promoted in courses on history, civics, and contemporary national and international affairs.

Students could be taught that hard work is important for the individual's and the nation's economic well-being and that performing one's job diligently is a source of pride and satisfaction. Children need to understand that there is no contradiction between industriousness and a reasonable degree of entertainment and pleasure. In history classes, for example, they might well learn about German immigrant farmers who settled on the frontier in the late eighteenth century and worked diligently Monday through Saturday, refreshing themselves on Sundays with vigorous entertainment. Students could be assigned to read and discuss biographies of Americans who made a success of their lives by hard work without sacrificing a reasonable degree of rest and entertainment.

School could be used to counter the growing disinclination of poor people to accept or retain low-paying jobs. The only thing "menial" about picking crops or washing floors is the stigma attached to these tasks by the popular culture. Attitudes toward "menial" work by affluent Americans, as well as the poor, need to be changed. Teachers and school books might emphasize the importance of holding a job as the responsibility of all worthwhile citizens. In order to combat the denigration of working-class jobs by the entertainment media and popular opinion, the contribution of every job to the community's welfare could be stressed. Requiring children to help clean their schools, a common practice in Japan, would instill the view that manual labor degrades no one, rich or poor. The importance not simply of holding down a job, but of working with care and skill in any occupation, should be stressed.

The duty of every citizen to contribute to the community's economic well-being by holding down a job will be rejected by the unemployed as hypocritical so long as there are not jobs available for all those willing to work diligently. A national policy of employment opportunities for all Americans, with the government as the employer of last resort, would show the jobless that Americans actually do value the importance of economic opportunity.

Many children of parents who have held jobs only sporadically do not possess the basic work habits absorbed by the children of regularly employed parents. Such practices as punctuality, good grooming, and obeying legitimate authority can be effectively taught to disadvantaged students. One such Michigan program dealt with teenage delinquents who were wards of the court and had an average of 3.9 arrests.[7] The youths were motivated to take part in the program by the promise of a private-sector job and the opportunity to avoid further court action. Prior to job interviews, advice was given on grooming and appropriate dress. During the youngsters' first weeks on the job, they were counseled concerning the following basic job behaviors and rewarded with pay increases for improvements:

- Getting to work every day and on time.
- Calling in ahead of time if ill or if going to be late.
- Following the employers' job regulations, including dress code and breaks.
- Good job performance.
- Cooperation in following directions.

At first, the program's participants were harassed by their peers for taking conventional jobs. But the use of earnings to purchase such highly valued items as clothes, radios, and cars soon made their friends envious. As problems arose on the job, the new employees were taught to work on solutions rather than simply quitting out of frustration. Compared to similar delinquents not enrolled in the program, the following year saw high levels of employment and low levels of arrests.

Disadvantaged job applicants are often passive in job interviews, failing to understand the purpose behind the interviewer's questions. They tend to answer with a "yes" or "no," rather than conveying information about skills, experience, or motivation. Conducting oneself more effectively in a job interview by responding fully to questions and by showing greater assertiveness and initiative has been found to be readily trainable and might be incorporated into courses taught in schools located in economically disadvantaged neighborhoods.[8]

In addition to teaching the value of hard work and appropriate job behaviors, schools could be used to combat the glorification of leisure, widespread in the entertainment media. It is often said that advertising reflects society's values. Today, much advertising plays on people's emotions and fantasies to promote a product. The cumulative effects of thousands of hours of television programing and ads during an individual's youth help determine the kinds of behaviors and social relationships that an individual will consider desirable.

There is preliminary evidence that films designed to enhance young children's critical viewing skills increase their skepticism about commercials.[9] Students might be taught that television advertising promotes sensual desires and recreation at the expense of the self-denial necessary to achieve long-term goals. They could be told, for example, that the Marlboro Man was designed by advertisers to appeal to the American male's desire to see himself as tough and virile and that cosmetic ads play on the viewer's desire to be more alluring. Children could be taught that they can enjoy themselves to a reasonable degree without allowing their values to be manipulated by emotion-based advertising.

Television itself could be used within the schools to promote work-oriented values and self-control. The denial of present plea-sures for future gains is seldom portrayed in television series. This omission can be corrected by showing films that portray individuals choosing large, delayed rewards over small, immediate rewards. Such films have been found to increase young children's subse-quent self-control, and youngsters are more strongly influenced if the protagonist verbalizes reasons for choosing the delayed re-wards.[10] Films that promote self-control, when supplemented by class discussion, would provide an excellent opportunity to strengthen work values.

One television show, *Mister Rogers' Neighborhood*, is an ex-emplary exception to the audiovisual gimmickry commonly em-ployed to capture children's attention. This program moves at a slower pace than most children's shows, with Rogers asking ques-tions designed to encourage reflection about focal topics. Prosocial themes include delay of gratification, persistence, and the impor-tance of competence at tasks.[11] A variety of shows that promote industriousness could be shown young students in school.

Greater stress on positive work values would be important at all levels of education. In vocational schools and colleges, there might be greater emphasis on inculcating professional values. In a pre-vious chapter we saw that our special education teacher, Betty Robbins, spends long hours preparing her classes because of her professional dedication. The commitment to excellence that Betty absorbed from teachers and colleagues made pride of accomplish-ment a central component of her self-identity. The satisfaction Betty receives from watching her students' success is strongly sup-plemented by the duty she feels to uphold the ideals of the teaching profession.

Such professionalism promotes work values by tying one's self-evaluation to competent and ethical job performance. Many profes-sionals who take pride in their standards of excellence never had a class in school that specifically emphasized the importance of care and integrity in job performance. Responsible job-related values often arise from watching valued teachers and colleagues treat membership in the profession as a privilege and source of respon-sibility.

Whether a dentist, electronic technician, or lawyer, commitment to professional codes of conduct reduces the temptation to give less than one's best on behalf of a client. The individual comes to feel that inappropriate performance disgraces the individual and may bring condemnation by colleagues. Thus, professionalism can be a powerful force to combat laziness and dishonesty.

The most socially valuable kind of professionalism combines a commitment to skilled performance with a strong sense of responsibility to the public. Without a strong dedication to the welfare of clients, professionals can appropriate their skills for unethical self-gain. For example, it is no secret that some talented surgeons increase their income by carrying out unneeded operations. And we have seen that the quality of American goods and services has been severely damaged by MBAs who use their expert knowledge of financial controls to increase short-term profit at the expense of product quality, research, and development. Business-school courses can be used more effectively to teach students a connection between self-worth and ethical job behavior.

Another way educators influence work values is by the effort they put into preparing courses. The teacher who spends little time readying lectures, who returns student essays without detailed comments, or who fails to show up for office hours sends the message that competence and hard work are viewed as unimportant.

The practices used to evaluate student performance influence the development of the personal work ethic. Lax grading criteria in elementary school, high school, and college teach poor work values by rewarding laziness. College courses in social sciences, education, and business too often are opportunities for an easy path to a college degree. Teachers at all levels of education could promote work values by insisting that a passing grade means the student has acquired an adequate knowledge of the subject and that a grade of "A" signifies excellence rather than an inflated reward given to a majority of students. Administrators and school board members can help by backing teachers against demands by students and their parents that minimal effort be rewarded with high grades.

This will be a difficult task for public schools and colleges whose continued fiscal strength depends on the good will of tax payers. Nor will the change be easy for those private grade and high schools and colleges that are heavily tuition dependent, requiring a large influx of new students each Fall to survive. But schools and colleges can engage in a kind of "creeping competence," slowly raising academic requirements while providing data to students and parents which show that employers give desired jobs to students who have been well educated.

Most academic subjects involve a combination of tasks with varying degrees of intrinsic interest and difficulty. Even if a student finds that an academic subject is generally interesting, the acquisition of a good understanding of the subject matter will require the study of some topics found to be dull and repetitive and other topics that, although interesting, are discouragingly difficult to master. Without the encouragement of grades or some other effective reward, many students will not acquire the knowledge or persistence necessary to deal effectively with the subject matter.

Some psychologists, educators, and proponents of the human potential movement have claimed that the use of grades, prizes, approval, and other rewards for high achievement causes children to lose interest in the academic subject. Experiments show that if you give a child a monetary reward each time the child performs a school task and then withdraw the reward, the child will be less interested in the task than before you started the reward process. [12]

One explanation of why this occurs is that the child is convinced that the task was carried out because of the anticipated reward rather than the enjoyment the task itself provides. [13] Another explanation is that individuals react negatively when others seem to be trying to control them. [14] So, the argument runs, if you give a student a grade or prize for learning history lessons, the student will lose interest in studying history for its own sake. Take away the reward and the student will pay less attention to the history lessons than if rewards had never been given.

What is seldom pointed out by opponents of the grading process is that such a loss of intrinsic interest as a result of reward occurs only under a limited set of circumstances. There is no loss of intrinsic interest in a task if the reward depends on the adequacy of performance. [15] Grades and other rewards that depend on high effort in academic subjects improve performance without diminishing intrinsic interest.

Rewarding high effort in school work can have several positive effects. A student who fails to study, say, biology because there is no reward for doing so misses the opportunity to discover that he or she may like the subject. As a psychology major at UCLA, I tried to get permission not to take the required course in the psychology of learning because it sounded uninteresting. Forced to take the course, I found the material fascinating and decided to specialize as a psychologist in the area of learning.

But whether or not greater study produces an increased enjoyment of the subject matter, reward for high effort does strengthen an individual's general industriousness.[16] We previously reviewed evidence indicating rewarded high effort in one academic subject increased the students' persistence in other academic subjects. Reward for high effort has been found to improve subsequent performance both in dull, repetitive tasks and in intrinsically interesting tasks.[17] Thus, grading practices can be used effectively to strengthen work values.

Another complaint against the use of grades is that children study only what is absolutely necessary for the test rather than learning the subject generally or how to use their new-found information creatively.[18] It is true that rewards can induce children to work hard to memorize trivia, which is one of the major flaws of Japan's educational system. Such narrowing of interest results from tests that emphasize rote memorization. Students' anticipation of essay questions that require the integration or extension of learned materials is especially useful in motivating the study of basic principles.

Children can be taught to work hard on creative tasks as well as on tedious tasks. In one experiment, a group of students received approval for solving a very simple problem, and another group for solving a more difficult problem that required testing a variety of hypotheses. Students who solved the more difficult problem subsequently tackled an entirely new problem with greater concentration and flexibility than the children who had received the easier problem.[19] The children had learned to be industrious and creative.

Teachers face the momentous task of trying to reverse strong habits of laziness ingrained by the popular culture. It is naive to expect a majority of teachers to display dedication without decent pay or respect from the community. True, many highly motivated individuals go into teaching despite the job's low pay and prestige value. But large numbers of talented individuals with an interest in teaching avoid the profession because of these drawbacks.

Few teachers are martyrs. Most want a comfortable standard of living as a payoff for the years of schooling required to obtain their teaching credentials and for the classroom pressures they endure each day. The hypocrisy of the community's stated high regard for teachers is apparent by low pay in a nation that shows respect for other occupations by generous financial compensation. Training teachers more carefully and holding them accountable to high standards will help improve the quality of their instruction. But the nation will attract and retain large numbers of talented teachers only if the pay is improved. As previously noted, Japanese elementary-school teachers receive greater pay and benefits, on the average, than middle-level executives. Better pay would, as in Japan, create greater competition for teaching jobs and allow the selection of more competent teachers.

Also important is the degree of respect shown teachers by students, parents, and administrators in daily interactions. A teacher who must spend most of his time trying to maintain discipline among unruly students cannot concentrate on education. From elementary school through college, a significant minority of students show their disrespect for teachers by socializing in class as if the teacher were not there. Local communities could increase the effectiveness of schools by insisting that students behave respectfully and by refusing to tolerate laziness by students or teachers.

Students who refuse to study or are disruptive should be expelled. Such individuals gain nothing from their incarceration in school, and interfere with the education of others. Removing chronic trouble makers will improve the learning atmosphere. In addition, apathetic students can be motivated by material rewards and by approval and recognition for academic success. As a high-school debate coach the President-to-be Lyndon Johnson used rallies, publicity, and awards to create the degree of enthusiasm for this academically-valuable activity that was normally reserved for sports.

* * *

Individuals begin their first full-time job with weak or strong work values learned from parents, teachers, friends, and the entertainment media. The kinds of behavior rewarded on the job influence the application of previously learned work values and the reinforcement or deterioration of these values. Reward for high effort helps to establish and maintain superior employee performance.

The decline of America's key industries occurred in part because managers and employees in large companies ceased to be rewarded for industriousness and innovation. Labor unions sought to protect their members from unreasonable, ever-increasing work loads by contractual rules that prevented the redefinition of jobs to meet changing needs. Past practice became the basis of job descriptions which, for practical purposes, were extremely difficult to change. Management bargained away their prerogative to define jobs instead of offering unions more rational ways to protect their members from the speedup.

Restrictive work rules defined the responsibilities for hourly workers so narrowly that pride of accomplishment was destroyed. Often, several individuals had to be called to complete different portions of an extremely simple task. Zealous hourly employees who overstepped these bounds found their diligence punished by co-workers guarding against the speed-up.[20] Doing little work for high pay became the creed of the unions and the members they represented.

Many managers wastefully kept surplus numbers of hourly workers permanently on the payroll to guarantee help during periods of peak production. Competing executives sought to demonstrate their importance by building personal kingdoms involving bloated numbers of managers and white collar workers. In many cases there was too little work to keep the inflated ranks of employees busy, and performing make-work at a lackadaisical pace became an ingrained habit.

The steel and auto manufacturers and their associated labor unions established conditions that discouraged employees with a strong work ethic from applying themselves earnestly. Salaries and hourly wages were much higher, on the average, than in other

233

American industries but were not influenced by how hard one worked. Those employees in whom parents had instilled a willingness to exert high effort for material gain learned that hard work simply did not pay off. Managers who took pride in their work and who called for greater quality control, modernization of equipment, and research into new products, were given the choice of shutting up or getting out by executives who placed short-term profits above long-term gain.

Even employees with strong work values are generally not willing to increase their effort without a reasonable anticipation of reward. By instituting policies that award money and status for improving the quality of products and services, companies can encourage individuals with a strong personal work ethic to put their beliefs in practice. Reward for increased effort also helps shape positive attitudes in employees with a low work ethic.

Consider the employees at the National Steel Corporation plant in Weirton, West Virginia. They received wages higher than average for America's best paid industry. But there were the same disincentives for hard work as in the rest of the industry. When the American steel companies were being decimated by imports during the early 1980s, the plant was scheduled to close.

Weirton's employees purchased the plant, and the corporate culture changed. Because the employees now owned the operation, they believed that waste and laziness hurt themselves. The workers accepted the necessary pay cuts that their compatriots in other steel companies often refused. They worked harder because they understood that the success of *their* company depended on personal effort. Little talk was now heard of enforcing work rules. Everyone had to pitch in to help the plant survive.[21]

Those Weirton employees in whom parents had instilled a strong work ethic were encouraged, for the first time at the plant, to put their values into operation. Others had weak work values that became stronger because of the positive relation between effort and reward. The plant started turning a profit. Although it is unclear whether the change in attitudes and behavior at the Weirton plant occurred soon enough to achieve ultimate success in a badly damaged industry, the lesson seems clear. Reward for high effort on the job strengthens work values and productivity.

In contrast to the poor performance of the large steel companies, modern small "mini-mills" are competing successfully with imported steel. The Nucor Corporation, which owns several of these profitable operations, rewards greater effort by offering a bonus for each ton of steel manufactured above a target figure.[22] Companies can compete more effectively by creating cultures that reinforce high effort rather than punish it.

Changing the corporate culture to produce long-term gains requires more than slogans. Employees observe whether managers practice what they preach. Executives in a prospering microcomputer company with 250 employees, located in the heart of the Silicon Valley, told employees that henceforth: "Attention to detail is our trademark; our goal is to do it right the first time. We intend to deliver defect-free products and services to our customers on time."[23] Numerous meetings were held to spread the new philosophy.

But the executives' behavior belied their stated values. In order to meet an announced release date for a new computer model, many units were shipped out containing defects. The company's actions spoke louder than words. Managers came to understand that the company cared little about product quality. One manager said: "We do have a zero-defect program: Don't test the product and you'll find zero defects."[24] This lack of commitment to product quality helped drive the company into bankruptcy.

Improvements in product quality, research, and development are encouraged by a solid company commitment that includes material rewards and strong approval for those who work diligently toward long-term goals.[25] Managers cannot expect employees to cooperate fully in attempts to improve productivity or product quality when the likely result will be layoffs or speedups.[26] One of the reasons for the major economic success of factories in Israeli kibbutzim is that workers can change to different tasks as needed without worrying about speedups or layoffs.[27] Quality circles and other procedures by which employees are encouraged to make productive suggestions are most effective when high effort earns recognition and increased pay.

Dedication to high standards of performance and product quality can be enhanced by increasing pride of accomplishment. It is significant that few managers in the premier industrial nation, Japan, have graduated from the equivalent of our MBA programs. In America, new MBAs are frequently made managers before they have a good knowledge of the products or services that the company provides.

After graduating with an MBA from a prestigious Eastern business school, Jack Peters became a top manager in a large private hospital. He makes decisions on budgeting and allocation of funds among the hospital's different departments, despite having only the most rudimentary understanding of the functions of these units. He lacks the first-hand experience to differentiate a department's true needs from a padded request. If future managers worked for a time at lower ranks within the company, as is the practice in Japan, they would have a better understanding for the company's products or services, the production process, and the attitudes of hourly-paid employees.

Pride of accomplishment can be strengthened by increasing the skill requirements of the job. The elimination of human skills by new machinery has worsened employee performance in many American factories. GM spent billions on automation during the 1980s only to find production costs remain among the highest in the industry. American workers felt they were mere attendants to the machines. They lost interest in the quality of their work and became inattentive and sloppy. Companies in the process of automation can help retain pride of accomplishment by selecting equipment that enhances rather than replaces operator skills.

Additional job enrichment techniques, when backed fully by management, have been found repeatedly to improve the care with which jobs are carried out.[28] These steps include one or more of the following:

- Giving employees a role in planning how tasks are to be carried out
- Giving objective feedback concerning job performance.
- Making the employees personally accountable for their performance.
- Giving employees greater authority to communicate directly with others on whom they depend for information and supplies.

• Giving them direct feedback from those who benefit from their product or service.

Job enrichment can be used to enhance a feeling of personal responsibility for carrying out jobs well. These techniques have been used effectively with jobs involving manual labor, clerical tasks, and higher level positions. The message employers need to send is that the success of the organization depends on the skills and motivation of all employees and that superior achievement in any job will be recognized and rewarded.

The private sector could also do much to strengthen the work values of poverty-stricken Americans for whom repeated failure and welfare have produced a culture of indolence. The best way to keep capitalism strong in America is to make it work for everyone, eliminating entrenched joblessness that distorts our economic system. Business is much better equipped to train poor people to become industrious than is the federal government, and might be encouraged to do so by moral suasion and favorable tax policies.

As previously noted, children who grow up in families with no one working on a regular basis usually develop weak work values. They frequently lack knowledge of appropriate ways to look for a job, to present themselves well when being interviewed, or to conduct themselves according to approved standards on the job. In 1967, the Ford Motor Company showed concretely what enlightened business people can do about these problems.

The company established recruitment centers in the Detroit ghetto, provided bus service to its factory, counseled new recruits on the importance of getting to work on time, and used a buddy system so a new employee would receive encouragement and advice from a knowledgeable senior employee.[29] The program was generally successful. Turnover among such employees was higher than among typical American workers, but each ghetto resident retained was a victory for the capitalistic system.

Television programing and advertising instill passivity and desire for immediate gratification, which the networks and cable systems have little incentive to change. Because top network executives are evaluated almost exclusively by the profits they generate, obtaining the networks' agreement to remedy the negative social effects of commercials and entertainment programing is a difficult problem. Even when there is overwhelming evidence of a seriously detrimental influence of television on viewers' moral values, as in the case of portrayed violence begetting viewer violence, networks have failed to show sustained improvement.

The market place restricts the actions that a public-spirited network owner might take to reduce the promotion of short-term, pleasure-seeking and indolence. Because most people watch television for light entertainment, a network that suddenly proclaimed itself devoted to uplifting the public's education, morality, and culture by offering only educational shows, theater, and the arts would sustain a large loss of viewers.

If a majority of viewers desired shows that were culturally or educationally uplifting, public-supported TV and occasional forays by the networks into better programming would produce a large audience. Competition for viewers would then produce better programs. The majority of viewers seem to be getting the type of programing they desire.

What then might a responsible network owner do, without losing viewers, to reduce television's role as a teacher of laziness? One relatively painless change would be to stop undercutting the respectability of working-class and middle-class jobs. As discussed in the chapter on laziness among poor Americans, the *work-avoiding poor* do not perceive obtaining a low-paying job as a success but as a reiteration of failure. Many poor people decline to take low-paying jobs that they believe are demeaning, based on attitudes reinforced by television series.

Television generally ignores working-class jobs or treats them as menial, and portrays their holders as buffoons. Recently, even middle-class white collar jobs have been receiving negative treatment. There is no evidence that the negative portrayal of working-class and middle-class jobs on television influences ratings. Perhaps programers and script writers simply feel that people who work a nine to five job are inferior and uninteresting.

Television can portray low paying jobs and their holders as worthwhile without losing audience. Would the *Bill Cosby Show* have been any less of a hit if Cosby had portrayed a carpenter or cab driver? Viewer identification with the the show's characters comes from how the characters interact as they face problems common to most families. Cosby's wit, humor, and portrayal of a loving relationship with the other characters makes the show special. Ratings would not have been harmed if Cosby and his wife held less prestigious jobs or if their children attended less prestigious colleges and were to help finance their educations by part-time work.

What of the sensuality promoted by commercials and entertainment programing? What would happen if one of the networks declared a moratorium on ads that promote a hedonistic life-style? No more sugared-cereal or candy ads presented during children's shows that, the evidence suggests, hook children on sweets and increase their general gluttony before they are old enough to understand what a commercial is. No more beer ads that encourage alcohol consumption by showing sports heroes enjoying the good life by drowning in the brew. No more use of soap operas and suggestive ads that glorify impulsive sexual behavior. No more voyeuristic shows like *Entertainment Tonight* that promote a preoccupation with self-indulgence by using sexually suggestive dress and movement as the primary component of the show, accompanied by the feigned prurient interest of the hosts.

Companies that sell sugared cereals, candy, beer, perfume and a variety of products by emphasizing hedonism would switch their ads to other networks and cable systems. Ad agencies, upset because their artistic freedom had been violated, would encourage additional sponsors to desert. Viewers who enjoy viewing innumerable daily episodes of sexual excess would watch the other networks. Local television stations that were affiliated with our born-again altruistic network would also abandon ship because of their own lessened ability to sell advertising time. The network programer would be forced to resign, taking a job working for Ralph Nader at a salary of $8,000 a year.

We should therefore be prepared to offer thanks to networks willing to take the modest step of treating working-class and middle-class jobs and their holders as worthy of sympathetic treatment. Such a change would require bravery in an industry suspicious of the public interest.

* * *

The federal government can help promote the industriousness of teachers and the effectiveness with which schools teach basic values and skills. The Japanese national government pays almost half that country's education bill, thereby promoting a uniformly high quality of instruction.[30] Such funding also makes the teaching profession attractive by providing salaries higher than comparable professional positions in the private sector.[31]

Starting salaries of Japanese teachers are generally greater than received by businessmen, engineers, and pharmacists, the reverse of the situation in the U.S. In Japan, it takes until mid-career for the salaries of these others to catch up to teachers, and beyond age fifty-three the teachers again have greater salaries.[32] It is little wonder that in Japan more than five applicants compete for each teaching position.

Among the Japanese, teaching is a prestigious job, entry into which requires superior college performance. According to a 1975 survey, Japanese *elementary-school* teachers have a higher status among the public than engineers and department heads of large corporations.[33] In return for high pay and status, Japanese teachers are expected to perform their jobs with the greatest diligence and to instill students with a dedication to group solidarity and hard work. The teachers themselves serve as excellent role models of industriousness. Since the community esteems teachers and education, students absorb strong work values.

By contrast, U.S. college students majoring in education have below-average aptitude scores. The lack of respect or decent pay for American teachers speaks louder than politicians' professions concerning the importance of education. Paying teachers far higher salaries and insisting that they earn their pay through dedicated work would greatly improve the education system.

College students, reared in a society that trains indolence and discourages the self-denial required to pursue long-range goals, are increasingly shying away from difficult majors in science and mathematics. Their places are being filled by foreign students, many of whom will return home bearing knowledge of the latest American technology. The lack of technically trained college graduates reduces the nation's capacity to compete economically with other industrialized nations.

Although pay in research jobs is lucrative, fewer American students than in the past are willing to accept the hard work required by college majors in science and math. Federal fellowship programs that used to encourage talented college seniors to choose the long haul toward a graduate scientific degree have been drastically cut. The annual total cost of these programs was less than that of a single jet fighter. The restoration and expansion of these fellowship programs would reward students for the long, hard work necessary to become first-rate scientists. Extending these programs, on a smaller scale, to high school and undergraduate college education would similarly encourage science-oriented students to continue their education.

Millions of youths attend college primarily because employers require a college degree. For many such jobs a college education provides few skills directly relevant to the required duties. To attract students, colleges frequently provide easy courses that make the four-year incarceration as pleasant as possible. Students are reinforced for laziness by the lax entry and grading standards.

There seems little value of keeping a majority of high school graduates (fifty-eight percent) in the involuntary servitude of college. Japan does quite well with half that number (twenty-nine percent).[34] A substantial proportion of American college students would be happy to take a good-paying job if it were available following high school graduation. The time such individuals spend in college reinforces their laziness and is a drain on the national economy.

Businesses might be encouraged to accept more high school graduates for good-paying jobs. But the problem is deeper than this. Many employers require a college degree because the high school diploma no longer signifies the attainment of basic skills in writing or math. High school education must be improved to equip students with the skills necessary for most entry-level jobs. Then businesses would be more willing to accept high school graduates for jobs that do not require advanced education.

State-supported universities (institutions with graduate programs, as opposed to two-year community colleges or four-year colleges) often publicly exaggerate the extent of their dedication to undergraduate education. To carry out their central mission of research and graduate education, universities need appropriations from tight-fisted state legislators and tuition moneys from undergraduates. The more undergraduate students that can be enrolled, no matter how lax the instruction, the greater the sum obtained from students and legislators.

A more sensible arrangement might involve leaving most undergraduate education to state and private two and four-year colleges. State Universities would then be able to focus their resources on research, graduate education, and preparing undergraduates for graduate education. Of course, this would only work if the universities received much greater federal funding for the valuable function of research and the training of researchers and professionals.

Changes in federal policies may also be needed to reorient American business toward long-term goals. One reason for America's economic decline is that ambitious executives, unencumbered by traditional work values, have sought to satisfy stockholders and earn hefty bonuses by maximizing their companies' short-term profit at the expense of future gains. To obtain immediate profits, top managers reduce the quality of products or services and lessen investment in research and new equipment. Executives face the choice of being rewarded for lazy and improvident behavior or getting fired if they work hard toward long-term objectives.

Current tax laws might be changed to encourage research and development. Congress could re-institute in an expanded form the investment tax credit that recently was eliminated. Businesses could be allowed to take a quick tax deduction equal to a substantial proportion of investment in new equipment and research. This would reduce the initial monetary cost of working hard toward future gains.

Tax breaks and anti-trust laws could be better formulated to encourage managers to work diligently to increase exports, thereby helping to reduce the trade deficit. An important ingredient in Japan's economic progress is the status earned by companies and their executives when products capture a large share of the world market. Reward in the form of tax breaks for greater exports would encourage American companies to work harder to keep prices down, improve product quality, and react effectively to changing consumer needs. A greater world market share for American products would mean more jobs and a smaller trade deficit.

The anti-monopoly laws could be strengthened to reduce the ability of a small number of companies to dominate an entire domestic industry. Monopolistic control of a product by a few companies, abetted by formal and informal import restrictions, allows corporate giants to profit in the short term by acting against their own and the nation's long-term interests.

A number of large American companies, including the three major auto manufacturers, support the research and development of foreign competitors by serving as domestic selling agents for the foreign companies. The Ford Motor Company, for example, uses its membership in a shared monopoly to take an average profit of over $1,000 per car rather than lowering the price to increase market share. Dominant American companies such as the major airline manufacturers improvidently trade advanced technology in return for foreign sales. Such near-sighted behavior often results in high prices at a cost to world market share.

If there were more competition in American industry, large companies would have to depend more on foreign sales and so would be less inclined to trade away technology to overseas competitors. With greater domestic competition, American companies would be hesitant to serve as selling agents for foreign products because other domestic companies would sell American products at lower prices, not having to pay transportation and import fees.

The success of American steel mini-mills shows that this nation's basic industries can compete effectively with foreign companies. With stronger anti-trust laws and substantial tax breaks for capturing an increased share of the foreign market, American companies would work harder to achieve foreign sales.

Another task in which the federal government might play a greater role is the strengthening of work values among the poor. Many conservatives attribute black poverty to a wanton lack of self-responsibility. Other minority groups, they point out, have overcome poverty. They favor destroying poverty by punishing the poor. Conservative politicians do not openly speak this way since they must constantly battle their anti-people, pro-business image. But their actions speak louder than words. Whatever the merits of a program for helping the poor, many conservatives try to cut its funding.

Most liberals emphasize the historic causes of poverty among blacks in the ghetto. They note that poverty is, in part, a legacy of the docility engendered by slavery and the associated suppression of black education and entrepreneurship. To redress this injustice, many liberals favor supplying the poor with all the necessities of life and most of the comforts. They also advocate that the poor be given access to job training and remedial education which the great majority, the claim runs, would actively pursue.

These arguments between liberals and conservatives over who is to blame miss the point. It does not really matter whether we wish to assess ninety percent of the blame for black ghettos on slavery and later discrimination and the remaining ten percent on lack of personal responsibility, or vice versa. To continue arguing about the historical causes that set off the present morass of poverty tells us little about how to strengthen work values today.

This nation faces a fundamental problem of lethargy among white and black poor Americans that will not go away either as a result of punishment or handouts. The liberals' approach of providing small amounts of money in poorly planned job-training programs did not work. President Johnson insisted on expenditures of funds without pilot projects or adequate organization.[35] The waste found in such programs is illustrated by what happened in Salem county, New Jersey. Cyndi Kurland, a former social work director sympathetic to the plight of poor Americans, remembered:

> There was a ruling that any mother with a child more than five years old had to come in for job training [the WIN Program enacted by Congress in 1967]. So they all came in and there were no jobs. They just came in and signed the forms. We also had the case of a community college taking anyone to study for a degree because of what are now termed Pell grants. They would just take the money. Eventually the students would just flunk out. There's no way they could pass. They just took a mishmash of classes. The purpose was to get

244

them in school so they would be employable. It did nothing to get them a job. If the college saw there was money coming they didn't care who or what the money was attached to. This really worked against the poor.[36]

Reviews of government sponsored job training programs, carried out by the Management Demonstration Resource Corporation, came to the conclusion that careful planning and repeated program evaluation are essential for success.[37] President Johnson obtained funding increases for poverty programs because he had a genuine concern for the welfare of poor people and because, at the time, helping the poor was good politics. Johnson said he was fighting a war on poverty; by great cash flows poverty would be defeated.

But Johnson spent much less money on poverty than his rhetoric indicated, in part because he chose to finance the Viet Nam War simultaneously. Johnson's insistence on increased spending without taking the time for careful planning, paired with his promise to the American people of too much too soon, helped create a backlash that destroyed sympathy for ghetto residents.

If Johnson produced hopes for an easy solution to poverty that could not be fulfilled, the Reagan administration lessened hope with a blanket condemnation of spending money to reduce poverty. Creative and carefully conceived training programs, such as many of those researched by the Management Demonstration Resource Corporation, were eliminated by a presidential administration dead set against the federal government's role in fighting poverty.

Welfare payments are a poor solution since they perpetuate a life style of passivity and dependence that is passed on from one generation to the next. Other than those who suffer the most severely incapacitating physical disabilities or mental illnesses, there seems no good reason for excusing anyone from earning a living *when given the opportunity.*

Simply cutting off welfare benefits, as suggested by conservative economists like Charles Murray, would indeed cause a larger number of unemployed people to look for jobs. But America's economy would not provide enough full-time jobs to employ the majority of the poor who now work sporadically. For many poor Americans, cutting off public assistance would replace welfare-produced in-

245

action with inaction based on failure to find a job. Moreover, by far the greatest portion of welfare benefits goes to mothers and the physically disabled. Thus, the threat of a welfare cutoff would mean little to poverty-stricken adult males.

State experiments that provide a combination of welfare and a supposed work requirement have been compromised by narrow political considerations. California's new GAIN (Greater Avenues for INdependence) program requires all welfare recipients to work off their welfare grants. The recipients will have access to free education and day care and will not be forced to take jobs beneath the skill level for which they have been trained, unless their performance is unsatisfactory.

Unfortunately, the law contains major loopholes that have been noted by *New Republic* columnist Mickey Kaus. No woman with a child younger than six can be forced to work, which may, in effect, provide an "incentive" for a single mother to bear more children. Poor people will be tempted to quit their jobs to go into the program and receive educational and welfare benefits to which they are not currently entitled. No one can be required to take a job at a wage that results in a net loss of welfare income, including the paid benefits for child support, transportation, and health insurance. Thus, many will have no incentive to take low-paying jobs.

The law forbids the use of welfare recipients in jobs that would normally be performed by union members or by government agencies where regular employees are on layoff. Thus, there will not be enough jobs to employ large numbers of the unemployed. Finally, the plan does not apply to young unmarried men who receive minimal welfare support and are the most difficult group for whom to find employment.

The new federal welfare law is another modest step in the right direction. By 1995, 20 per cent of eligible welfare recipients (mostly mothers with children over the age of three) must take part in programs involving education, job training, or work. These participants will be eligible for transportation and child-care funds. However, the majority of the California law's exclusions and disincentives to work are also contained in the federal legislation.

Moreover, the modest funding of a billion dollars a year guarantees a limited impact.

Kaus has offered a plan to strengthen the work ethic of those made passive by welfare. He proposes ending welfare benefits and substituting a guaranteed job for anyone willing to work:

> Replace all cash-like welfare programs that assist the able-bodied poor (. . . but not Medicaid) with a single, simple offer from the government—an offer of employment for every American citizen who wants it, in a useful public job at a wage slightly below the minimum wage. If you could work and needed money, you would not be given a check (welfare). You would not be given a check and then cajoled, instructed, and threatened into working it off or "training it off" (workfare). You would be given the location of several government job sites. If you showed up, and worked, you would be paid for your work. If you didn't show up, you [wouldn't] get paid. Simple.[38]

Kaus notes that if mothers with young children are expected to work, there will have to be federally paid child-care services. Many mothers on welfare who go into training programs currently make private arrangements to care for their children, but a substantial proportion will still need to place their children in government-paid programs. The cost of these programs could be reduced by training poor women currently on welfare as child-care providers.

Kaus further points out that the plan would cover large numbers of poverty-stricken men who now receive minimal welfare benefits and who are learning to be lazy, in part, because of the lack of available jobs. Such employment would give poor people a supervisor who could give a job reference to help hard workers obtain better paying jobs in the private sector.

Conservatives often argue against public "make-work" jobs which in some cases accomplish little for the local community. Not all large federal job programs are accurately described as make-work. During the Great Depression, the WPA gave large numbers of Americans employment and job skills that were later transferred to jobs in private industry. Moreover, the WPA helped communities nationwide through construction projects and the improvement of highways. Writer Nicholas Lemann has called for a reinstitution of the WPA with salaries set lower than in private industry in order to encourage people to take industry jobs when available.[39]

Even make-work jobs that had no obvious benefits for the community would have great value if they strengthened the personal work ethic among poor people by rewarding increased effort. Replacing welfare with government-guaranteed jobs would, in the long run, increase American productivity. More important, it would restore the dignity and sense of purpose for many who have lost sight of the American dream.

Additional steps could be taken by the government to increase the industriousness and job skills of the poor. Economically disadvantaged children tend to do poorly in school because their parents and the local community fail to reward academic achievement or to inculcate them with a belief in the value of education. Most such children value cash if not education. Students attending elementary and high schools in impoverished neighborhoods could be paid for good attendance records, with the amount of payment dependent on academic performance. Such a program is probably not politically feasible on a large scale, but its value might be tested by demonstration projects supported by private foundations.

Too many unmarried women become pregnant in high school and drop out without having learned basic job skills. Unwed motherhood and welfare have become a socially accepted part of the economically disadvantaged culture. Changing such ingrained behavior will not be easy. Simple advertisements on television for birth control would probably have little influence when used alone, as indicated by the ineffectiveness of one well-funded and carefully carried out media campaign.[40]

A combination of steps can be far more effective. The provision of birth-control information at school combined with the availability of nearby clinics that supplied birth-control devices proved highly effective in a three-year experiment in Baltimore's inner city. Pregnancy rates at a junior high and senior high school decreased by thirty percent, in comparison to a substantial increase at similar schools in the area.[41]

Birth control information and contraceptive devices could be made available free of charge in community clinics. Black civic and church leaders could encourage birth control as responsible behavior for promoting the economic emancipation of blacks.

There seems little reason for individuals with moderate physical disabilities to receive welfare. They can be trained for the many jobs that they are fully capable of carrying out. Government and charity-supported sheltered workshops are currently available for physically disabled individuals. Giving handouts to people with handicaps who come around begging simply decreases self-esteem and reinforces dependency. Private employers might be given tax breaks for hiring the handicapped. Again, the federal government could serve as the employer of last resort.

Institutionalized mentally retarded or mentally ill individuals often lose their sense of self-worth because they are treated like small children. Television is frequently used as a baby sitter because it makes individuals placid and reduces the need to deal with their problems.[42] Mentally disabled individuals and psychiatric patients, like the rest of us, learn to be passive by watching television.

Paying institutionalized individuals to do some of the work now performed by the staff would strengthen work attitudes and give their lives a greater sense of purpose. Institutionalized mentally retarded adults who had held useful jobs in their facility for a period of over five years were found to miss the work considerably after being taken away from their jobs for two weeks during which time they were given a variety of entertainments throughout the day.[43] Paying for one's keep by a useful job increases self-respect and gives one's life greater meaning through service to the community.

Americans have traditionally been an optimistic people, looking to the future to create an economically and ethically sound society while paying scant attention to the lessons of the past. In a time of prosperity it has been easy for most Americans to dismiss as doomsayers those who perceive flaws in the nation's economic fabric and who decry the public's acceptance of an enjoy-now, pay-later philosophy.

Today, Americans cling to the complacent assumption that economic gains will continue to accumulate automatically. The unparalleled federal debt and international trade deficit, the perilous condition of the nation's Savings and Loans Associations, and the ruinous debt faced by major corporations resulting from junk-bond take-overs occurred because the public refused to ask who would pay tomorrow for today's self-indulgence. Most Americans are no longer saving prudently, working hard at school or on the job, or worrying about who is financing their present pleasures.

The American economy cannot continue to be inflated indefinitely by consumption-oriented spending unless supported by improved productivity based on hard work. If the nation continues on its present path the best that can be hoped is that the coming economic decline will occur slowly, without a major shock that will create great hardships.

The preceding suggestions for increasing Americans' work values stem from a diversity of evidence that effective rewards for increased effort teach industriousness. Greater diligence in school and on the job will not solve all of our economic problems but will certainly help. The sense of purpose provided by working hard toward long-term goals would enrich many lives spiritually as well as materialistically.

Notes

Introduction

1. Gould, S. J. Hen's Teeth and Horses Toes, New York: Norton, p. 122.

Chapter 1. Americans Used to Try Harder

1. Erickson, P. D., "Winthrop v. Reagan," *The New Republic*, October 20, 1986 15.
2. As noted by Maccoby, M., "The managerial work ethic in America," in Barbash, et al., Eds. *The Work Ethic: A Critical Analysis* (Madison, WI: Industrial Relations Research Association, 1983), 183–196.
3. Rodgers, D. T., *The Work Ethic in Industrial America: 1850–1920* (Chicago: University of Chicago Press, 1978).
4. Ibid.
5. Hector St. John de Crevecoeur quoted in Croly, H., *The Promise of American Life* (New York: Macmillan, 1912).
6. Breen, T. H., "New World Symphony," *New York Review of Books*, January 29, 1987, 27–29.
7. Stratton, J. A., *Pioneer women: Voices from the Kansas Frontier* (New York: Simon & Schuster, 1982), 57–76.
8. Ibid.

9. Cowen, R. S., "Less Work for Mother?" *Invention and Technology,* 2, Spring, 1987, 57.

10. Stratton, Ibid., 75.

11. Ibid., 146.

12. Ibid., 157–170.

13. Parker, S., *Leisure and Work* (London: George Allen & Unwin, 1983) 14–15; Tilgher, A., *Work: What It Has Meant to Men Through the Ages* (New York: Harcourt, Brace, & Co., 1930).

14. Rodgers, Ibid., xxx.

15. Sowell, T. *The Economics of Politics and Race* (New York: William Morrow and Company, 1983), 54–56.

16. Stratton, Ibid.

17. Ibid., 149.

18. Ibid., 155–156.

19. Rodgers, Ibid., 176.

20. Ibid.

21. Tyler, G., "The Work Ethic: A Union View," in Barbash, et al., Ibid.

22. Nevins, A., *Ford: The Times, the Man, the Company* (New York: Charles Scribner's Sons, 1954), 20.

23. Dickson, P., *Work Revolution* (London: George Allen & Unwin, 1977), 1–8.

24. Shaiken, H., *Work Transformed: Automation and Labor in the Computer Age* (Lexington, MA: D. C. Heath and Company, 1986), 23–24.

25. Lacey, R., *Ford: The men and the machine* (Toronto, Canada: McClellend and Stewart, 1986), p. 109.

26. Turkel, S. *Working.* New York: Avon, 1975, pp. 221–222.

27. Lacey, Ibid., pp. 128–129

28. Bender, F. L., Ed., *Karl Marx: The Essential Writings* (New York: Harper & Row, 1972), 69.

29. Ibid., 73.

30. Dickson, Ibid. 6.

31. Lacey, Ibid., 129.

32. Rodgers, Ibid., 178.

33. Owen, J. D., *The Price of Leisure: An Economic Analysis of the Demand for Leisure Time* (Montreal: McGill-Queen's University Press, 1970), 90.

34. Allen, F.L. Only Yesterday. New York: Bantam, 1959, pp 70–71.

35. Ibid., 79.

36. Lacey, R., Ibid., 285

37. Fox, S., *The Mirror Makers* (New York: Vintage Books, 1984), 96.

38. Ibid., 85.
39. One of the founders of modern behaviorism, Watson had been hounded out of academia because of adultery. The presidents of esteemed Eastern universities deemed it permissible that their professors preach that humans were governed by base drives, but they were not about to forgive a professor for any such weakness.
40. Fox, Ibid., 86.
41. Sargent, S. S., *The Great Psychologists: Their Theories, Discoveries, and Experiments* (New York: Barnes & Noble, 1958), 84, 134.
42. Fox, Ibid., 87–114.
43. Israel, L., *Estee Lauder: Beyond the Magic* (New York: Macmillan, 1985), 16–17.
44. Allen, Ibid., 75.
45. Israel, Ibid., 32–33.
46. Fox, Ibid., 138–139.
47. Allen, F. L. *Since Yesterday: The 1930's in America* (New York: Harper, 1940).
48. Yankelovich, D., *New Rules: Searching for Self-Fulfillment in a World Turned Upside Down* (New York: Random House, 1981), 21.
49. Harrington, M., *The New American Poverty* (New York: Holt, Rinehart, & Winston, 1984), 224–225.
50. Ibid., 211.
51. Maccoby, Ibid., 189.
52. Cherrington, D. J., *The Work Ethic: Working Values and Values That Work* (New York: Amacom, 1980), 82–86.
53. Ibid., 80–82.
54. Ibid., 88.
55. Israel, Ibid., 49.
56. Ibid., 48–49.
57. Glennon, L. M., & Butsch, R. "Growing Old On Television and With Television," in D. Pearl, L. Bouthilet, & J. Lazar, Eds., *Television and Behavior: Ten Years of Scientific Progress and Implications for the Eighties* (Washington, DC: U.S. Government Printing Office, 1982), 266.
58. Ibid., 266.
59. Ibid., 267.
60. *New York Times*, Business Section, June 15, 1986, 29.
61. Strohmeyer, J. *Crisis in Bethlehem: Big Steel's Battle to Survive* (Bethesda, MD: Adler & Adler, 1986), 113.
62. Levitan, S. A., & Johnson, C. M., "The Survival of Work," in Barbash et al., Ibid., 13.

63. Prokesch, S., "Managerial Class Gets Roughed Up. *New York Times*, Section 12, March 22, 1987, 11.
64. Strohmeyer Ibid., 143.
65. Snelbecker, G. E., *Learning Theory, Instructional Theory, and Psychoeducational Design* (New York: McGraw-Hill, 1974).
66. Korman, A., & Korman, R. W., *Career Success/Personal Failure*: Alienation in Management (Englewood Cliffs, NJ: Prentice-Hall, 1980), 13.
67. Hampton, D. R., Summer, C. E., & Webber, R. A., *Organizational Behavior and the Practice of Management*, 4th Ed. (Glenview, IL: Scott, Foresman and Company, 1982), 766–768.
68. Gross, Murray G., *The University: The Anatomy of Academe* (New York: McGraw-Hill, 1976), 127.
69. Yankelovich, D., "The New Naturalism, in *Saturday Review*, April 1, 1972, 35.
70. Yankelovich, (1981), Ibid., 175.
71. Halberstam, D., *The Reckoning* (New York: William Morrow & Co, 1986).
72. Yates, B. The Decline and Fall of the American Automobile Industry (New York: Empire Books, 1983), 232.
73. Barnet, D. F. & Schorsch, L., *Steel: Upheaval in a Basic Industry* (Cambridge, MA: Ballinger Publishing Company, 1983), 55, 64.
74. "One More Chorus of the *Steelyard Blues*" (January 12, 1987), *Business Week*, January 12, 1987 81; "Steel Wills" in *Time*, August 11, 1986.
75. Haddad, W., *Hard Driving*: My Years with De Lorean (New York: Random House, 1985).
76. Fox, Ibid., 257.
77. Yankelovich (1981), Ibid., 41.
78. Halberstam, Ibid., 23.
79. Lacey, Ibid., 575–586, 627.
80. Haddad, W., Ibid.
81. Shaiken, Ibid., 237
82. Ibid., 46.
83. Ibid., 122.
84. Ibid., 224.
85. Sanger, D. E., "Trying to Get America Into Competitive Trim, in *New York Times*, Section 12, March 22, 1987, 17.
86. Personal interview, March, 1987.
87. Shaiken, H., "When the Computer Runs the Office, in *New York Times*, March 22, 1987, E3.

88. Ibid.
89. Quoted in Sirota, D., & Wolfson, A. D., "Job Enrichment: What Are the Obstacles?" *Personnel*, 1972, *49*, 8–17.

Chapter 2. Laziness Among Affluent Americans

1. Stratton Ibid., 228.
2. Ibid., 227.
3. Ibid., 228.
4. Yankelovich (1981), Ibid., 182.
5. "A Non-Existent Nest Egg? *New York Times*, March 8, 1987 F1; Kilborn, P. T., The Sudden Wilting of Reagan's Rosy Economy, *New York Times*, July 27, 1986, F1.
6. Rasky, S. F., "A New Generation of Non-Savers," *New York Times Business Section*, November 2, 1986, F12.
7. Bennett, R. A., "Pick a Card, Any Card, Every Card," *New York Times*, November 30, 1986, F1.
8. Glaberson, W., "A Sense of Limits Grips Consumers," *New York Times*, March 15, 1987 F14.
9. "A Bankruptcy Boom," *New York Times*, February 15, 1987, F1.
10. $7,000 Is Spent Per Capita, *Wilmington News Journal*, July 31, 1986, A12.
11. Rasky, Ibid., 1.
12. Garten, J., *New York Times*, Business Section, July 20, 1986, 3.
13. Reinhardt, U. E., "Reaganomics, R. I. P.," *The New Republic*, April 20, 1987, 24–27.
14. "Owe, No!," *The New Republic*, November 24, 1886, 7.
15. Baumol, W. J., A Modest Decline Isn't All That Bad, *New York Times*, February 15, 1987, F2.
16. United States National Commission on Excellence in Education, *A Nation at Risk: The Imperative for reform*. Washington, D. C.: Government Printing Office, 1983, 21. Stevenson, H. W., Stigler, J. W., & Shin-ying, L., *Achievement in Mathematics*, 1986; "School Education: Its History and Contemporary Status," in H. Stevenson, H. Azuma, & K. Hakuta, Eds., *Child Development and Education in Japan*, New York: Freeman 201–216.
17. *Japanese Education Today*, U.S. Department of Education, (Washington, D.C.: U.S. Government Printing Office, 1987), 35.
18. Stevenson, Stigler, & Shin-ying, Ibid.
19. White, M., *The Japanese Educational Challenge* (New York: Free Press, 1987), 2.

20. Inagaki, T., "School Education: Its History and Contemporary Status," in Stevenson, Azuma, & Hakuta, Ibid., 3–12; *Japanese Education Today*, Ibid., 63; Stevenson, Stigler, & Shin-ying, Ibid.

21. White, Ibid.

22. Stevenson, Azuma, & Hakuta, Ibid., 209.

23. *A nation at risk*, Ibid., 18.

24. Adler et al., *The Effects of Television Advertising on Children* (Lexington, MA: Lexington Books, 1982).

25. Zuckerman, D. M., Singer, D. G., & Singer, J. L., "Television Viewing, Children's Reading, and Related Classroom Behavior," *Journal of Communication, 30*, 1980, 166–174.

26. Liebert, R. M., & Poulos, R. W., "Television and Personality Development: The Socializing Effects of an Entertainment Medium," in A. Davids, Ed., *Child Personality and Psychopathology: Current Topics*, Vol. 2. (New York: John Wiley & Sons, 1975), 61–97.

27. "Breakthrough Also a Warning," *Wilmington News Journal*, May 13, 1987, A10; NSF Chief Cites Technological Challenge, *University of Delaware Update*, November 3, 1986, 1; "Scientists From Overseas," *The New York Times, Business Section*, October 5, 1986, F1.

28. Snelbecker, Ibid., 492.

29. I personally observed this practice.

30. Korman, A. K., Wittig-Berman, U. W., & Lang, D., "Career Success and Personal Failure: Alienation in Professionals and Managers," *Academy of Management Journal, 24*, 1981, 342–360.

31. Oxnam, R. B. "Why Asians Succeed Here," *New York Times Magazine*, November 30, 1986, 86.

32. Cherrington, Ibid., 61–62.

33. Glassman, J. K., "The Wreck of General Motors," *The New Republic*, December 29, 1986, 23.

34. Prokesch, S., "America's Imperial Chief Executive," *New York Times*, October 12, 1986, F1.

35. Kleinfield, S., *Staying at the Top: The Life of a CEO*, (New York: New American Library, 1986), 131–132.

36. Bhadwati, J. N., & Irwin, D. A., "Fair Trade Could Trap the Democrats," *New York Times*, Business Section, June 22, 1986, 3.

37. "The New Export Champs," *New York Times*, December 7, 1986, F1.

38. Yates, Ibid., 15.

39. Meyer, G. W., & Stott, R. G., "Quality Circles: Panacea or Pandora's Box, *Organizational Dynamics, 13*, 1985, 34–50.

40. Ibid.; Wayne, S. J., Griffin, R. W., & Bateman, T. S., "Improving the Effectiveness of Quality Circles," *Personnel Administration*, 29, 1986, 79–88.
41. Jaeger, A. M., "Organization Development and National Culture: Where's the Fit?" *Academy of Management Review*, 11, 1986, 178–190; Schrank, Robert, Ten Thousand Working Days (Cambridge, MA: MIT Press, 1978, 87).
42. Tsurumi, Made in America, managed in Japan, *New York Times*, Nov 16, 1986, F3.
43. Yates, Ibid., 235
44. *Time*, August, 1983, 44.
45. "EPA Grades Best Cars for Mileage; Top Slops Again Go to Imports." *Wilmington News Journal*, September 22, 1986. A3.
46. Braunstein, J., "GM Must Find Its Identity." *Wilmington News Journal*, November 4, 1986, B6.
47. Bohn, E., "U.S. Steel Changes Name to USX Corp," Associated Press release published in *The News-Journal*, Wilmington DE, July 9, 1986 B6.
48. Farnsworth, C. H., "The U.S. Giveaway," *New York Times*, December 7, 1986, F1.
49. Prokesch, S., "Stopping the High-Tech Giveaway," *New York Times*, March 22, 1987, F8.
50. Ibid.
51. Farnsworth, Ibid.
52. Ibid., F13.
53. Christopher, R. C., "Don't Blame the Japanese," *New York Times Book Review*, October 19, 1986, 77–78.
54. Yates, Ibid., 238.
55. Hamilton, R.F., & Wright, J.D., *The State of the Masses* (New York: Aldine, 1986), 275.
56. Clark, C., "The Work Ethic: An International Perspective. In Barbash et al., Ibid., 131–133.
57. Hamilton & Wright, Ibid., 275–278.
58. Mowday R.T., Porter, L.W., & Steers, R.M. Employee-organization linkages: The Psychology of Commitment (New York, Academic Press, 1982, 95).
59. Hamilton & Wright, Ibid., 280.
60. Interview, February, 1983.
61. de Grazia, S., *Of time, work, and leisure* (New York: The Twentieth Century Fund, 1962), 55.

62. Shaiken, Ibid., 140.
63. Personal interview, April, 1984.
64. Interview, November, 1982.
65. Glazer, M. P., & Glazer, P. M., "Whistleblowing," *Psychology Today*, August, 1986, 39.
66. Ibid.
67. "Feeling the Crunch From Foreign Chips," *Time*, October 27, 1986, 72.
68. Schneider, K., "Looking Abroad to Fill Our Bellies," *New York Times*, August 3, 1986, F1.
69. "Big farms to Get Huge U. S. Subsidies," *New York Times*, July 27, 1986 19.
70. "Big farms to Get Huge U. S. Subsidies," Ibid.; "Spending Smarter," *The New Republic*, February 2, 1987, 5–7.
71. "Going to Seed" *The New Republic*, August 25, 1986.
72. Whiting, R., "East Meets West in the Japanese Game of Besuboro," *Smithsonian*, September, 1986, 112–113.
73. Eisenberger, R., & Shank, D. M., "Personal Work Ethic and Effort Training Affect Cheating," *Journal of Personality and Social Psychology*, 49, 1985, 520–528.
74. Frank, B., "Do Something Drastic About Spies," *The Wilmington News Journal*, October 6, 1986, A6.
75. Barron, J., *Breaking the Ring* (Boston: Houghton Mifflin, 1987), 171
76. Ibid., 55, Blum, H., "Spy Ring: the Untold Story of the Walker Case," *The New York Times Magazine*, June 29, 1986.
77. Barron, Ibid., 123.
78. Ibid., 188.
79. Egelko, B., "Spy Gets 365 Years in Prison," *Wilmington Evening Journal*, August 29, 1986.
80. Barron, Ibid., 103, 173.
81. Blum, Ibid.
82. The following account of the William Summerlin affair is taken from Broad, W. & Wade, N., *Betrayers of the truth* (New York: Simon & Shuster, 1982), 153–157; Hixson, J., *The Patchwork Mouse* (New York: Anchor Press, 1976)
83. Dr. Good denied the Fall 1973 alleged incident; Broad and Wade, Ibid., 157.
84. Hixson, Ibid., 7–8.
85. Ibid., 36.
86. Ibid., 108.
87. Ibid., 21.

Chapter 3. Laziness Among Poor Americans

1. Morley, D.E, *Pictures From the Water Trade* (Boston: Atlantic Monthly Press, 1985)
2. Ibid., 61.
3. Kaus, M., "The Work Ethic State," *The New Republic*, July 7, 1986, 22
4. Personal Interview, July, 1886.
5. Kaus, Ibid., 25.
6. Auletta, The Underclass (New York: Random House, 1982, 27).
7. Ibid., 161.
8. Murray, C., *Losing Ground: American Social Policy, 1950–1980* (New York: Basic Books, 1984), 55; Harrington, Ibid., 139.
9. Harrington, M., Ibid., 130, 136–137.
10. Ibid., 138.
11. Levitan, S. A., & Johnson, C. M., "The Survival of work," in J. Barbash et al., Ibid.
12. Freeman, R. B. (July 20, 1986). *New York Times* Business Section, July 20, 1986, 2.
13. Wilson, W. J., & Neckerman, K. M., "Poverty and Family Structure: The Widening Gap Between Evidence and Public Policy Issues," in. S. H. Danziger & D. H. Weinberg, Eds. *Fighting Poverty: What Works and What Doesn't* (Cambridge, MA: Harvard University Press, 1986), 232–259.
14. Lemann, Nicholas, "The Origins of the Underclass," *Atlantic Monthly*, Part 1: June, 1986, 31–55; Part 2: July, 1986, 54–68.
15. Morley, Ibid., 35–37, 43.
16. Personal Interview, July 1986
17. Banfield, E. C., *The Unheavenly City: The Nature and Future of Our Urban Crisis* (Boston: Little, Brown, 1970), 53.
18. Liebow, E., *Tally's Corner: A Study of Negro Streetcorner Men* (Boston, MA: Little, Brown & Company, 1967), 63, 211
19. Ibid.
20. Ibid., 34–35.
21. Ibid., 57–58.
22. Ellwood, D. T., & Summers, L. H., "Poverty in America: Is Welfare the Answer or the Problem? in. Danziger & Weinberg, Ibid., 100–101.
23. Murray, C. Losing Ground: American Social Policy, 1950–1980 (New York: Basic Books, 1984, 125).
24. Kaus, Ibid, 23.

25. Liebow, Ibid.,

26. Curland, Cyndi Louise, Personal interview, May, 1986.

27. Ibid.

28. Auletta, Ibid., 72.

29. Ibid., 73.

30. Kaus, Ibid., 23.

31. Stark, E., "Young, Innocent and Pregnant," *Psychology Today*, October, 1986, 35.

32. Statistics sometimes used to counter this view show that the average number of children by mothers receiving federal child support payments is 2.2, only slightly above the national average. And the average length of time the assistance is received is only thirty months. See Rodgers, H. R., Jr., *The Cost of Human Neglect: America's Welfare Failure* (Armonk, NY: M. E. Sharpe, Inc., 1982), 74. These figures are sometimes used to portray the welfare mother as very similar to other mothers except for poverty.

    But with statistics we must always be careful not to compare apples with oranges. The average woman *stops* having children after the first two. It is inappropriate to compare the *total* number of children borne by the average woman with the number of children of welfare mothers who are still of child-bearing age. Since many mothers currently on welfare will bear more children, welfare mothers do have *more* children than average.

33. Kaus, Ibid., 22; Rodgers, Ibid., 74.

34. About one-third of all families receiving this aid at any time are repeaters, many of them having received such aid several times in the past. Further, four in ten mothers receiving welfare payments in 1961 were found to have been raised in homes that also received such aid. See Rodgers, Ibid., 74–75. Moreover, the number of welfare mothers counted as repeaters at any time is diluted by the large number of women bearing children for the first time. Therefore, during a welfare mother's lifetime, she is likely to be on welfare repeatedly.

35. Auletta, Ibid., 225.

36. Andrisani, P. J., "Internal-External Attitudes, Personal Initiative, and the Labor Market Experience of Black and White Men," *Journal of Human Resources*, 12, Summer, 1977, 308–338. G. J. Duncan and J. N. Morgan ["Sense of Efficacy and Subsequent Change in earnings: A Replication," *Journal of Human Resources*, 16, 1981, 649–657] reported weaker results and therefore challenged Andrisani's arguments. However, Andrisani [*Journal of Human Resources*, 16, 1981,

658–666] cogently noted that even though the replication's apparent effects were weak using the same two-year follow-up period, within an additional two years the effects had become comparable in size to his own results. D. A. Evans and F. B. Tyler [Is Work Competence Enhancing for the Poor? *American Journal of Community Psychology, 4*, 1976, 25–33] reported a very small-scale study supporting these results.

37. Ibid., 60.
38. Liebow, Ibid., 55.
39. Auletta, Ibid., 33.
40. Quoted in Banfield, Ibid., 221–222.
41. Auletta, Ibid., 11.
42. Ibid., xvii.
43. Kaus, Ibid., 27.
44. Auletta, Ibid., 76.

Chapter 4. Laziness Among Television Viewers.

1. Comstock, G., "Television and American Social Institutions," in Pearl, Bouthilet, & Lazar, Ibid., 334–348.
2. Ibid., 339.
3. Patterson, T. E., & McClure, R. D. (1976). *The Unseeing Eye: The Myth of Television Power in National Politics* (New York: Putnam, 1976), 55.
4. Csikszentmihalyi, M., & Kubey, R., "Television and the Rest of Life: A Systematic Comparison of Subjective Experience," *Public Opinion Quarterly, 45*, 1981, 302–315.
5. Brody, G. H., Stoneman, Z., & Sanders, A. K., "Effects of Television Viewing on Family Interactions: An Observational Study," *Family Relations, 29*, 1980, 216–220.
6. Anderson & Lorch, Ibid., 10–11.
7. Liebert, R. M., Sprafkin, J. N., & Davidson, E. S. *The Early Window: Effects of Television on Children and Youth* (2nd ed.). New York: Pergamon Press, 24.
8. Brody, Stoneman, & Sanders, Ibid.
9. Gerbner, G., Morgan, M., & Signorielli, N., "Programing Health Portrayals: What Viewers See, Say, and Do," in Pearl, Bouthilet, & Lazar Ibid., 291–307.
10. Ibid.
11. Culhane, J., "Report card on *Sesame Street*," *New York Times Magazine*, May 24, 1970.

12. Anderson & Lorch, Ibid., 22.
13. Culhane, Ibid.
14. Ibid.
15. Ibid.
16. Ibid.
17. Zuckerman, Singer, & Singer, Ibid., 166–174.
18. Culhane, Ibid.
19. Evertson et al., *Classroom Management for Elementary Teachers* (Englewood Cliffs, NJ: Prentice-Hall, 1984), 119.
20. Ibid., 142–143.
21. Morgan, M., & Gross, L. "Television and Educational Achievement and Aspirations," in Pearl, Bouthilet, & Lazar Ibid., 78–90.
22. Such studies also do not tell us whether heavy TV watching causes failure in school or whether the repeated withholding of teachers' approval that results from failure leads children to rebel by refusing to do homework, spending more time in front of the TV [Morgan, & Gross, Ibid.]. Quite possibly, the causation works in both directions. Heavy television watching may result in poor school performance, *and* poor school performance may make television an inviting alternative to study. Longitudinal studies, involving repeated observations over time on children's watching habits and school performance, are needed to sort out cause and effect.
23. Hornik, R., "Television Access and the Slowing of Cognitive Growth," *American Educational Research Journal*, 15, 1978, 1–16.
24. One experiment, [Anderson, D. R., Levin, S. R., & Lorch, E. P., "The effects of TV Program Pacing on the Behavior of Preschool Children," *AV Communication Review*, 25, 1977, 154–166] that failed to find an effect of watching *Sesame Street* on subsequent persistence contains serious methodological deficiencies. Seventy-two four-year-old children were shown a single forty minutes of film clip of thirty-six rapidly-paced bits strung together from *Sesame Street*, another group was shown seventeen slower bits from the show, and a third group was read stories by a parent. Then, persistence was tested on two brief tasks. Task persistence was reported not to differ among the three conditions, and the researchers concluded that watching *Sesame Street* did not influence task persistence. The innovation of varying the pace of bits from the same show was very clever. Such a procedure gets at the influence of a show's pace while controlling for any effects of the act of watching or the general content of the show.

Unfortunately, the strength of any effects may have been minimized by limiting the treatment to a single sitting, and by the assessment of the effects immediately after the viewing. A lessening of task persistence that may result from repeatedly watching such a show may have been masked in this study by presenting the show on only one occasion. Further, by presenting the persistence task immediately after the show's presentation, the long-term effects of watching may be masked by temporary effects. By analogy, exercising a muscle increases the muscle's long-term strength but reduces its short-term capacity due to fatigue. The children who listened to stories for forty minutes may have become *temporarily* restless, thereby reducing task persistence, while increasing their long-term patience. Further, even if watching *Sesame Street* reduces task persistence in the long run, it may have an immediate *temporary* effect of satiating children on fast pacing and thus increasing their toleration for taking greater time to work on a slower paced task.

Even though the study was limited to a single presentation of *Sesame Street* bits and the impact assessed immediately after, it is tantalizing that the two groups that watched Sesame Street did show substantially greater distraction than the control condition on some critical measures of task persistence, although the differences were generally not statistically reliable. It would be valuable to repeat the study using more children in each group, a greater number of presentations of the films, and a greater separation in time between the treatments and the assessment of their effects.

25. Friedrich, L. K., & Stein, A. H., "Aggressive and Prosocial Television Programs and the Natural Behavior of Preschool Children," *Monographs of the Society for Research in Child Development, 38* 1973; *4*, ser. no. 151.

26. A subsequent similar study [Friedrich-Cofer et al., "Environmental Enhancement of Prosocial Television Content: Effects on Interpersonal Behavior, Imaginative Play, and Self-regulation in a Natural Setting," *Developmental Psychology, 15*, 1979, 637–646] which failed to include fast paced cartoons, did not find a reliable improvement in persistence as a result of watching *Mister Rogers' Neighborhood* versus neutral films. Thus, the diverse prosocial content over several weeks of viewing does not appear to have a positive effect on task persistence.

27. Salomon, G., *Interaction of Media, Cognition and Learning* (San Francisco: Jossey-Bass, 1979), 181–182.

NOTES

28. Ibid., 182.
29. LeConte, P., "The Psychologist as TV Guide," *Psychology Today*, August, 1986, 55.
30. Rose, M., *Re-working the Work Ethic: Economic Value and Sociocultural Politics* (New York: Schocken Books, 1985), 104.
31. Atkin, C. K., 1982, Ibid., 193.
32. Adler et al., Ibid., 33.
33. Ibid., 37.
34. Ibid., 34.
35. Liebert, R. M., Sprafkin, J. N., & Davidson, E. S. (1982). *The early window: Effects of television on children and youth* (2nd ed.). New York: Pergamon Press, 18.
36. Adler et al., Ibid.
37. Barcus, F. E., & McLaughlin, L., *Food Advertising on Children's Television: An Analysis of Appeals and Nutritional Content* (Newtonville, MA: Action for Children's Television, 1978).
38. Ibid.; Gerbner, Morgan, & Signorielli, Ibid., 295.
39. Barcus, & McLaughlin, Ibid.
40. Ibid., 15.
41. Ibid.
42. Ibid., 16.
43. Atkins, Ibid., 195.
44. Oskamp, S. *Applied Social Psychology.* Englewood Cliffs, NJ: Prentice-Hall, 1984, p. 316.
45. Liebert, Sprafkin, & Davidson, Ibid., 150–151.
46. Barcus, & McLaughlin, Ibid.
47. Atkin, Ibid., 196–197.
48. Gerbner, Morgan, & Signorielli, Ibid., 291–307.
49. Atkin, Ibid., 194.
50. Gerson, W. M., "Mass Media Socialization Behavior: Negro-white Differences," *Social Forces, 45*, 1966, 40–50.
51. Stark, Ibid., 28.
52. Sullivan, A., "Flogging Underwear," *The New Republic, 198*, January 18, 1988, 20–24.
53. Fraser, K., "As Gorgeous As It Gets," *The New Yorker*, September 15, 1986, 50.
54. Israel, Ibid., 109.
55. Ibid., 113.
56. Fraser, Ibid., 50.
57. Sullivan, *Ibid.*, 20.

58. Harvey, S. E., Sprafkin, J. N., & Rubinstein, E., "Prime Time Television: A Profile of Prosocial and Aggressive Behaviors," *Journal of Broadcasting*, 23, 1979 179–189; Liebert, & Poulos, Ibid., 61–97; Poulos, R. W., Harvey S. E., & Liebert, R. M., "Saturday Morning Television: A Profile of the 1974–75 Children's Season," *Psychological Reports*, 39, 1976, 1047–1057.
59. Liebert, & Poulos, Ibid., 61–97
60. Roberts, in Pearl, Bouthilet, & Lazar, Ibid., 220.
61. Byrne, D., & Lamberth, J., "The Effect of Erotic Stimuli on Sex Arousal, Evaluative Responses, and Subsequent Behavior," in *Technical report of the Commission on Obscenity and Pornography* (Vol. 8) (Washington, DC: U. S. Government Printing Office, 1970).
62. Roberts, E. J. In D. Pearl, L. Bouthilet, & J. Lazar (Eds.), Television and Behavior: Ten Years of Scientific progress and implications for the eighties (pp. 209–223). Washington, D. C.: U. S. Government Printing Office, 222
63. Experimental research indicates that highly explicit pornographic films elicit a strong physiological sexual response in young adult males. Repeated exposure to pornography materials for a number of days decreases the magnitude of this response considerably [Howard, J. L., Reifler, C. B., & Lipzin, M. B. (1970). "Effects of Exposure to Pornography," in *Technical report of the Commission on Obscenity and Pornography*, Vol. 8, (Washington, DC: U. S. Government Printing Office, 1970), 97–132] This is consistent with findings in Denmark that as restrictions on pornographic books, magazines, and movies were progressively lifted, each new class of material placed on the market produced a marked increase in sales, followed by a decline to a level less than during the time of prohibition. Thus, "The frustration of the pornographic promise results not in continued excitement, but in boredom." [Sonenschein, D., quoted in Howard, Reifler, & Lipzin, Ibid., 97].

This decreasing interest in pornography with greater exposure does not tell us about the effects of such materials on attitudes and behavior. A single session of presentation of sexually explicit slides had no effect on the following week's self-reported sexual behavior of married couples who had volunteered to take part in the experiment. Of course, there might have been a greater effect had there been exposure to such materials over a longer period of time or if younger single individuals had been studied whose attitudes toward sex may be less settled. One experiment reported that single college students had more liberal attitudes toward premarital sexual intercourse two weeks after seeing a single pornographic film. But this small amount of evidence is far from conclusive.

Chapter 5. Industriousness Among the Japanese

1. Benedict, R., *The Chrysanthemum and the Sword: Patterns of Japanese Culture* (Cambridge, MA: Houghton Mifflin, 1946), 44–45.
2. Ibid., 44.
3. Zuckerman, S., "Bombs and Morals," *The New Republic*, November 17, 1986 42.
4. Halberstam, D., Ibid., 113.
5. The account of MacArthur's governance of postwar Japan is taken from Halberstam, D., Ibid., 112–130.
6. Fallows, J., "The Japanese Are Different From You and Me," *The Atlantic Monthly*, September, 1986.
7. Fallows, J., "Letter From Tokyo," *The Atlantic Monthly*, August, 1986.
8. "A Baffling Trade Imbalance," *Time*, August 11, 1986.
9. White, M., *The Japanese Educational Challenge: A Commitment to Children* (New York: Free Press, 1987), 2.
10. Shaiken, Ibid., 156.
11. Oxnam, R. B. Ibid., 72.
12. Irish, J. S., "A Yankee Learns to Bow," *New York Times Magazine*, Part 2. June 8, 1986, 122–126.
13. Coleman, S., "The Tempo of Family Formation," in D. W. Plath, Ed., *Work and Lifecourse in Japan* (Albany, NY: State University of New York Press, 1983), 192.
14. Ibid., 190.
15. Miyake, K., et al., "Issues in Socioemotional Development," *Child Development*, Ibid., 239–261.
16. Azuma, H., "Why Study Child Development in Japan?" in *Child Development*, Ibid., 7–8.
17. Miyake et al., Ibid.
18. Ibid.
19. Benedict, Ibid., 262.
20. Ibid.
21. Ibid., 263.
22. Azuma, Ibid., 4.
23. Benedict, Ibid., 273–274.
24. Ibid., 262–263; Miyake, *et al.*, Ibid.

25. Benedict, Ibid., 286.
26. Hess, et al., "Family Influences On School Readiness and Achievement in Japan and the United States: An Overview of a Longitudinal Study," in *Child Development*, Ibid., 161.
27. *Japanese Education Today*, U.S. Department of Education (Washington, DC: U.S. Government Printing Office, 1987), 3.
28. White, Ibid., 68.
29. *Japanese Education Today*, Ibid., 27.
30. *Japanese Education Today*, Ibid., 45.
31. Fallows, September, 1986, Ibid.
32. White, M. I., & LeVine, R. A., "What Is An *ii ko* (good child)," in *Child Development*, Ibid., 55–62.
33. Befu, H., "The Social and Cultural Background of Child Development in Japan and the United States," in *Child Development*, Ibid., 13–27.
34. Morley Ibid., 61–65.
35. Irish, Ibid.
36. Benedict, Ibid.
37. Ibid., 235.
38. Ibid., 249.
39. Morley Ibid., 111.
40. Oxnam, Ibid., 86–87.
41. Benedict, Ibid., 179.
42. Morley Ibid., 196.
43. Ibid., 188–190.
44. Benedict, Ibid., 177–194, 238; Morley, Ibid., 188–189.
45. Woronoff, J., (1986). *The Japan Syndrome: Symptoms, Ailments, and Remedies* (New Brunswick, NJ: Transaction Books, 1986), 25.
46. Ibid., 69.
47. Morley, Ibid., 250.
48. Ibid., 123–124.
49. Chira, S., "South Korea: The Next Wave," *New York Times Magazine*, December 14, 1986.
50. Fallows, September, 1986, Ibid, 38.
51. Ibid.
52. Ibid., 41.
53. Burgess, J., U.S. Literacy Gap Disparaged, *Wilmington News Journal*, September 24, 1986, A2.
54. "Nakasone Still Scrambling to Clarify His Remarks," *The Wilmington News Journal*, September 25, 1986, A2.

55. Kashiwagi, K. "Personality Development of Adolescents," in *Child Development*, Ibid., 147–166.
56. Bhadwati, & Irwin, Ibid.
57. "A Baffling Trade Imbalance," Ibid.
58. Garten, J. E., "Taming the Swings of the Yen and Dollar," *New York Times, Business Section*, July 20, 1986, 3.
59. Harrington, Ibid., 57; Author notes that an Office of Technology Assessment study indicates foreign hourly employment costs are rising much more rapidly than our own.
60. Christopher, R. C., *Second to None: American Companies in Japan* (New York: Crown Publishers, 1986), 16.
61. Woronoff, Ibid.
62. Christopher, Ibid.
63. Fallows, August, 1986, Ibid.
64. Ibid., 16.
65. Christopher, Ibid., 33.
66. Ibid., 184.
67. Ibid.
68. Christopher, R. C., "Don't Blame the Japanese," *New York Times Book Review*, October 19, 1986, p. 77.
69. Christopher, 1986, Ibid., 43.
70. Christopher, 1986 Ibid., 168.
71. Fallows, 1986, Ibid.
72. Pearlman, J. K. (December 14, 1986). "Save the Lectures, Give Us Some Help," *New York Times*, December 14, 1986, p. F3.
73. Woronoff, Ibid., 55.
74. Ibid.
75. Chira, Ibid., 34.
76. Morley, Ibid., 70–76.
77. Azuma, Ibid., 9.
78. Christopher, Ibid., 77.
79. "Locals Luring Foreigners," *New York Times, Business Section*, July 26, 1986, 1.
80. Christopher, Ibid., 224.
81. Yoffie, D. B., "Helping Industry Fight the Good Fight," *New York Times*, August 10, 1986, F2.
82. Befu, Ibid., 23.
83. Benedict, Ibid., 115.
84. Ibid., 145–176; Morley, Ibid., 184–185.
85. Morley, Ibid., 184–185.
86. Ibid.

87. "Shultz Criticizes Reagan Decision on Wheat Sales," *Wilmington News Journal*, August 5, 1986 A3.
88. "A Baffling Trade Imbalance," Ibid.
89. Woronoff, Ibid., 84.
90. Krugman, P. R. (August 10, 1986). "Just a Fancy Form of Protectionism," *New York Times*, August 10, 1986, F2.
91. Ibid., Schmid, R. E., "Protectionism Costs Consumers," *Wilmington News Journal*, February 14, 1987.
92. Schmid, Ibid.
93. Bhagwati & Irwin, Ibid., 3; Krugman, Ibid.
94. Aurbach, S., "Tariffs Ordered to Even Score in Trade with Japan," *Wilmington News Journal*, March 28, 1987, Al; "Possible Targets for New Duties," *Wilmington News Journal*, March 28, 1987.
95. Christopher Ibid., 77.
96. DeVos, G., & Suarez-Orozco, M. M., "Child Development in Japan and the United States: Prospectives of Cross-cultural Comparisons," in *Child Development*, Ibid., 289–298. Hatano, G., & Inagaki, K., "Two Courses of Expertise," *Child Development*, Ibid., 262–272.
97. Morley Ibid., 67.
98. Ibid., 67.
99. Benedict, Ibid., 292.
100. Hofstede, G., *Cultures consequences: International Differences in Work-related values*, (Beverly Hills, CA, Sage: 1980); Hofstede, G., "Cultural Dimensions in Management and Planning," in Hampton, D. R., Summer, C. E., & Webber, R. A. *Organizational Behavior and the Practice of Management*, Fifth Ed. Glenview, Illinois: Scott-Foresman, 1987, pp 401–422.

Chapter 6. America's Industrious Minority

1. Greenberg, J., "Equity, Equality, and the Protestant Ethic: Allocating Rewards Following Fair and Unfair Competition," *Journal of Experimental Social Psychology*, 14, 1978, 217–226; Greenberg, J., "Protestant Ethic Endorsement and the Fairness of Equity Inputs," *Journal of Research in Personality*, 13, 1979, 81–90.
2. Hooker, K., & Ventis, D. G., "Work Ethic, Daily Activities, and Retirement Satisfaction," *Journal of Gerontology*, 39, 1984, 478–484.
3. McLeod, "The Oriental Express," *Psychology Today*, July, 1986.
4. Butterfield, F., "Why Asians Are Going to the Head of the Class," *New York Times*, Section 12., August 3, 1986, 18.
5. McLeod, Ibid.

6. Oxnam, Ibid, 74.
7. Butterfield, Ibid.
8. Oxnam, Ibid., 74–75.
9. Chance, P., "Imported Apple Pie," *Psychology Today,* July, 1986.
10. Butterfield, Ibid., 19–20.
11. Ibid., 18.
12. McLeod, Ibid.
13. Shaiken, Ibid.
14. Cherrington, Ibid., 120–128.

Chapter 7. Learned Industriousness

1. Wenrich, W. et al., "A Trans-response Effect of Partial Reinforcement," *Psychonomic Science,* 1967, 9, 247–248.
2. McCuller, R., Wong, P. T. P., & Amsel, A., "Transfer of Persistence from Fixed-ratio Bar-press Training to Runway Extinction," *Animal Learning and Behavior, 4,* 1976, 53–57.
3. Eisenberger et al., "Transfer of Effort Across Behaviors," *Learning and Motivation, 10,* 1979, 178–197; Eisenberger et al., "Transfer of Persistence Across Behaviors," *Journal of Experimental Psychology: Human Learning and Memory, 5,* 1979, 522–530.
4. Eisenberger, R., Terborg, R., & Carlson, J., "Transfer of Persistence Across Reinforced Behaviors," *Animal Learning and Behavior, 7,* 1979, 493–498.
5. Eisenberger, R., & Leonard, J. M., "Effects of Conceptual Task Difficulty on Generalized Persistence," *American Journal of Psychology, 93,* 1980, 285–298.
6. Eisenberger, et al., *Transfer of Effort,* Ibid.
7. Boyagian, L. G., & Nation, J. R., "The Effects of Force Training and Reinforcement Schedules on Human Performance," *American Journal of Psychology, 94,* 1981, 619–632.
8. Rubinstein, E. A., et al., "Television Viewing Behaviors of Mental Patients: A Survey of Psychiatric Centers in New York state," New York: Brookdale International Institute, 1977, ii.
9. Ibid., 14.
10. Eisenberger et al., *Transfer of Persistence,* Ibid.
11. Nation, J. R., & Woods, D. J., "Persistence: The Role of Partial Reinforcement in Psychotherapy," *Journal of Experimental Psychology: General, 109,* 1980, 175–207.
12. Eisenberger et al., *Transfer of Persistence* Ibid.
13. Eisenberger & Leonard Ibid.

14. Eisenberger, et al., "Generalized Self-control of Effort and Delay," Twenty-sixth Annual Psychonomic Society Meeting, Boston, MA, November, 1985.
15. Eisenberger, R., Mitchell, M., & Masterson, F. A., "Effort Training Increases Generalized Self-Control," *Journal of Personality and Social Psychology, 49,* 1985, 1294–1301.
16. Eisenberger, R., Masterson, F. A., & Adornetto, M., "Appetitive Effort Training Increases Self-control Involving Stress," Twenty-seventh Annual Psychonomic Society Meeting, New Orleans, LA, November, 1986.
17. Eisenberger, R., & Adornetto, M., "Generalized Self-control of Delay and Effort," *Journal of Personality and Social Psychology, 51,* 1986, 1020–1031.
18. Owen, D., "Where Toys Come From," *The Atlantic Monthly,* October, 1986.
19. Johnson, P. H., "Achievement Motivation and Success: Does the End Justify the Means?" *Journal of Personality and Social Psychology, 40,* 1981, 374–375.
20. Ainslie, G., "Specious Reward: A Behavioral Theory of Impulsiveness and Impulse Control," *Psychological Bulletin, 82,* 1975, 463–996.
21. Eisenberger, R., & Masterson, F. A., "Required High Effort Increases Subsequent Persistence and Reduces Cheating," *Journal of Personality and Social Psychology, 99,* 1983, 593–599.
22. Eisenberger, R., Masterson, & Over. S., "Maintenance-feeding Effort Affects Instrumental Performance," *Quarterly Journal of Experimental Psychology, 34B,* 1982, 141–148.
23. Eisenberger, R., & Shank, D. M., "Personal Work Ethic and Effort Training Affect Cheating," *Journal of Personality and Social Psychology, 49,* 1985, 520–528.

Chapter 8. Marathonists

1. Olsen, S., *Young Henry Ford.* (Detroit, MI: Wayne State University Press, 1963), 5–8.
2. Ibid., 14–15.
3. Ibid., 15–16.
4. Nevins, Ibid., 49–50.
5. Lacey, Ibid., 11.
6. Olson, Ibid., 24–25.
7. Nevins. Ibid., 48.
8. Ibid., 54.

9. Ibid., 82–83.
10. Olson., Ibid., 33.
11. Ibid.
12. Ibid., 45.
13. Ibid., 46.
14. Ibid., 58.
15. Ibid.
16. Ibid., 78–80.
17. Ibid., 57.
18. Lacey, Ibid., 50.
19. Ibid., p. 93.
20. Allen, F. A., *The Big Change: America Transforms Itself 1900–1950* (New York: Harper & Brothers, 1952), 110.
21. Ibid., 113.
22. Ibid., 121.
23. Boyer, R. O., *Labor's Untold Story* (New York: United Electrical, Radio and Machine Workers of America, 1955).
24. Boyer Ibid., 265–266; Lacey, Ibid. 343–344.
25. Farago, Ibid., 48.
26. Farago, Ibid., 51.
27. Blumenson, M., *Patton: The Man Behind the Legend, 1885–1945* (New York: William Morrow & Company, 1985).
28. Ibid., 29.
29. Ibid., 45–46.
30. Ibid., 49–54.
31. Ibid., 60.
32. Ibid., 34.
33. Ibid., 70.
34. Farago, Ibid., 105.
35. Farago, Ibid., 65
36. Patton, G. S., "The Secret of Victory," published in Province, C. M., *The Unknown* Patton (New York: Hippocrene Books, 1983), 136
37. Blumenson, Ibid., 74.
38. Ibid., 73–75.
39. Ibid., 141.
40. Ibid., 82.
41. Ibid., 89.
42. Ibid., 92
43. Ibid., 94.
44. Farago, Ibid., 68.
45. Blumenson, Ibid., 97–98.

46. Farago, Ibid., 71.
47. Ibid., 74.
48. Ibid., 73.
49. Blumenson, Ibid., 114; Farago, Ibid., 90.
50. Blumenson, Ibid., 116.
51. Province, Ibid., 9.
52. Ibid., 62.
53. Blumenson, Ibid., 135.
54. Ibid., 152.
55. Patton, Ibid.
56. Ibid., 136.
57. Farrago, 9.
58. Blumenson, Ibid., 181–184.
59. Farago, 9.
60. Ibid., 323.
61. Patton, Ibid., 135.
62. Blumenson, Ibid., 280.
63. Hooker, K., & Ventis, D. G. (1984). Work ethic, daily activities, and retirement satisfaction. *Journal of Gerontology, 39*, 478–484, p. 478.

Chapter 9. Sprinters

1. Tom Wolfe's spirited book *The Right Stuff* (1979, New York: Ferrar-Straus-Giroux) managed to capture Yeager's talents and personality in an accurate short chapter that anticipated Yeager's own more detailed account (Yeager, C., & Janos, L., *Yeager: An Autobiography,* 1985, Toronto: Bantam Books).
2. Yeager & Janos, Ibid., 53, 67.
3. Ibid., 45.
4. Ibid. 82.
5. Ibid., 84.
6. Watson's candid sketch of his research on the trail of the mechanism of heredity provides excellent insights into the style and causes of his industriousness: Watson, J. D., *The Double Helix,* (New York; Atheneum, 1968). An extensive account of recent genetic discoveries and the personalities of the scientists involved is H. F. Judson's, *The Eighth Day of Creation.* (New York: Simon & Schuster, 1979), 117–118.
7. Ibid., 35
8. Ibid., 163.

9. Ibid., 77.
10. Ibid., 21–30, 80.
11. Ibid., 77.
12. Ibid., 43, 56, 68.
13. Judson, Ibid., 117–118.
14. Ibid., 142.
15. Ibid., 20–21.
16. Ibid., 81, 86.
17. Ibid., 229.
18. Ibid., 493, 581.

Chapter 10. Explorers

1. Because she has been so secretive about her life, the information on Estée Lauder's life is limited. Lee Israel's short unauthorized biography (*Estée Lauder: Beyond the magic*, 1985, New York: Macmillan) shows good detective work. My discussion is based on this work, a sketch of Estée Lauder promoting her products that appeared in *The New Yorker* (Fraser, K., *As gorgeous as it gets*, September 15, 1986), and Lauder's self-serving autobiography (*Estée: A success story*, 1985, New York: Ballantine). In cases where Israel's book conflicts with Lauder's, I have used Israel's account as the more impartial.
2. Lauder, Ibid., p. 92.
3. Fraser, Ibid., p. 42.
4. Lauder, Ibid., pp. 77–79.
5. Lauder, Ibid., p. 68.
6. Lauder, Ibid., p. 74.
7. Estée claims that the basic scent for Youth Dew was created by her uncle for a Russian princess and perfected by herself (p. 101). Because of the objectivity of Lee Israel's book, her account is used in the text.
8. Israel, Ibid., p. 43.
9. Lauder, Ibid.
10. Fraser, Ibid., p. 44.
11. Lauder, Ibid., p. 56.
12. Lauder, Ibid., p. 66.
13. Fraser, Ibid., p. 47.
14. Fraser, Ibid., p. 43.
15. Fraser, Ibid., p. 50.
16. Fraser, Ibid., p. 51.
17. Fraser, Ibid., p. 52.
18. This analysis of Henry Hill's learned industriousness is based on an

excellent biography by Nicholas Pileggi entitled *Wise guy: Life in a Mafia Family.* (New York: Simon & Schuster, 1985).

Chapter 11. Teaching Americans to Try Harder

1. Croly, Ibid.
2. Oxnam, Ibid., 88.
3. Seligman, M. E. P., *Helplessness: On Depression, Development, and Death* (San Francisco: Freeman, 1975).
4. Comstock, Ibid.
5. Owen, Ibid., 74.
6. "Kibbutz: A Commune That Works," *Business Week*, September 6, 1969, 120.
7. Mills, C. M., & Walter, T. L., "Reducing Juvenile Delinquency: A Behavioral-employment Intervention," In J. S. Stumphauzer; (Ed.), *Progress in Behavior Therapy with Delinquents* (Springfield, IL: Charles C. Thomas, 1979), 287–301.
8. Barbee, J. R., & Keil, E. C., "Experimental Techniques of Job Interview Training for the Disadvantaged: Videotape Feedback, Behavior Modification, and Microcounseling," *Journal of Applied Psychology*, 58, 1973, 209–213.
9. Liebert, Sprafkin, & Davidson, Ibid., 158–159
10. Yates, G. C. R., "Influence of Televised Modeling and Verbalization on Children's Delay of Gratification," *Journal of Experimental Child Psychology*, 18, 1974, 333–339.
11. Friedrich, & Stein, Ibid., 11.
12. See reviews by: Deci, E. L., & Ryan, R. M., "The Empirical Investigation of Intrinsic Motivational Processes," in L. Berkowitz, Ed., *Advances in Experimental Social Psychology*, Vol. 13 (New York: Academic press), 40–80; Deci, E. L., & Ryan, R. M., *Intrinsic Motivation and Self-determination in Human Behavior* (New York: Plenum Press, 1985); Geen, R. G., Beatty, W. W., & Arkin, R. M., *Human Motivation: Physiological, Behavioral, and Social Approaches (Boston: Allyn & Bacon, 1984).*
13. Lepper, M. R., Greene, D., & Nisbett, R. E., "Undermining Children's Intrinsic Interest with Extrinsic Rewards: A Test of the Overjustification Hypothesis," *Journal of Personality and Social Psychology*, 28, 1973, 129–137; Lepper et al., "Consequences of Superfluous Social Constraints: Effects on Young Children's Social Inferences and Subsequent Intrinsic Interest," *Journal of Personality and Social Psychology*, 42, 1982, 51–65.

14. Deci & Ryan, Ibid., 1980, 1985.
15. Ibid.
16. Condry, J., "Enemies of Exploration: Self-initiated Versus Other-initiated Learning," *Journal of Personality and Social Psychology*, 35, 1977, 459–477.
17. Most of the studies we discussed examined the transfer of rewarded high effort from one dull task to another or from one interesting task to another. But rewarded high effort on a dull, repetitive task can also transfer to an intrinsically more-interesting task. For example, Boyagian and Nation (Ibid.) found that reward for pressing a pad with high force increased the subsequent performance by college students on an anagram task. And another study reported that preadolescent children who had been rewarded for accuracy on a monotonous reading task produced more-accurate subsequent drawings and stories than did students who had been rewarded for simply completing the reading task (Eisenberger, R., Mitchell, M., McDermitt, M., & Masterson, F. A., "Accuracy Versus Speed in the Generalized Effort of Learning-disabled Children," *Journal of the Experimental Analysis of Behavior*, 42, 1984, 19–36). Therefore, generalized high effort influences intrinsically-interesting tasks, as well as dull, repetitive tasks.
18. Amabile, T. M., *The social psychology of creativity* (New York: Springer-Verlag, 1983); Condry, Ibid.
19. Eisenberger et al., "Transfer of Effort" Ibid.; Eisenberger, R., Frank, M.. & Park, D. C., "Incentive Contrast of Choice Behavior," *Journal of Experimental Psychology: Animal Behavior Processes*, 1, 1975, 346–354.
20. Strohmeyer, Ibid.
21. Ibid.
22. Zerzan, J., "Anti-work and the Struggle for Control," *Telos*, 50, Winter, 1981–1982, 187–193.
23. Reynolds, P. C., "Imposing a Corporate Culture," *Psychology Today*, March, 1987, p. 34.
24. Reynolds, Ibid., 36.
25. Ibid.
26. Meyer & Stott, Ibid.
27. Golomb, N., "The Relations Between the Kibbutz and its Industry," in A. Cherns, Ed., *Quality of the Working Life and the Kibbutz Experience* (PA: Norwood Editions, 1980).
28. For example: Herzberg, F., "The Wise Old Turk," *Harvard Business Review*, September-October, 1974, 70–80; Sirota & Wolfson, Ibid.

29. Lacey, Ibid., 539.
30. *Japanese Education Today*, Ibid., 7–8.
31. Ibid., 15.
32. Ibid., 16.
33. Ibid., 17.
34. Fallows, J., "Gradgrind's Heirs," *The Atlantic*, March, 1987, 19.
35. For Lyndon Johnson's propensity for throwing money at problems without adequate planning, see Robert Caro's book: The Years of Lyndon Johnson; Vol 1: The Path to Power (New York, Knopf, 1982).
36. Personal interview.
37. Auletta, Ibid., 246–248.
38. Kaus, Ibid., 30.
39. Lemann, Ibid., 60.
40. Solomon, D. S., "Health Campaigns on Television," in Pearl, Bouthilet, & Lazar, Ibid., 308–321
41. Stark, Ibid.
42. Rubinstein, E. A., "Television and Persons in Institutions: Health Campaigns on Television," in Pearl, Bouthilet, Lazar Ibid., 322–330
43. Clelland, C. C., & Swartz, J. D., "Work Deprivation as Motivation to Work," *American Journal of Mental Deficiency*, 73, 1969, 703–712.

Suggested Reading

The classic study of the effects of early industrialization on the work ethic is Daniel Rodgers' *The Work Ethic in Industrial America: 1950-1920* (Chicago, University of Chicago Press, 1978). The rise of the leisure ethic in the 1920's is described with lucidity and verve in Frederick Lewis Allen's *Only Yesterday* (New York: Bantam, 1959). Diminished work values and lackadaisical performance among industry business executives and union members in the decades following the Second World War are recounted in *Crisis in Bethlehem: Big Steel's battle to survive* by John Strohmeyer (Bethesda, MD: Adler & Adler, 1986).

Recent attitudes toward jobs and work are analyzed in Daniel Yankelovich's *New Rules: Searching for Self-Fulfillment in a World Turned Upside Down* (New York: Holt, Rinehart, & Winston, 1981) and David Cherrington's *The work ethic: Working values and values that work* (New York: Amacom, 1980). The study that touched off widespread concern about the lack of rigor in American education is *A Nation at Risk: The Imperative for Reform*, the report of the United States National Commission on Excellence in Education (Government Printing Office, 1983).

A vivid and eloquent description of life styles and negative attitudes toward work that emerge from long-term unemployment is given in Elliott Liebow's *Tally's Corner: A study of Negro Streetcorner Men* (Boston, MA: Little, Brown, & Company, 1967). Mikey Kaus has written a clear and penetrating analysis concerning how government assistance might be redirected to promote strong work values (*The Work Ethic State, New Republic* (July 7, 1986). Experimental findings regarding the relationship between reward for high effort and the development of the work ethic are presented in an article in the *Journal of Personality and Social Psychology* (Eisenberger & Shank, 1985, Volume 45, Pages 520–528). Strohmeyer's previously mentioned book includes a valuable study of one steel plant that was scheduled for closing but was saved, in large part, by incentives for high employee effort.

Index